MEN INTO
SPACE

MEN INTO SPACE

by
John C. Fredriksen

BearManor Media

2013

Men Into Space

For information, address:

BearManor Media
P. O. Box 71426
Albany, GA 31708

bearmanormedia.com

Typesetting and layout by John Teehan

Published in the USA by BearManor Media

ISBN—1-59393-231-6
978-1-59393-231-2

TABLE OF CONTENTS

To Neil Alden Armstrong (1930-2012)

The first human being to stride
across another world.

Preface

THIS BOOK IS INTENSELY AND INTENTLY PERSONAL, wherein the afterglow of a halcyon childhood, an embedded sense of wonderment, and a lingering, cheery optimism about the future all co-mingle. Yet I eschew dispassionate objectivity, for what follows emanates more from a pained psyche than anything else. It is with an acute sense of loss that I, a prodigy of both the Space Age and Cold War, wince every time an *American* astronaut boards a *Russian* rocket to dock at the *international* space station. A deep rumbling within me asks: what happened? To my generation, this construct obliterates the cherished expectations for spaceflight cultivated during my youth which, in turn, formed such a pervasive part of attaining sentience in the late 1950s. Since the anti-climactic demise of the Apollo Moon project two decades later, the once-fabled United States space program has devolved into a polite fiction, with taxpayers reluctant to underwrite future endeavors. In truth, lack of money, lack of leadership, and endemic public apathy have unraveled what for us Baby Boomers averred America's leadership in science, and incontrovertible proof that Mankind was vaulting toward the heavens. But, aside from a few rovers on Mars and fewer fly-bys of the outer planets, nothing dramatic has transpired since the last time humans left their footprints on an alien world. Today the public greets even these scientific milestones with a collective shrug, being sedated by a hedonistic obsession for computer games, websites, and blogs, replete with myriads of beeping, blinking, hand-held monstrosities that eviscerate attention spans and vitiate curiosity about the universe they inhabit. In a real and very perilous way, the ethos of *sense* has been sacrificed on the altar of *self*.

Disillusionment alone compels me to reflect on past events, casting mind and memory back to what I consider more efficacious times. In September 1959, I was a precocious First Grader and a glassy-eyed space wonk who avidly devoured the books of Willy Ley, Werner von Braun, and Hans Haber, the spaceflight cartoons of Walt Disney, and the Soviet-laden documentaries of David L. Wolper. However, when *Men Into Space* debuted that same month, it instantly become my first favorite show, and to say that I was transfixed is an understatement. This program was also my formal introduction to sci-fi (I watched *Science Fiction Theater* sometime earlier, but was too young to comprehend it) and for a year I giddily immersed myself in the exploits of Colonel McCauley every Wednesday night–the only time I could stay up to 9 p.m.–and had pleasant dreams of space thereafter. Moreover, I consumed every episode with a fervor that would make the Taliban flinch and have remained a NASA groupie ever since. My parents also paid heavily for CBS's mid-week lineup, for I badgered them to buy me the numerous tie-in toys and games from the series. *My very own space helmet!* Life was good, secure, and continually stoked the possibilities of "space" in lofty, impression-able minds. I freely confess buying into it--hook, line, and ray-gun.

Seeing this series on DVD for the first time in fifty-two years reignited the glow, for I savored my reunion with that old space savant Colonel McCauley and enjoyed recounting his fearless ex-ploits. *Men Into Space* is significant for several other reasons, most notably in being the first "hard-science" sci-fi show and thereby de-void of aliens, madmen, and tentacle-faced, brain-sucking cretins that might have boosted ratings. The show expired after only one season and is all but forgotten, but it indelibly imprinted on me the necessity of paying attention to space. No television show, before or since, ever spoke to me with such urgency. Suffice to say, one had to be a youthful denizen of the late 1950s not merely to watch *Men Into Space* but, rather, *experience* it. To that same end, this compilation is much less a treatise than the celebration of a bygone era and the boundless confidence and optimism it exuded. I was transformed by this show, it forever altered my attitude towards science, and I hope to render it justice in the pages that follow.

I am indebted to numerous individuals for helping to bring this project to fruition. First and foremost are Drs. Michael Neufeld and Margaret Weitekamp of the National Air and Space Museum, Smithsonian Institution, who granted me access to a forthcoming essay on the topic. Thanks also go out to Anastacia Lundigan, daughter of actor William Lundigan; Kristine Krueger of the Margaret Herrick Library; William H. Rosar of the Society of Film Music; Mary K. Huelsbeck of the Wisconsin Center for Film and Theater Research; Melvin H. Schuetz of Baylor University, Jean Marie Stine of Renaissance Books; Jerry Arcieri of Landov Media; Roy Scarfo; and finally, Jim Mayberry of the New Mexico Museum of Space. Finally, kudos to editor Ben Ohmart of BearManor Media for indulging me in this guiltiest of guilty pleasures. May readers find it a close encounter of note.

Synopsis photos are courtesy of the Wisconsin Center for Film and Theater Research unless otherwise marked.

Teutonic tutor: to many Americans, Werner von Braun personified
the "space race" of the 1950s. Author's collection.

Space Was New/The Future Was Now

MANKIND, AS A SENTIENT SPECIES, is insatiably curious about its surroundings and, regardless of the dangers and labors involved, invariably explores and exploits them. That a starry curtain overhead, to which our ancestors ascribed mystical qualities and superhuman deities, lay beyond their grasp did not stop vivid imaginations from contemplating what paraded nightly before them. Consequently, astronomy, astrology, mythology, calendars, and accurate navigation at sea all arose from this fascination with twinkling lights drifting across an ebony cloak. Awareness of the sky, its fantastic denizens like the Sun, the Moon, the stars, and more elusive apparitions like comets and supernovas, only increased once nascent technology in the form of telescopes allowed closer scrutiny.[1] Moreover, the notion of visiting alien worlds and contacting the locals is equally ancient and, by the late 19th century, was being mass-marketed to a curious public by such visionaries as Jules Verne and H. G. Wells. With the dawn of the 20th century, astronomy had advanced to where modern notions of "space" held scientific merit, and more accurate concepts of our galaxy and the universe arose. Growing awareness of Mankind's own puniness in relation to all this knowledge likewise came painfully to the fore. Moreover, new forms of mass media like radio, pulp magazines, and cinema in particular allowed for more striking visualizations of the future, which more often than not invoked spaceflight. Some of the earliest motion pictures invoked sojourns to other worlds and, with the invention of sound, the popularity of space operas like *Flash Gordon* and *Buck Rogers* abounded. On the scientific front, the romantic fictions of Verne and Wells were gradually abetted by erudite studies by Russian Konstantin Tsiolkovsky, American Robert Goddard,

1

and Hungarian/German Herman Oberth, all of whom advocated the practical applications of rocket science. The future, as an intellectual commodity, was fast becoming an undercurrent of popular culture.[2]

It was not until the end of World War II that German V-2s, the first expression of modern rocketry, took to the sky with malevolence. Afterwards, the United States and Soviet Union absconded with captured missiles *and* scientists to erect research programs of their own. In doing so, they casually disregarded this underlying stratum of Nazi science and, in light of national priorities, simply looked the other way.[3] Moreover, the weapons each side promulgated, coupled with mastery of atomic fission, highlighted the paradox that Man had finally acquired many of the very technologies heretofore dismissed as the stuff of pulp novels. This equation carried an ominous wrinkle: humanity could now use such devices to either explore the Heavens or immolate itself on Earth. Fortunately, Eisenhower's policy of "Massive Retaliation" and the evolving Cold War paradigm of "Mutually Assured Destruction" held Soviet aggression at bay for nearly half a century, ensuring that humanity's final charge off a cliff never materialized.[4] Space, however, remained a contested arena for both sides to flex their missile-muscles, which they did with relish. Commencing in 1947, the first reports of flying saucers from other worlds further muddied the waters and Man's wonderment about the universe gradually yielded to fear of the unknown.[5] The future had arrived suddenly and with a thudding vengeance, presenting Mankind with increasingly stark choices.

In its own way, the 1950s was uniquely positioned for the propagation of spaceflight. Interest in science fiction movies was a driving force for the genre throughout this decade, with interplanetary travel a recurring theme in popular titles, such as *Destination Moon, Riders to the Stars, Conquest of Space, Forbidden Planet*, and others. It was also a golden age of science fiction writers, such as Robert Heinlein, whose novels, like *Starship Troopers*, embodied wholesale expeditions to other worlds, battles with intractably hostile aliens, and all the other engaging conventions of soap opera. Popular outlets, such as *Collier's* magazine, also commissioned collaborative efforts between scientists like Willy Ley and visionary artists like Chesley Bonestell to enhance and popularize awareness of spaceflight. The publishing industry took their cue from all these developments and churned out children's books that were lavishly illustrated and scientifically

Noted space artist Chesley Bonestell provided ZIV with several concept designs which guided the program's overall look. Courtesy Bonestell.org.

accurate–that is, to the extent that space was "known." However, it fell upon the broadcast milieu to disseminate the means and enunciate justifications for exploring outer space as a national goal. Television itself was not exactly new and, in fact, its earliest manifestation harkened back two decades earlier. However, the electronics revolution occasioned by World War II, coupled with perfection of the transistor, resulted in sets that not only performed better, but were less costly and within easy reach of a burgeoning bourgeois. In sum, technology, mass production, and conscious consumerism rendered television sets a *de rigueur* status symbol for muddled middle America.[6] Given its leisurely reach into millions of households on a daily basis, TV proved an ideal medium for discussion of all things space and then in a comfortable arena ideal for mass persuasion.

Television programming was still in its infancy in 1949 when the Dumont Network pioneered science fiction shows by broadcasting *Captain Video and His Video Rangers.* This low-tech venture was shown live five times a week, but found loyal viewership among youthful space enthusiasts throughout its six-year run. Undaunted, the American Broadcast Corporation (ABC) devised its own space soap for the kiddie crowd with *The Space Patrol,* which appeared Saturday mornings. A more serious outing along these lines was *Tom Corbett, Space Cadet,* which was considered a tad more somber and scientifically "accurate" than contemporaries. This televised tableau was gradually joined by other series, such as *Commando Cody, Sky Marshal of the Universe* and *Rocky Jones, Space Ranger,* neither of which made lasting impressions. In truth, TV's first wave of science fiction programming was melodramatic, episodic, and deliberately aimed at children to promote sugar-laden products. Scientific veracity was of secondary concern, if at all. A host of lesser, shorter-lived titles continued surfacing and disappearing at various intervals, but all had decayed from orbit by 1955.[7]

Fortunately, the mantle of space promotion was picked up by none other than Walt Disney, visionary filmmaker and first-rate hopeless romantic, who was typically obsessed by the promise of spaceflight. He found his avatar in the person of Dr. Werner Von Braun, a handsome, charismatic *junker* previously associated with the Nazi V-2 program and whose transgressions were absolved through Cold War expediency.[8] In fact, Von Braun was only one of several high-visibility German expatriates taking to the airwaves to expound the virtues of science throughout the decade. Some, like Hans Haber, were former Luftwaffe members while others, such as Willy Ley, fled the Nazi regime beforehand and immigrated. Together with the telegenic Von Braun, they were completely fluent in heavily German-accented English and exuded an urbanity and technical expertise that average Americans found daunting. In sum, these Teutonic tutors proved the most persuasive space salesman and were emblematic of an age. Furthermore, Disney harnessed their message by producing elaborate TV cartoons about spaceflight in which these *Experten* also starred. These shows were viewed by 42 million Americans at home and are regarded as classics of the genre.[9] Disney further disseminated the promise of space through elaborate and technically sophisticated theme parks like Tomorrowland. The public enthusiastically embraced his vision of the future and flocked in droves to Disneyland to behold it. Less spectacularly, the relatively new field of plastic models introduced scores of rocket and satellite kits to a generation of children eager to build them, and toy manufacturers were not long in following suit. All told, this is one of very few instances in history where popular culture dovetailed perfectly with national interests and space awareness mounted.[10] By mid-decade, the nation was awash in everything "space" and the public felt secure–even smug–in believing that America was the unchallenged leader in its promotion. More importantly, when satellites and spacemen finally debuted, few doubted they would be anything but our own.

Such endearing warm fuzzies about space evaporated on October 4, 1957, when the Soviet Union orbited its iconic Sputnik, Earth's first artificial satellite. At a stroke, space exploration and science, long held as a comfortable novelty, was instantly transformed into a dire necessity. Sputnik was, in essence, a beeping ball and many held it up as some kind of technological Pearl Harbor when, in fact, the United States could have easily launched a similar device in 1956 had the funding been requested.[11] Consequently, space had become prioritized and became the latest arena of the ongoing showdown between the free world and communist totalitarianism. The United States, resolving not to be surprised again, channeled millions of dollars not simply into space technology, but in science education across the board. The National Air and Space Administration (NASA) arose to embody and direct the nascent space program. Politicians and military figures also lectured the public on the strategic expedience of being first in space to forestall a Soviet nuclear attack from on high or a possible conquest by our ideological adversaries. Outperforming the communists into space became a vocal national mantra while Hollywood, its finger firmly on the pulse of popular culture, cranked out another round of space-oriented science fiction movies, contributing to the furor.[12] Still, by 1957, television lacked bonafide space programs to capitalize on the craze and, just as nature abhors a vacuum, network executives began casting about to fill the void.

Frederic W. Ziv, the legendary head of ZIV Productions, sounded the possibilities of a space-oriented program for CBS immediately in Sputnik's wake.[13] Unlike the children-oriented science fiction programming of a few years previous, the tenor of the times now demanded an approach that was rigorously scientific to appease more mature audiences. Ziv, who prized flaunting the technical expertise assisting his programs, also believed that obtaining Department of Defense cooperation facilitated access to their extensive and elaborate space facilities. At length, his show acknowledged help from the Air Force Air Research and Development Command, the Office of the Surgeon General, and the School of Aviation Medicine. ZIV's credibility was further enhanced when Air Force technical experts were brought into the scripting and consulting process, receiving credits in the end titles. Noted space artist Bonestell was likewise recruited to provide various "space concepts" to assist the program's visual feeling and special effects. The prolific composer David Rose, who had already contributed some memorable ZIV scores, was again tapped to provide more. Individual episodes were budgeted at $50,000 each, sizable by ZIV standards, while a further $100,000 was earmarked for construction of a realistic "moonscape" sound stage on Santa Monica Boulevard (which occasionally also doubled as an asteroid), along with various life-size rocket and space station interior sets.[14]

The entire project was handed off to producer Lewis J. Rachmil, who toiled endlessly securing the requisite technical advice and permission to shoot on location at various research facilities. In this manner, Cape Canaveral and Edwards Air Force Base, among others, frequently appeared as backdrops, lending greater credence to the series. Dramatic stock footage of missiles launching was also acquired and spliced into most episodes. Where mock ups were used, they were constructed and filmed by special effects experts Jack Rabin, Irving Block, and Louis DeWitt, which proved adequate considering the budgetary constraints. The spacecraft models themselves were large, three-stage affairs in the Bonestell tradition, but crew capsule itself was envisioned as cramped and crammed with dials and other equipment, much as the Apollo Moon vehicles they presaged. Zero-gravity sequences were also concocted through an elaborate system of cranes and pulleys devised by rigging expert Peter Foy, and conveyed a sense of weightlessness outside the ship.[15]

Another futuristic lunar landscape by Bonestell depicting an initial foray on the Moon's surface. Courtesy Bonestell.org.

These and various "Moon walking" scenes were filmed at higher speeds to enhance the illusion of zero- or low-gravity. Not to be outdone, the U.S. Navy lent genuine full-pressure suits, designed for high altitude, for the pilot episode. However, these were dark blue and photographed poorly against the blackened set. By the second episode, newer suits of silver-colored nylon costing $3,152 each–hugely expensive in those days–were acquired.[16] In sum, this new show, requiring two years of research and preparation, was the most complicated, expensive, and technically astute series ZIV attempted since the highly successful *Sea Hunt*. But even this fabled emphasis on realism had dramatic limits, and concessions were made by allowing engine noises and explosions in the vacuum of space and dispensing with zero-gravity effects in most cabin interior shots.

ZIV made an even greater concession in its quest for full military cooperation, striking a Faustian pact in the process. The Air Force retained supervisory control of scripting and insisted that all episodes depict the American space effort in a strictly realistic vein. No bug-eyed monsters or mad scientists were permissible, so story lines invariably turned on conflict arising from faulty equipment or personality clashes among crewmen. In Rachmil's words, this arrangement precluded "little green men from Mercury and insects with tractors for feet."[17] Ironically, ZIV was uniquely positioned to inculcate this approach, having just concluded *Science Fiction Theater*, television's first sci-fi anthology. This landmark show was produced by Ivan Tors, a Hungarian expatriate, who delighted in presenting audiences with thoughtful, scientific-based themes.[18] Authenticity served as the show's common denominator and Chuck Fries, who headed up production, characterized it as "high drama in low orbit":

> What made everybody want to do it back then was it seemed like an anticipation of things to come, as if we were doing a documentary about the future. Remember: Sputnik had happened and the Space Age was just getting under way... We had technical advice from the United States Air Force, among others, and that meant we had realistic-looking space suits and other hardware. The show was an entire future history of the space program before it ever, in reality, got started.[19]

Given acute public interest in the space race, both ZIV and CBS entertained high hopes for the series—and possibly a second season. The new show, initially labeled *Moon Probe* and then simply *Space*, ultimately premiered as *Men Into Space* on Wednesday night, September 30, 1959, nearly two years after *Sputnik*. And–to rub salt in the wound–this occurred 17 days after the Soviet Lunik II probe became the first Man-made object to orbit the Moon. The format adopted by ZIV was usual in featuring only one recurring character, Colonel Edward McCauley, who interacted with a different cast in every show. McCauley was played by veteran actor William Lundigan, longtime spokesman for Chrysler and a host of several TV shows; hence, a well-known and apparently well-liked commodity. The role of Mary McCauley originally went to rising star Angie Dickinson, but when she departed to star in *Rio Bravo* opposite John Wayne, the insufferably cute Joyce Taylor replaced her. Perennial child actor Charles Herbert also signed to appear as their son in a handful of episodes. The only other recurring actors were Tyler McVey and Russ Conway, irregularly cast as Generals Norgrath and Devon, respectively.[20] Notable guest stars such as Robert Vaughn and James Coburn, who went onto to greater fame in the following decade, also made guest appearances.

At length, thirty-eight 30 minutes episodes were shot, mainly addressing the problems inherent in Moon landings, runaway rockets and satellites, insubordinate crewmen (usually scientists), and technical malfunctions, all of which had to be resolved by the ever-resourceful McCauley. To underscore the hazards of spaceflight, cast members were sometimes "dead" before such issues were resolved. Moreover, the depiction of requisite devices such as three-stage rockets, pressurized Quonset huts for habitation, portable solar screens for power, telescopes on the Moon, atomic engines, and radio dish antennas for scanning the galaxy were conspicuously displayed. Episodes incorporating such technical exotica also employed an authoritative narrator who explained what was happening to viewers. For example, scenes aboard the space station brought commentary that artificial gravity was created and maintained by rotating the main wheel. All told, the show portrayed the American space effort–at that time actually lagging behind the Russians–as technically proficient and in capable hands.[21] Coming at the time it did, *Men Into Space* was a salve on the national consciousness and provided its audience with badly-needed escapist fare, if even within the bounds of reality.

In many respects, *Men Into Space* proved amazingly prescient regarding the difficulties and dangers awaiting humans aloft. Meteor strikes, lack of oxygen, construction accidents in zero gravity, balky thrusters, medical emergencies (including a punctured lung, appendicitis, and a heart attack), leaking fuel tanks, collisions while refueling, disposal of radioactive wastes, and uncontrolled rocket tumbling were all presented in dramatic fashion. Other, less-anticipated perils such as "Moon quakes," micro-meteorite showers, and tipping over in soft lunar soil were also posited as plausible scenarios. The series further pioneered the view of women as central to space research and Moon colonization, although ZIV's hidebound approach to gender roles is hysterically funny by today's standards.[22] Curiously, the Soviets were portrayed not merely as competitors, but compatriots in exploration and, for the most part, responsible partners under trying circumstances. Coming at the height of the Cold War, the emphasis on cooperation is surprising and welcome.

Two other episodes also strayed from the established fold for flirting with the possibility of alien life. That McCauley was a military figure and not a civilian scientist further demonstrates the trust and popularity of that branch in handling such vital assignments. It is no coincidence that on April 9, 1959, the Mercury 7 astronauts, publicly introduced for the first time, were all pilots and officers, so the notion of delegating all the heavy lifting in space to guys in uniform–and not white coats–was an accepted reality.[23]

William Lundigan, joined by Gene Barry of *Bat Masterson*, graced the cover of *Life* magazine just prior to the fall 1959 television season. Courtesy Getty Images.

For all the care and attention paid to detail, *Men Into Space* remained low-budget fare with straitjacketed storylines and special effects bordering on mundane by today's standards. The series launched with reasonably good ratings, but critics instantly rendered verdicts that were–no pun intended–less than stellar. One media maven noted, "At times the picture resembled a snip out of an old George Pal flicker. The results, while not entirely unsatisfactory, proved that even the most painstaking authenticity may manufacture something of a dud."[24] The public gradually reached the same conclusion for, on January 27, 1960, *Variety* reported that *Men Into Space* tracked 32nd out of 35th in ratings and was most likely slated for cancellation. A month later, Gulf Oil withdrew its sponsorship, leaving one critic to crow, "Now that presumably half of the sponsor resistance has disappeared, "Space" has far less to hold it in orbit." The bad news finally arrived in April when no less than 55 shows of the current broadcast season were cut by the networks, including *Men Into Space*.[25] This was despite the fact that producer Rachmil had tempted CBS executives with a final episode concerning a flight to Mars, hence the promise of future exploration to other planets in the Solar System in a new season. The axe finally fell on September 7, 1960, although that same year the series was nominated for a Hugo Award in the category of "Best Dramatic Presentation," only to lose to *The Twilight Zone*. A year later, John Sinn, president of newly-created ZIV-United Artists, Inc., defended their approach to the show this way: "We took a foresighted look up to the tallest dream and highest mechanical aspiration of man and underscored the view with an accurate, detailed, informative presentation of the dramatic facts behind the drama."[26] From a ratings standpoint, close but no cigar (-shaped flying object).

Overall, *Men Into Space* was quickly forgotten, save for cult members like myself, although the space suits and rocket ship interiors were recycled in the film *Phantom Planet* and several episodes of *Outer Limits*. A tie-in novel by Murray Leinster also appeared in October 1960, one month following its cancellation. As a final slap, cosmonaut Yuri Gagarin became the first human to orbit the Earth in April 1961, another stunning setback. But in July 1969, Neil Armstrong and Buzz Aldrin finally alighted on the Moon—and in a manner not dissimilar from what Colonel McCauley routinely performed a decade earlier. Success here signaled America's victory in the space race and the culmination of all those other-worldly aspirations underscoring popular culture in the 1950s. In conclusion, *Men Into Space* and the ethos it conveyed were all part of a lengthy, but ultimately triumphant, national process.[27]

As previously stated, I lapped up all this *astro-angst* as a child and retained a morbid curiosity for space that continues today. I vividly recall being glued to the tube Wednesday nights and this fixation was probably symptomatic among my age group at the time. I have since learned from reading essays by Matt Novak and Roger D. Launius that public support for the manned Moon program never exceeded 50 percent, even at the height of this period.[28] I am surprised by this assertion, but they obviously never canvassed any 6-year olds from 1959-1960, for the verdict would have unanimously been in favor! Yet, when viewed through the prism of half a century, I think that the real problem with *Men Into Space* was making everything look routine, almost effortless. Real spaceflight was and remains expensive, complicated, and dangerous. The research and development responsible for all the marvelous hardware involved is also governed by common denominators of time and money, with an occasional dash of serendipity. Skylab and the space shuttle were impressive in their own right, but, aside from the Apollo landings, few technical facets portrayed by this series, including a manned Moon base or manned reconnaissance of Mars, have been realized. The handful of nations with viable space programs talk boldly, yet it may be years, even decades, before another project on the scale of Apollo transpires. The United States, for its part, will not field another viable spacecraft, Orion, until 2020. Suffice it to say, the diminution of America's *manned* space program represents the loss of something golden, and with it, a good part of who we are as a people.[29] Sad commentary, perhaps, but failure has become an option.

At the time of the Apollo triumph, national expenditures on NASA amounted to only one percent of the gross national product; today, it amounts to only half that and further cutbacks are planned. Early this morning, the $2.5 billion rover *Curiosity* successfully debuted on the Martian surface, further demonstrating our over-reliance on unmanned technology. So robots rule the roost, leaving humanity to play second banana on the galactic stage–where is the outrage? Are we so engrossed in worldly affairs, so indifferent to our long-term survival that we marginalize, what is *literally* for mankind, the final frontier? Overcrowding, pollution, depletion of natural resources and fresh water, coupled with the aggressive, violent nature of the species in question, all bode ill for our continued existence here. Who dares contemplate the singular reality that, should Man ultimately fail to "slip the surly bonds" and colonize other worlds, this beloved planet may yet become our collective grave? The ultimate triumph in space may take centuries to achieve, even a millennia. Yet, given the track record of human civilization, what alternatives have we? Our leaders have failed us–ultimately, so will our planet.[30] May future generations rekindle that sense of awe, the ability to dream a better future, and a fixed determination to cross the gulf separating imagination from reality as we did, and joyously so, in the 1950s. If *Men Into Space* encapsulates the essence of a departed, heroic ideal, it is also a good measure of everything we have lost as a space-faring culture.

www.FightforSpace.com

Bibliography

Benford, Gregory. *The Wonderful Future that Never Was*. New York: Hearst Books, 2010.

Brosterman, Norman. *Out of Time: Designs for the Twentieth Century Future*. New York: Harry N. Abrams, 2000.

Corn, Joseph J. *Yesterday's Tomorrows: Past Visions of the American Future*. Baltimore, MD: Johns Hopkins University Press, 1996.

Dregni, John, and David Dregni. *Follies of Science: 20th Century Visions of Our Fantastic Future*. Denver, CO: Spark Press, 2006.

Wilson, Daniel H., and Richard Horne. *Where's My Jetpack? A Guide to the Amazing Science Fiction Future That Never Was*. New York: Bloomsbury USA, 2007.

William Lundigan

CAST AND CREW

WILLIAM LUNDIGAN was born in Syracuse, New York, on June 12, 1914, the son of a shoe salesman whose building was shared by an early radio station. The youngster was intrigued by this new medium, pursued it in his spare time, and by sixteen he was producing and performing in radio plays of his own. Lundigan subsequently studied law at the University of Syracuse and partly supported himself by working as a radio announcer. The lanky, six-foot-two-inch Irishman was also patently handsome and possessed a deep, sonorous voice ideal for radio. It so impressed Charles R. Rogers, head of production at Universal Studios, who happened to hear Lundigan on the air waves, that he sought the young man out and arranged a Hollywood screen test. He passed with flying colors and his first movie, *Armored Car*, appeared in 1937. Lundigan continued on with bit parts until 1939, when Warner Bros. signed him for major roles in *Dodge City* and a handful of other top-flight titles, such as *The Fighting 69th* (1940). A star on the ascent, Lundigan transferred his fortunes to M-G-M the following year, only to resume his trademark "nice-guy" roles in several mediocre titles and also wrangled roles in two Andy Hardy pictures. In 1943, the United States was at war and Lundigan, after performing in *Salute to the Marines* with Wallace Beery, disregarded an old athletic injury and enlisted in the Marine Corps. Studio head Louis B. Mayer was so incensed that he cancelled Lundigan's contract and the actor never again toiled for M-G-M. This meant little to Lundigan at the time, for he passed through basic training at Quantico, Virginia, then underwent instruction as a combat photographer.[31] He was assigned to a unit commanded by Captain Thayer Soule, who recalled:

Bill Lundigan, straight from Hollywood, where he had played feature roles, burst on the school as our most handsome, most vibrant personality. He had a quick eye for pictures, worked hard, and never asked favors. Time and again hints were dropped that I should go easy on Lundigan, let him off this or that, but Bill didn't want that. He took things as they came.[32]

Lundigan was subsequently billeted with the 3rd Battalion, 1st Marines, and part of the crack 1st Marine Division, the victors of Guadalcanal. Like any Leatherneck, he was no wallflower when it came to combat. On September 15, 1944, he landed on the island of Peleliu, 500 miles east of the Philippines, defended by 10,500 crack Japanese troops, which degenerated into one of the bloodiest slugfests of the Pacific arena. Lundigan survived the ferocious fighting unhurt, but his 1st Marine Division was so badly mauled that it rotated out of line to refit for several anxious months. During this interval, he narrated Louis Hayward's award-winning documentary *With the Marines at Tarawa* (1944) with that unmistakable voice of his. Lundigan next saw action at an even bigger struggle, Okinawa, which was invaded on April 1, 1945, and took eighty-two days to secure. He was in the thick of things and his Hollywood notoriety occasioned some good-natured jostling. According to Sterling Mace:

Off to the side a camera crew was setting up their gear, and in their midst was the actor William Lundigan, another California type turned Marine. "Say," Eubank gawked, "I seen that guy in that *Dodge City* picture...and what was that other one? The *Fighting 69th*, too!" 'Hey, Hollywood!' some marines whistled and shouted, giving the young actor their approval. Lundigan simply nodded back good-naturedly, then resumed his job with the camera team.[33]

Much of Lundigan's Okinawa footage ended in up the 1945 documentary *Fury in the Pacific* (1945). Once the war ended, his back injury required him to spend time in a U.S. Navy Hospital. He was then honorably discharged as a corporal on October 5, 1945, the

Lundigan as astronaut Richard Stanton in *Riders to the Stars*. Author's collection.

proud recipient of two Bronze Stars. That year, he also married dancer Rena Morgan.

Work was scarce for many actors who had served during the war, but Lundigan eventually appeared in *Dishonored Lady* and *The Fabulous Dorseys* in 1947. He then signed on with 20th Century-Fox, performed in noirish *Follow Me Quietly*, the racially sensitive *Pinky*, and the soaring *I'd Climb the Highest Mountain*, all of which he capably handled. However, the closest thing to a memorable role came in 1953 while playing against the type as villainous Joe Duncan in *Inferno*, opposite Rhoda Fleming and Robert Ryan. Lundigan undoubtedly relished that, for once, he broke typecasting as a perpetual do-gooder, and his biting performance underscores his acting range. Unfortunately, he reverted back to the usual good-guy types in a string of forgettable B pictures. As he later conceded, "My mistake was being so damned cooperative. Not only did I accept bad pictures, but I accepted lousy parts in those bad pictures."[34]

In 1954, Lundigan had his first brush with science fiction by playing astronaut Richard Stanton in Ivan Tors' potboiler *Riders to the Stars*. He played opposite Martha Hyer and B-flick icon Richard

Carlson, who also directed. Here both men are tasked with piloting spacecraft to capture meteorites in flight for study back on Earth, with some unsavory consequences. Lundigan's role also required him to project a consummate professional pilot image around Carlson, yet still exude personal feelings in his private moments with Hyer. He subtly nuanced the role, lent dramatic credibility to an otherwise unmemorable film, and neatly anticipated the role he fulfilled in *Men Into Space* five years later.[35] By this time, Lundigan's film

Lundigan as Captain Fred Gunderman in the *Science Fiction Theater* pilot "Beyond." Author's collection

career was fading, but television beckoned, so he typically shifted gears and went on his merry way. His smooth, affable disposition and reputation for being easy to work with held him in good stead in 1954 when he signed on co-host of the dramatic series *Climax!* with Mary Costa. The show enjoyed a four-year stint and, between 1956 and 1957, he also hosted the variety program *Shower of Stars.* Concurrently, Lundigan also served as spokesman for the Chrysler's Corporation, which flew him 100,000 miles around the country to various auto shows, dealer conventions, board meetings, and the like. It is estimated that he personally addressed, hand-shook, and cajoled 560,000 people over a four-year period, receiving an astronomical $100,000 yearly for a task few actors would undertake.[36] Thus, by mid-decade, Lundigan was one of the most familiar and best-liked faces of the televised milieu, which played a big role in events still unfolding.

In 1955, Lundigan accepted his second science fiction role when Tors apparently recommended him to Frederic W. Ziv for his new weekly anthology, *Science Fiction Theater.* The show in question was actually the series pilot, cryptically titled "Beyond." Now cast as Major Fred Gunderman, Lundigan was a test pilot that apparently saw an unidentified flying object while flying and bailed out. Experts on the ground spend the rest of the show trying to convince him that he was hallucinating, but the subject is left tantalizingly open once the wreckage of his aircraft is examined and found highly magnetized after colliding with an object riding a magnetic beam. Again, Lundigan performed credibly as a military officer who refused to buckle under pressure and he was apparently growing comfortable with the type.[37] Moreover, by 1958, his growing cache with American audiences led to numerous offers for a television slot of his own, including a western and a detective show. He remained uncommitted until approached by ZIV for a reality-based space program, which intrigued him. "What helped me to make up my mind was the fact that this was not some Buck Rogers type show," he asserted. "It was not a science-fiction series, but a science-fact series. You might even say it's a combination of a public service show and a dramatic series."[38] Lundigan, whose wide-ranging career had taken him to virtually every venue, characteristically sought out something new.

As star of *Men Into Space*, Lundigan stepped into the shoes of Colonel Edward McCauley and drew upon his own military experience to render the character capable, but believable. He naturally projected the authority of a senior Air Force officer with his commanding voice and figure. McCauley could be gruff, did not suffer fools gladly, and demanded results from those around him. A project as essential as the American space program required no less from a man designated its chief pilot and ace troubleshooter. On the other hand, McCauley was also a good judge of human psychology and openly empathetic, for after dressing down reckless subordinates, he invariably slapped their shoulder, smiled, and told them not to forget. During the best episode of the series, "Mission To Mars," McCauley forfeits a perfect Mars launching to rescue some stranded Soviet cosmonauts, which underscores his basic decency and humanity. Lundigan interpreted his role with low-key restraint and an understated world-weariness belying an otherwise heroic stereotype direct from central casting. McCauley, unlike James T. Kirk of a later age, was more an eminence grise and a restraining influence on the youthful hotspurs he commanded. In sum, he was a commander that any military man wanted in a clinch–stern, unyielding, yet willing to sacrifice himself for others. Colonel McCauley inspired a generation of youthful space-niks, including the present writer, with his weekly exploits.

On a lighter side, McCauley's character exuded something of a romantic streak, for he repeatedly wished to be the first human to contact alien life. Moreover, and consistent with 1950s sensibilities, he was also devoted and doting to his wife and children despite the impossible pressures of directing a space program. Through it all, McCauley always managed a smile, maintained an even keel emotionally, and when it came time to flaunt his masculine dominance, did so over another American fixture–the barbecue grill. The only salient other point I will raise is that he drove a 1959 Buick with fins bigger than any rocket's. Welcome to the Fifties! Lundigan also sought to flesh out McCauley's character and render him three-dimensional, fought with writers to make him less infallible, and suggested that he commit an occasional mistake. According to Rachmil, "We've made McCauley more human, I think, because Bill has complained: I'm no hero, so take me off the hook."[39] Reporting to the set, the actor also found the daily routine far more demanding than he ever imagined:

I thought my old job with my auto sponsor was rugged, but working on this show is much tougher physically. There's lots of climbing and 'flying' over special sets in heavy space equipment and helmets. The sweat pours out of you from the moment you put on the uniforms on until you take them off. And some of our working days have been 18 hours long. I lost 9 or 10 pounds during the shooting of the first three shows.[40]

Lundigan as Colonel Edward McCauley, star of *Men Into Space*.

The advertising run up for *Men Into Space* was also considerable and, shortly before it debuted, Lundigan appeared on the cover of *Life* magazine, hovering over Gene Barry, star of ZIV's *Bat Masterson*, on the Moonscape. Critics may have panned the show, but it drew fairly strong ratings initially and certainly won over millions of youthful viewers already smitten by this space thingy. The latter led to certain difficulties for Lundigan, beset as he was by legions of rabid nine-year-old fans, each of whom knew light-years more about space than their hero. "It's all I can do to drive a car...I can't answer their questions," he insisted. "I excuse myself and pretend to answer the phone. Or else I wind up asking the questions–and sure enough, the boys know the answers."[41] Prior to signing on as McCauley, ZIV executives promised Lundigan that they would maintain quality scripts and hire top-flight directors, but he became increasingly exasperated by what he considered mediocre writing and directing. In the words of wife Rena, "He ended up being very disappointed in the way it was handled."[42]

After *Men Into Space* was cancelled, Lundigan made his final foray into science fiction by starring in the Tors production of *The Underwater City* (1962), which garnered no laurels, and then focused on character parts for the remainder of the decade. This tack produced supporting roles in such unmemorable fare as *The Way West* (1967) and *Where Angels Go, Trouble Follows* (1968). A conservative Republican, Lundigan and several like-minded celebrities openly campaigned for Barry Goldwater in the 1964 presidential election and he also accompanied USO tours to Vietnam with his good friend John Wayne. "I'm a square, conservative Irishman," he insisted, "and I make no apologies for it."[43] One can only wonder about the thoughts racing through his mind in July 1969 when astronauts Armstrong and Aldrin actually walked on the Moon, much as he had "done" a decade earlier. Lundigan continued making guest star appearances on shows like *Marcus Welby, M.D.* well into the early 1970s until he died of Emphysema in Duarte, California, on December 20, 1975, aged 61. Previously, he received a star on the Hollywood Walk of Fame, leaving the imprint of his Marine Corps badge in the cement. Despite that his career spanned forty years and included over 100 feature films, several television series, and innumerable guest shots, William Lundigan is all but forgotten today. He nonetheless bequeathed an *oeuvre* of work both estimable and admirable.[44]

JOYCE CROWDER was born in Taylorville, Illinois, on September 14, 1932. She was attracted to singing at a young age and began winning amateur contests at the age of 10. By 15, she started appearing in night clubs and received a recording contract from Mercury Records. Around this time, she adopted the stage surname Taylor to honor her hometown. A visit to Hollywood brought the attractive young lady to the attention of eccentric RKO producer Howard

Joyce Taylor. Author's collection

Hughes, who signed her on as a starlet in 1952, but he only allowed her a bit part in the forgettable *Beyond A Reasonable Doubt* (1956). Three more years in oblivion lapsed before her contract expired and, now freelancing, Taylor accepted a role in *Men Into Space* for ZIV. She was tapped to replace Angie Dickinson, who appeared in the pilot and then moved on to *Rio Bravo* with John Wayne. Now cast as Mary McCauley, wife of America's leading astronaut, she made the most of a rather limited role in ten episodes. On the surface, Taylor appears as simply another contented fifties *hausfrau*, but even the indomitable Colonel McCauley yields to her wifely wiles and divulges whatever she needs to know. She also kept an immaculate house, cooked lavish meals for any occasion, and was hubby's biggest fan and cheerleader. Given the sensitivities of the age, Mary was a domestic diva that any American wife could relate to. It is a major failing of the program's story arcs that writers failed to develop the McCauleys' personal lives in a richer and more fulfilling vein. The colonel's nighttime confessions of anxiety and fears for his men would have allowed Mary an outlet to emote more than wifely empathy–not more cooking.

Overall, Taylor enjoyed her stint with the space age and especially working around William Lundigan. "He was *precious*, just wonderful. He was a big tease, always joking around. I shouldn't even tell you the things they did to me on that show!" At one point, Lundigan clandestinely arranged to have a bedroom scene shot almost entirely in the dark with himself arrayed in pajamas. Taylor panicked on the set after viewing what lay in store for her and ran off to grab the director's arm, producing hysterical laughter. He explained they did it just for laughs and she exclaimed, "Thanks a lot! Why does the joke always have to be on me?? I was *very* shy, that's why they always teased me so much."[45] Shortly before the cancellation of *Men Into Space*, Taylor parleyed her reputation in a major role in *The FBI Story* (1959), then filmed what was probably her most memorable role as Princess Antilla in George Pal's disappointing flop, *Atlantis, the Lost Continent* (1960). Taylor seemed to have an affinity for fantasy titles and she made subsequent appearances in *Beauty and the Beast* (1961) and *Twice-Told Tales* (1963) alongside Vincent Price. A handful of other movies and television appearances kept her occupied until she retired from the business in 1971 to concentrate on raising her family. As Mary McCauley, Taylor cut a comely visage for any space-weary astronaut to return home to, despite describing herself to *TV Guide* as the "possessor of an earthy quality, very plain."[46] Since her retirement, she resides in the same Midwest from which she sprang.

CHARLES HERBERT SAPERSTEIN was born in Culver City, California, on December 23, 1948, and life proved pretty uneventful until he was discovered on a bus by a Hollywood talent agent at the tender age of four. He subsequently won a slot on the local television show *Half Pint Panel* in 1952, exuding a genuine talent for acting. Herbert subsequently appeared in numerous programs and in 1955 landed a bit role on *Science Fiction Theater*, his introduction to the

Charles Herbert.

genre. Thereafter, he appeared in numerous horror and sci-fi films, such as *Monster that Challenged the World* (1957), the *Colossus of New York* (1958), and the timeless classic *The Fly* (1958) opposite Vincent Price. He had also become one of the highest-paid child actors in Hollywood and also his family's sole provider. A year later, ZIV Productions signed him up to appear as precocious Peter McCauley, son of astronaut Edward McCauley, in *Men Into Space*. He was seconded by Del Russell, who was his younger brother, Johnny. Thus disposed, Herbert starred in six episodes that by and large eluded his youthful memory. "I was supposed to work three, four days, something like that, and they were going to pay me $750 for the week," he recalled, "But we got in all done in one day so I ended up getting $750 for one *day*. And that's the only thing I remember about *Men Into Space*!"[47] He was convincing in his role, even during this limited regimen, and went onto bigger–but not necessarily better–things.

The peripatetic child star continued on with films and television shows as the new decade dawned and even landed his own fantasy adventure, *The Boy and the Pirates*, in 1960. Ultimately, he appeared in 20 motion pictures, 50 televised episodes, and several commercials. Unfortunately, Herbert, forever typecast as a tyke, saw work more or less dry up after reaching the age of twelve. The fact he never enjoyed meaningful education during his youth, coupled with his parents' dereliction by squandering his life savings, militated against a rational adulthood. Herbert embraced wanderlust, drug use, and licentiousness throughout adolescence, and four decades elapsed before he reclaimed himself. Since then, he has teamed up with fellow child star Paul Peterson on behalf of former and present child actors. Today, Herbert makes personal appearances at numerous science fiction/horror conventions throughout the country, though he harbors no affection for the genre. "Maybe it's because all the work I did in it!" he insists.[48]

LEWIS J. RACHMIL was born in New York City on July 3, 1908, and he graduated from the Yale University Art School in 1930 before serving with the Long Island branch of Paramount Studios. Moving west in 1935, he worked in Hollywood as an art director, a production manager, a production designer, and set decorator, at all of which he proved very proficient. In 1940, he received an Oscar nomination for his art direction in *Our Town* (1940) and over the next decade he also labored as an associate producer. Rachmil rose to full producer with *The Devil's Playground* in 1946, and six years later he produced the televised series of *Hopalong Cassidy* based on the movie series, which he also produced. He remained associated with B pictures for the rest of the decade until Frederic W. Ziv tapped him to serve as producer of *Men Into Space*. This was ZIV Productions' most ambitious program to date and, given Rachmil's background in art and his consummate acquaintance with low-budget fare, he

Lewis J. Rachmil.

proved an ideal selection. They placed scientific accuracy above all other considerations, which posed an entirely new set of challenges for the company and Rachmil in particular. According to Maurice Unger, a ZIV production manager, two years of negotiations transpired between studio heads and Madison Avenue executives before the concept was packaged and sold to CBS. "When we first began to work on Space," he conceded, "I knew there was no Bible on this stuff. Our problem would be how to get down that first pill of fantasy."[49] No one inculcated this dilemma more than Rachmil himself, who spent a full year devouring books and magazine articles about space, especially those relating to manned flight, before production even commenced. His first major creative decision was securing the services of noted space artist Chesley Bonestell, who provided numerous pieces of concept art and received top billing. Given the emphasis on special effects that, by necessity, were low-budget, he approached an accomplished trio of technicians, Jack Rabin, Irving Block, and Louis DeWitt, to deliver the goods. In terms of story content, Rachmil also decided that venues further out than the Moon loomed beyond audience comprehension. He explained:

> According to the best thinking, it takes 258 days to get to Mars from Earth; then you have to stay on Mars 455 days to await proper position of the planets in their orbits for the return trip–more than 900 days and 690,000,000 miles altogether. The average person simply does not comprehend this. In fact the average person does not understand why an airplane leaves the ground. You see what we are up against.[50]

Thus, the Moon remained a dramatic leitmotif for most stories. However, a final episode bringing Colonel McCauley tantalizingly close to Mars–with the promise of actually landing there in a second season–was filmed, but CBS refused the bait and the series waned. On June 6, 1960, Rachmil was nonetheless elected vice president in charge of production at ZIV-United Artists.[51] Thereafter, he returned to filmmaking over the next two decades, producing such memorable titles as *633 Squadron* (1963), *Inspector Clouseau* (1968), and *Footloose*

(1984). He died in Beverly Hills, California, on February 19, 1984, aged 75 years. *Men Into Space* was a mere footnote in his long and distinguished career, but Rachmil never flinched from tackling projects deemed too challenging by others. The totality of his career, including 100 films and television shows, amply testifies to that.

CHESLEY BONESTELL was born in San Francisco, California, on January 1, 1888, and he reputedly painted his first space painting at the age of 17 after observing Saturn through the San Jose Lick Observatory. He next briefly studied engineering at Columbia University in New York City, quit before graduating, but nonetheless secured work on the new Chrysler's Building. Back home, Bonestell provided conceptual drawings for the new Golden Gate Bridge. However, his passions were astronomy and painting, so in 1938, he relocated to Hollywood as a matte painter, earning $1,500 a week. Here he contributed to such noted titles as *The Hunchback of Notre Dame*, *Citizen Kane*, and *The Magnificent Ambersons*. In 1944, he achieved a minor breakthrough, artistically speaking, by painting a series of astronomical scenes for *Life* magazine rendered so realistically they appeared to be photographs. One canvas, a view of Saturn from the moon Titan, is still regarded as a timeless depiction within this genre. It certainly cemented Bonestell's reputation as the world's leading exponent of astronomical art. He followed up this success by providing around fifty covers for all the major science fiction magazines along with illustrations for *Scientific American*, *Coronet*, *Pic*, and *Mechanix Illustrated*. His renown accelerated exponentially in 1949 after collaborating with rocket expert Willy Ley on the popular book *The Conquest of Space*, which launched a host of similar titles and imitators. Commencing in 1950, Bonestell created otherworldly mattes for a host of George Pal's science fiction movies, such as *Destination Moon*, *When Worlds Collide*, *War of the Worlds*, and *Conquest of Space*. More importantly, his work with German expatriate Werner Von Braun in a special series of *Collier's* magazines, 1952-1954 , created such a public stir that it accelerated popular interest in the nascent American space program. In truth, Bonestell's deft brush strokes conveyed an inexorable sense, not merely of space flight's possibility, but rather its inevitability.[52]

Chesley Bonestell. Courtesy New Mexico Space Museum.

In 1958, Bonestell was approached by ZIV producer Lewis J. Rachmil to provide "concept art" pieces for the new series *Men Into Space*. These consisted of his typical three-stage rocket in various flying attitudes coupled with dramatic lunar landscapes. Most of these were reproduced in a *Lucky Strike* cigarette advertisement published for the series. When the show finally aired, the missile props and Moon landscape sound stage likewise drew inspiration directly from Bonestell's futuristic vision. However, his sharply jagged vista representing the lunar surface was ultimately disproved by the Apollo landings, having been flattened by eons of meteoric bombardment.[53] Bonestell continued on as the dean of astronomical art until dying in Carmel, California, on June 11, 1986. In light of his indelible contributions to the visualization of space, he received a bronze medal from the British Interplanetary Society, a Special Achievement Hugh Award, and induction into the International Space Hall of Fame. A crater on Mars and an asteroid designated 3129 Bonestell were likewise named in his honor.

Bibliography

Miller, Ron, and Frederick C. Durant III. *Worlds Beyond: The Art of Chesley Bonestell*. Norfolk, VA: Donning, 1983.

_____. *The Art of Chesley Bonestell*. London: Paper Tiger, 2001.

Schuetz, Melvin H. *Chesley Bonestell Space Art Chronology*. Parkland, FL: Universal Publishers, 2001.

Wachhorst, Wyn. "The Dream of Spaceflight: Nostalgia for a Bygone Future." *Massachusetts Review* 36, no. 1 (Spring 1995): 7-43.

DAVID ROSE was born in London, England, on June 15, 1910, and emigrated with his parents to Chicago while a child. After studying at the Chicago College of Music at the age of 16, he joined the Ted Fio Rito dance band and three years later signed on as a pianist for NBC Radio. Rose spent the next decade as an arranger, conductor, and musician before relocating to Hollywood in 1938. There, he assembled the David Rose Orchestra for the Mutual Broadcast System and he was briefly married to actress Martha Raye. In 1941, Rose was signed on by M-G-M, where he met and married his second wife, Judy Garland. During his tenure at M-G-M, he composed what became his signature theme, "Holiday for Strings," which sold over a million copies. During World War II, Rose served in the U.S. Army as a conductor and in 1944 his composition "So in Love," which was featured in the Danny Kaye film *Wonder Man*, received an Oscar

David Rose. Author's collection.

nomination. He was also tapped to supply music for the stage production of *Winged Victory* and subsequently expanded it for the film version in 1944. He also divorced Garland that year after M-G-M head Louis B. Mayer insisted that she get an abortion to maintain her "girl next door" image. Rose, meanwhile, worked equally hard at acquiring one of the largest collections of miniature steam trains in the world, frequently giving guests a ride.[54]

After the war years, Rose began testing the new medium of television and he commenced providing music for *The Red Skelton Show*, for which he wrote for two decades. In 1957, he recorded his second Number One single, "Calypso Melody," another million seller. Up through the 1950s, he also composed memorable themes for various ZIV Production shows, including *Highway Patrol*, *Sea Hunt*, and *Men Into Space*. The man tasked with actually acquiring ZIV musical scores from Rose, former DECCA Records executive Herb Gordon, was apparently an astute operator. According to Chuck Fries:

> Along the way, Herb had picked up a quirky and valuable skill: he knew how to record music in a garage in Pasadena with top people...and he knew how to get excellent theme songs–all without any association or contract with the American Federation of Musicians, and without paying residuals. That was how ZIV Television worked for eight to ten years without having any contact with the musicians' union at all.[55]

The *Men Into Space* opening score consists of only three notes, dramatically rendered, then repeated in a higher octave. It is ear-catching and anticipates the effect that the *Outer Limits* attempted in 1963. However, Rose's end theme is soaring, and perfectly captures the majesty and exuberance of space flight as envisioned in 1959. He remained active over the ensuing decade and composed the famous theme to *Bonanza* and several Fred Astaire television specials. In 1962, he also enjoyed a pop single when his famous theme "The Stripper" became his third Number One hit and million seller. During the 1970s, Rose wrote and performed all the music to *Little House on the Prairie* and remained active as a symphonic conductor up through the 1980s. He died in Burbank, California, on August 23, 1990, having accumulated six golden discs, four Emmys, 22 Grammys, and two Oscar nominations over the previous 65 years. His prolific largesse includes no less than 50 albums, 36 film scores, and 24 television themes. In consequence, Rose also received a star on the Hollywood Walk of Fame for Recording.[56]

CONVAIR *ATLAS*

Cue the stock footage! One of the most familiar and comfortable visages of space-related programs from this period is that of the Convair Atlas ICBM taking off–or, in the case of films like *Angry Red Planet* (1959), usually landing backwards! This iconic missile system was the first American weapon of its class and, as such, has an intriguing developmental and deployment history.

The German V-2 of World War II was hardly the war-winning weapon Hitler envisioned, but the improved capabilities promised by greater size and refinement were obvious. Missile technology may have still been in its infancy, but the United States and Soviet Union hurriedly employed captured V-2s and German scientists during the initial stages of the Cold War. In 1946, the U.S. Army Air Force awarded Consolidated Vultee (Convair) a contract to develop their MX-774 design into a long-range ballistic missile, but the project fell victim to budget cuts a year later. The Americans basically ignored this vital field of strategic weaponry until 1950, when the Korean War beckoned and defense spending blossomed. Convair, which had continued design studies on its own since 1946, now promulgated the new MX-1953, a huge, five-engine rocket capable of lobbing heavy fusion warheads for several thousand miles. However, once the first H-bombs became available after 1954, they proved much lighter than predicted and a scaled-down, three-engine version of MX-1953, christened B-65, arose. This was hardly the popular "three-stage rocket" of 1950s lore, then too technologically challenging and expensive to design, so the new weapon, designated Atlas, was a "one-and-a-half stage" weapon. In other words, the Atlas possessed a single main engine that remained operational up through its ascent while two smaller "booster rockets" on either side fired until their fuel was exhausted, then were jettisoned. In 1955, the Atlas project received the highest national priority after the Soviets had already perfected their R-7 ICBM, the rocket which ultimately hoisted Sputnik aloft in 1957.

As a rocket, the Atlas stood 91 feet high, possessed a diameter of 10 feet, and produced 300,000 pounds of thrust that hoisted it 70 miles into space. The first model flight-tested, Atlas A, performed its maiden flight on June 11, 1957, and was destroyed following an onboard failure. A second attempt also failed and it was not until December 17, 1957, that an Atlas rocket finally completed its flight

Convair *Atlas*. Author's collection.

downrange. Subsequent test models designated B through C continued launching with various degrees of success until the Atlas D version finally deployed as America's first long-range ballistic missile in 1959. As a liquid-fueled weapon, it proved awkward to prepare and difficult maintain and was gradually phased out by the solid-fueled Minuteman I missile by 1965. However, the Atlas D gained a measure of immortality by launching John H. Glenn and the remaining Mercury Program astronauts into orbit. The Atlas booster continues in service as a launch vehicle today, over fifty years since stock footage of it appeared on *Men Into Space*. Ironically, the newest Atlas V variant, introduced in 2002, uses a Russian-designed and -built RD-180 motor as its first stage, signifying a far different world than the one which occasioned its rise.[57]

Bibliography

Neufeld, Jacob. *The Development of Ballistic Missiles in the United States Air Force, 1945-1960*. Washington, DC: Office of Air Force History, 1990.

Sheehan, Neil. *A Fiery Peace in a Cold War: Bernard Schriever and the Ultimate Weapon*. New York: Random House, 2009.

Waller, Chuck, and Joel Powell. *Atlas: The Ultimate Weapon: By Those Who Built It*. Burlington, ON: Apogee Books, 2005.

EPISODES

"Moon Probe"

(Aired Sept. 30, 1959)

Starring: Angie Dickinson (Mary McCauley), Charles Herbert (Pete McCauley), Paul Burke (Major Billy Williams), Paul Richards (Air Force Liaison Officer), H. M. Wynant (Joe Hale), John Vivan (Ground Controller), Robert Cornthwaite (Reporter), Stacy Harris (Reporter), William Phipps (Technical Officer), Edward Kenner (Communications Officer), James Anderson, Charles Maxwell, Susan Dorn, Ashley Cowan, John Bleifer, Jacques Gallo, Robert King, Sam Capuano, Moody Blanchard

Script: Arthur Weiss

Directed by: Walter Doniger

The story you are about to see has not happened—yet. These are scenes from that story, a story that will happen as soon as these men are ready. This is a countdown—a missile is about to be launched. It will be the XMP-13, XMP meaning "experimental moon probe"—a missile that will carry three human beings into outer space.

Zero day—3:15 PM—zero hour—a carefully selected group of top-flight newspaper people have been assembled from all parts of the nation. Thoroughly briefed on every detail of the flight, they will be centered in a special room adjacent to the blockhouse to witness the story they are about to write.

Several cars, full of bustling reporters, pull up in front of a towering rocket gantry. After a few seconds of awe-inspired viewing, the accompanying Air Force officer explains that the next time they see the rocket, it will be from the control room's televised conference room, to which they are now heading. Once inside, he lectures them, "One final reminder: this is not a secret effort, but no releases except as scheduled. There are hotlines to all the wire services-New York, Los Angeles, Paris, Tokyo, Rome–everything you need." One assertive reporter corners him, insisting, "Colonel, what we need is to see McCauley." The colonel assures them that time has been set aside for that purpose, then he recites a detailed checklist of what must transpire beforehand. At that same moment, Mary McCauley and her son Pete enter the room and are greeted by the colonel. The woman is instantly queried by a reporter and Mrs. McCauley nervously declares that, "As long as I've known my husband, he's been reaching for the sky. And I like to think this flight means going just a little higher." A full court press is then held for Colonel Edward McCauley, the mission commander, who debuts alongside Major Joe Hale, his communications officer, and Major Billy Williams, the navigational officer. McCauley politely explains that they will be gone two days, their top speed will exceed 25,000 miles per hour and, when pressed if they will attempt a landing, he reluctantly replies, "No, we don't have the know-how. Yet." Another reporter brusquely inquires if he is scared, which occasions an equally brusque response: "No comment. If there's a mountain, somebody has to climb it. The mountains on the moon just happen to be a few hundred thousand miles higher. Let's... call it a way of life." Still another chimes in, "Going to the Moon–a way of life?" McCauley instantly responds, "Let's say science is a way of life." The meeting abruptly halts once the loudspeaker announces the countdown at one hour and fifteen minutes to launching. McCauley hugs his infant son, pulls an eagle symbol from his shoulder, and tells him, "Pete, wear the eagle until I get back." Mary also gives him a final, nervous embrace before the men depart to their rendezvous with destiny.

Many years of research, the careful planning of our best scientists, went into making this flight possible–a journey into the unknown.

McCauley and crew clamber up the gantry, enter the XMP-13, then strap themselves for launching. The countdown lasts for what seems an eternity and the ground controller looks up with relief as the rocket leaps skyward, trailing plumes of fire and smoke. "Come on, baby, don't hold back on us!" he bellows. Curiously, McCauley and crew begin reciting "Mary Had a Little Lamb" in the face of crushing G-forces to demonstrate each is still conscious and functioning. The rocket continues climbing, dropping its first stage booster and the crew struggles with their poem, now broadcasted back to the press room. Mary takes Pete by the hand, tells him "Let's help," and begins reciting the poem along with him. The air force officer comes over and soothingly assures her, "Mary, they're going to make it." "I know they will," she timidly responds. Suddenly, incoming telemetry reveals that XMP-13 is off course by several degrees while at an altitude of 25,000 miles. McCauley then radios that they have no third-stage power. Technicians soon discern that the second-stage had burned itself out, but failed to separate from the crew module, leaving it powerless and drifting helplessly through the void. "Now without that power," the officer explains, "they cannot correct their course." An electrical short in the cabin also sends McCauley scrambling to fix it in zero gravity and he floats over to extinguish the blaze.

McCauley, aware of the fact that at an altitude of 25,000 miles, free from the Earth's gravitational pull, he is in free-fall, moved with the greatest caution. The slightest push could send him off in the opposite direction.

Within minutes, the ground controller updates McCauley's condition. "Control to XMP," he declares. "You are drifting at 25,600 miles per hour, seven degrees off planned trajectory." A journalist asks the Air Force officer what "drifting" means and the latter asks them, "Do you know what infinity means? Well, that's exactly what he means–they can't stop themselves." Mary's faith in her husband, however tested, remains unshakable. "He said he would be back in two days," she insists. "He will be."

Destination infinity. Was that to be the fate of the XMP-13? Speed, 25,600 miles per hour, no power, no way to alter its course. Magnetic shoes will counteract weightlessness, but what repairs will counteract the malfunction?

Back on the ship, McCauley speculates that the spent booster must be hung up on one of four release latches and he seeks permission to venture outside for a look. Ground control reluctantly agrees and allows him to leave the XMP-13. Back on earth, a curious reporter asks how this can be accomplished safely and the officer explains, "Not only did the rocket reach escape velocity, but so did Colonel McCauley, either inside or outside that nosecone. Now as far as we know, there is nothing that can knock him off that ship– no wind, no air pressure. He's in a vacuum."

McCauley suits up, leaves the airlock, thoroughly investigates the booster's four latches and discovers that Number 3 is hung up. He concludes their only recourse now is to cut through the latch with a blow torch. Repairs are proceeding well, but McCauley no sooner cuts the latch free than it lashes out, cutting his support line and tossing him from the XMP-13. As he drifts off into the inky ether, Majors Hale and Williams struggle to get their craft back under control while radar tracking systems plot the wayward colonel's trajectory. To enable them to keep a fix on his position, he keeps repeating "McCauley" every 30 seconds, never knowing if they are receiving him. The ground controller gets on the radio and states, "Transmit data to all minitrack stations in the free world, no, request it worldwide. All stations to track him and report back here. We must not lose him." McCauley's plight is broadcasted on stations around the world and in several languages while all nervously await his fate. Fortunately, the entire globe cooperates in tracking him, but the public-relations colonel cautions his audience, "There is no friction out there to stop him. It's a hundred million miles to the inner planets, a thousand million miles to the outer ones, and billions of miles beyond. He'd just keep going."

McCauley, a man lost in space. Helpless, repeating his name, getting no answers. Not even knowing if he's being heard. What goes on in the mind of such a man? How long will it be? Is it a matter of hours, miles, or is it an eternity?

Fortunately, Hale and Williams restore power to the crippled XMP-13, then request instructions on how to reach the colonel. A few bursts of 80-pound thrust nudges them to his last known location, where he is observed, floating helpless, but alive. "Keep it on course, Joe," Major Williams pleads. "If we pass any closer he'll end up the tail pipe!" The rocket is gingerly nursed alongside the wayward astronaut, Williams tosses a safety line to him, and McCauley is reeled in to safety. "I got him, Joe!" William exults, patting his commander heartily. "Request instructions for reentry–Colonel McCauley is safe," Hale dutifully reports. Cheers erupt back at the newsroom and Mary McCauley gratefully emotes her relief.

A few days later, McCauley reports back to his superior, stating that Mary and Pete are fine and notes, 'You know, he wouldn't give me back my eagle!" The officer informs him that an intense debriefing awaits, and also declares that McCauley's mishap affords conclusive proof that rockets can be repaired in space. "Now you've proved that beyond any doubt!" he gushes. McCauley, fondling a model of the XMP-13, momentarily reflects on his ordeal and adds, "Something else was proved, too, and not let's forget it. For one half-hour the world made one human life more important than anything else." Putting the model aside, he says, "Let's go."

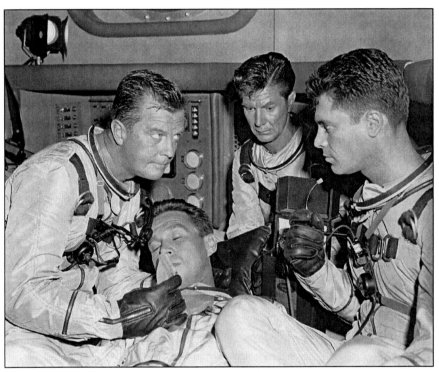

Courtesy Landov Media.

"Moon Landing"

(Aired October 7, 1959)

Starring: Charles Herbert, Joe Macoss (Major Patrick Donon), Don Oreck (Major Mason Trett), Karl Swenson (Senator Jim Sloan), Paul Lambert, Dean Harens, Ernestine Barrier, Jack Mann, Edward Paul, Andrew Glick

Script: James Clavell

Directed by: Walter Doniger

Technical Advisor: Lieutenant Colonel Frank P. Ball, U.S.A.F.

> *What you are about to see is Man's first attempt to reach the Moon. This story is not true; it hasn't happened yet. These are scenes from that story. It will happen when men such as these name the day. This is the story of that day—of Man's first Moon landing.*

A high-level board meeting convenes with Senator Jim Sloan prying last-minute details about the first attempted Moon landing. Major General Roberts subsequently introduces him to the intended crew, Colonel McCauley, Majors Donon and Trett, and Doctor Russ Russell. Colonel McCauley explains that the mission will be brief, only two days out and back, with an attempted landing at the *Sinus Roris* plateau. "As chairman of the president's space committee," Sloan interrupts, "I have to answer a great many questions. Why there?" McCauley declares that day temperature there will be a comfortable 50 degrees, plus the plateau is flat and "seems like the perfect place for a first landing." Still skeptical, Sloan switches to a more practical line of inquiry and asks if the colonel realizes how many billions of dollars are being spent to get him there. "Yes, Sir, I do, and I believe it's a good investment," McCauley continues. "You know, the practical applications to Moon conquest are enormous." The senator then queries the Moon-struck Dr. Russell if they are ready, drawing an emphatic response. "Well, nothing stands still, Senator. Life began in the sea, then groped onto the land, intelligence, and time, then staggered into the sky. Now we're leaping into space. *We are ready.* Space flight is only a natural and inevitable step in evolution. We have to go sooner or later. We might as well make it sooner." McCauley smilingly interjects, "He's quite a philosopher, Sir, but he's right." The meeting adjourns amicably, then General Roberts stands and informs McCauley, "Your mission is to go into orbit around the Moon. If conditions are favorable, you will land. It's your decision. The mission, as planned, will be short and quick. Takeoff, 23:59 hours." Senator Sloan asks the general if they can simply call it midnight, "just this once?" The general, eager to please his sponsor, smiles and acquiesces. "Takeoff, midnight–just this once."

Back at home, young Pete McCauley is playing in the yard with friends in his imaginary rocket ship. As he launches off, his father approaches with Doctor Russell and tells him, "Ground control to pilot–clean up for lunch." The children happily ask the two men to coach their softball team tomorrow, but with the moon landing planned, they take a rain check. Pete is disappointed, but his father reminds him that he has never broken a promise.

The next day, as the crew begins donning their space suits, they engage in some good-natured grousing. McCauley happily tells Doctor Russell to "Stop griping–wrap him up real pretty, will you?" Russell states that when his aged mother heard it was very cold on the Moon, she insisted that his crewmates dress warmly. The colonel, meanwhile, pulls out a model rocket ship from his locker. "Are you making them as well as flying them?" Trett jests. McCauley explains that, because he had to pass up a Little League game, the kit is a "peace offering" to son Pete. Trett also mentions his wife is nervous, yet pulling a "stiff upper lip" routine for his benefit. "I don't know whether it's tougher to sit at home or go," McCauley reasons. "*I don't think I could sit.*"

On launch day, Moonship Alpha thunders off the gantry atop sheets of flame and a jittery Senator Sloan asks General Roberts how he remains so calm. "Oh, we send birds aloft every day with men in them–not to the Moon, sure, but still aloft. The first time for everything is petrifying, but then after that it's routine. You've got to make it routine to play... to play this game." En route, the ship functions fine, but Doctor Russell experiences twinges of pain in his neck. McCauley unstraps himself and investigates, then Major Donlon jabs, "Who needs him anyway—*deadweight.*" The crew then watches in awe as they approach their destination and orbit only 100 miles above the surface. McCauley is surprised to find the topography more rugged than anticipated, yet pronounces it "fantastic." They then circle around the Moon's dark side, ejecting flares to continue observing. "Almost an anti-climax to find out it's just like the other side, isn't it," the colonel mutters. Russell, still in discomfort, whispers how long he has gazed at the Moon and how very much he wanted to be among the first humans there. "Well, Russ, you got your wish," McCauley assures him, and begins landing maneuvers. "Okay, nice and easy now..." he notes as they descend. Tension mounts as the shortening distance to the surface is called off, but the landing proves uneventful. Moon Probe Alpha settles amidst euphoria back at Ground Control, with General Roberts yelling, "We did it!" However, within seconds, the rocket begins tilting in soft sand and McCauley orders an emergency relaunch. Doctor Russell is slammed violently to the floor before he can reach his seat.

It was necessary for Colonel McCauley to once again orbit above the Moon before he could determine the next phase of this mission.

Back in orbit, the crew attends to Doctor Russell. He appears shaken, but otherwise all right. "I sure wish you'd learn to drive this thing," Russell hoarsely jokes. "*Quiet,*" McCauley tells him. The colonel next informs Ground Control of his close call and asks to land at another location. Permission is granted and this second attempt is successful. "McCauley to Ground Control–we've landed. We'll stay aboard half an hour ready for instant takeoff. Right now, it seems to be holding." Senator Sloan, greatly relieved, telephones the White House and news of the landing, now formally announced, triggers outcries of joy around the world. McCauley, Trett, and Doctor Russell then don space suits and venture onto the surface. Major Trett remains behind under orders to launch immediately if the ship lurches again. The men, especially Doctor Russell, are awestruck by the rugged landscape encompassing them. "It's unbelievable," Russell weakly murmurs. "Is it worth it, Russ?" McCauley asks. "Whatever the price," he assures the colonel. "All the hours I've looked at it–now to be here." However, Ground Control informs them that, due to excessive use of fuel, the return time has been moved up in order to rendezvous with tankers in space. The team busily unloads equipment and Doctor Russell's telescope, and he pronounces, "Telescopic observation from the Moon is infinitely better than that made from Earth. No doubt when we can erect a suitably-sized telescope, we will be undoubted able to... determine whether or not the canals on Mars are a natural geological phenomenon or..." Russell suddenly collapses and McCauley and Dolon rush over and return him to the ship. The colonel notices a trickle of blood coming from the doctor's mouth. Inside, it is determined that, when Russell slammed into the floor during the emergency blast off, a rib broke and punctured one of his lungs. "Russ," McCauley asks, "why didn't you tell us?" The doctor painfully explains, "I wanted to land... I waited so long." Beholding Earth for the last time, a blue orb suspended against a billion stars, Russell pronounces it, "like a jewel... a diamond... do me a favor... leave me here." The doctor expires and General Roberts instructs McCauley to fulfill his last request. Two men solemnly carry the body out to a nearby crater and the colonel somberly recites a passage from Psalm 8: *"When I consider thy Heavens and the work of thy fingers, the Moon and the stars which thou has ordained, what is man that thou art mindful of him?"* Its mission completed, Moonship Alpha triumphantly blasts off for home–minus one member.

Back on Earth, Colonel McCauley pays his respects to Doctor Russell's mother, who is a model of restraint. "Ed, Russ died doing his job. He wouldn't have had it any other way, so you mustn't fret," she informs him. The colonel comforts her, noting, "Your son would be as proud of you as you are of him, Mrs. Russell." She assures him, "I was proud of Russ before he went to the Moon. I'm happy he saw it. He wanted that more than anything else...and what other man has ever had so bright a monument?" McCauley smiles and departs as Mrs. Russell gazes wistfully at her son's celestial tomb.

"Building a Space Station"

(Aired October 21, 1959)

Starring: Don Dubbins (Lieutenant William Smith), Christopher Dark (Captain Lester Forsythe), Nancy Hadley (Paula Smith), Bartlett Robinson (General Robert Hicks), Don Kennedy (Captain Donald Michaels), Jack Mann (Major Hall), Michael Galloway, Walter Stocker

Script: Meyer Dolinsky

Directed by: Otto Lang

Technical advisor: Lieutenant Colonel Frank P. Ball, U.S.A.F.

The story you about to see hasn't happened—yet. These are scenes from that story, that will one day be a reality, when men will build a space station that will be used as a research center for the advancement of space travel. A station built by men such as these— men of flesh and blood and families. A new breed of adventurers, standing on the threshold of the unknown.

The task of so complex an undertaking as that of building Man's first station in space must, of course, rest on many shoulders. Head of the project, General Robert Hicks, United States Air Force—Colonel Edward McCauley, in charge of training the men who must complete the mission. The mission: to assemble these sections of the space station over a thousand miles from our Earth.

Colonel McCauley concludes a gathering of seven officers, only three of whom will accompany him aloft to construct the first space station in orbit. He seems pleased with the candidates, but, while walking to his office, General Hicks stops him. The general espouses concerns about Lieutenant Smith, a junior officer. "He handles himself pretty well," McCauley assures him. "Oh, I have nothing against the boy, but you never can tell what a kid will do in a crisis," the general insists. "Give it some thought before you pick your final crew." Later, McCauley commences training his men, suspended in the air by wires, on the fine art of assembling complicated machinery in simulated zero-gravity conditions. They fumble about, dropping their rabbit legs (wrenches), and drawing some pointed commentary from their superior. He also alerts Captain Forsythe that there is a large tear in his space suit, bellowing, "That only happens once up there. Even a pinhole, then you're dead–like that!" Some ground personnel then comment about the "wacky"' colonel leading a mission without equipment. McCauley, striding over, declares, "You'd like to volunteer? I'm the wacky colonel who's going up there." The two discretely decline his invitation and one states, "All I can say, colonel is keep your hands on that rabbit's foot!" General Hicks also arrives and is surprised that McCauley has selected Lieutenant Smith despite his inexperience. "He seems like the best man for the job," the colonel reiterates, and is confident any technical problems will be resolved. "Guess the next move, general, is to go up and try it," McCauley states. The colonel beams when Hicks announces that their launch is slated for a week from that day.

Back on the base, Lieutenant Smith meets up with his very pregnant wife Paula, who is naturally apprehensive over his dangerous mission. Colonel McCauley walks by the expecting couple and congratulates them, but jocularly warns Paula, "Wait till that kid start crying at 2 AM and all of a sudden he'll turn out to be *your* son." She shoots him a pensive look as he departs, then McCauley stops, pats her hand, and assures her, "I know, Paula." Elsewhere, preparations are made to put the program in motion.

Sections of the space station have been loaded into these cargo rockets, which will be sent up into orbit around the Earth at an altitude of one thousand seventy-five miles.

Cargo Rockets 1 and 2 are successfully placed in close proximity to each other, at which point McCauley's crew also ventures upward. The flight appears routine, so the observation ports are activated to observe the cargo rockets. Lieutenant Smith, dumbstruck by the starry void before him, blurts out, "Just look at that, will you." The colonel, smiling, seconds his wonderment by stating, "You can almost reach out and grab a handful of stars–the feeling is always the same..." Forsythe and Michaels likewise express their approval, but McCauley, mindful of his six-hour air supply, breaks up the "board session" and orders the cargo ships unloaded. "And remember," he informs them, "we're working against time." The colonel, Michaels, and Smith then suit up and, assisted by jet guns, float over to begin completing the space station's initial section.

Soon, man would know whether or not he would one day be able to live in outer space, depending on the success of Colonel McCauley and his crew.

Work proceeds apace and is slightly ahead of schedule until, as interior sections H-1 and H-2 are gingerly nursed together, the sleeve of Smith's suit becomes wedged between them. "Bill, don't move!" Michaels warns him as he alerts the other two men. McCauley quickly floats over and, assessing the situation, declares, "You're in trouble. Your suit is punctured–the air lock coupling is the only thing saving you. We open that and you're done for." As a precaution, McCauley has Smith tied firmly to the section, but, completely unnerved, Smith begins whining over his impending doom. The colonel angrily assures him, "Okay, if it will make you feel any better, when it happens it will be over so fast you'll never know it!" McCauley orders Smith to remain motionless while he and Michaels return to the ship. Ground Control is informed of the mishap and the decision is made to launch a fourth rocket with an "iron lung" device to keep him alive. Smith, his air supply dwindling, again pleads with the crew to abandon him and McCauley angrily cuts him off, barking, "Lieutenant Smith, I am in charge of this mission. You will do as you're told... besides, *why don't you shut up and save your air.*" He instructs Forsythe to bring the lieutenant some additional oxygen and warns, "Don't build up the pressure too much or you'll blow the puncture." Unfortunately, the trajectory of the incoming rescue A-3 rocket places it on a collision course with the space station. McCauley assures them that they are willing to risk it, but Hicks insists, "If it doesn't respond to guidance in the next two minutes, it will have to be detonated!"

Despite Ground Control's best effort, rocket A-3 fails to correct its course, so Hicks orders it destroyed in mid-flight. Anxious moments tick by as McCauley figures out what to do next, especially after the general orders him to return to Earth exactly as scheduled, abandoning Smith. "General," McCauley sputters, "General Hicks–" The colonel is cut off abruptly when Hicks reminds him, "You heard the orders, colonel." Not knowing exactly why, McCauley suits up to make a final visit to the doomed man. "What's the colonel doing out here?" Smith shrilly protests. "What do you want to do, stall around until everybody gets it? It's all over for me!" McCauley ignores him and closely examines his sleeve. It dawns on him that the same clamp used to secure oxygen tanks to the ship's hull might also seal off Smith's suit long enough to cut him free. He pats the young man on the shoulder, then departs. "How much time," the colonel asks Michaels. "Five minutes," comes the response. "Tell Smith not to move!" he insists. Acquiring a clamp, McCauley returns and begins fitting it around Smith's sleeve. "Bill, it's a long shot," he warns the lieutenant. "I'm going to cut your space suit between the clamp and the ship. Say your prayer that you don't get a leak in your suit." The colonel carefully cuts through the fabric, but the clamp works and Smith's arm is freed. "We cut him loose. We're bringing him back," the colonel exults. "Inform Control." The two men float Smith back to the ship where, having fainted from excitement, they work to revive him. "He's all right–he's passed out," the colonel says. "He's coming to now." McCauley then glances at the chronometer, which gave Smith only 10 more seconds of oxygen outside. The dazed lieutenant gradually opens his eyes and the colonel declares, "I'll strap him in and we'll head for home." The rocket departs, leaving the completed spaceship section floating in orbit.

Back on Earth, Colonel McCauley and General Hicks engage in another round of seemingly serious banter. "No, I'm sorry, colonel, I still have to say he's too young for the job," Hicks insists. McCauley counters, "Well, I don't know, general, he handles himself pretty well. On the other hand, you may be right, he is pretty young–you don't know what he'd do in a crisis." The two men happen to be talking about Lieutenant Smith's newborn son, crying in his cradle, and the beaming young parents nearby smile and embrace.

"Water Tank Rescue"

(Aired October 28, 1959)

Starring: John Shepodd (Lieutenant Rick Gordon), Joan Taylor (Carol Gordon), Paul Langton (Major Warnecke), Gar Moore (Captain Hal Roberts), Stephen Talbot, Richard Travis, Peter Walker, Barry Brooks

Script: Ib Melchior

Directed by: Otto Lang

Technical advisor: Major Charles A. Berry, U.S.A.F.

The story you are about to see has not happened yet. These are scenes from that story that will happen when men will colonize the Moon and discover how to live there. But before they accomplish this, they must have materials and supplies to sustain themselves on the Moon's hostile environment. In an undertaking such as this, it is inevitable that lives will be risked and new dangers faced. This is the story of a group of men who tried to conquer death on the Moon.

Head of Project Moonbase: Professor George Grayson. In command of the flight: Colonel Edward McCauley. The crew: Lieutenant Rick Gordon, Lieutenant Frank Werner, and Captain Hal Roberts. The mission: to land on the Moon and bring down the cargo pods from three robot satellites that have been sent up and are orbiting around the Moon.

In the comfortable surroundings of Lieutenant Rick Gordon's home, the lieutenant waxes optimistically that theirs is only the first of many supply missions to come. Carol Gordon pensively turns to Colonel McCauley for assurance, declaring, "I'm glad the first flight is with you, Ed." The colonel smiles and diplomatically intones, "Don't thank me. I just pick the best man for the job." Their precocious son, Tommy, also begins badgering McCauley for his "Astronaut Aptitude Test," a set of simple questions which he easily passes. "I can't fool you, can I?" the colonel concedes with a grin. "No, sir!" comes the eager retort. As McCauley departs for home, Carol presses him for assurances on Rick's health and he states, "You don't have to worry about Rick. As far as medical science can tell, he's a perfect specimen, believe it or not." When Tommy anxiously asks if the mission will be a "milk run," the colonel smiles and says, "That's right, it's just a milk run."

Back at base, preparations are being made to launch the MR-2 and its crew is summoned for a final assembly. Mimicking all these procedures at home is wide-eyed Tommy Gordon, calling out sequential commands, much to his mother's distress. "Gee, I wish it was me–all the way to the Moon. Wouldn't that be great, huh, Mom?" "Yes, Tommy," she whispers. The improvised countdown proceeds apace with Tommy bellowing out commands. "They'll be all by themselves–way, way out there," he declares. His mother, watching the rocket lift skyward, is overcome with anxiety and tells Tommy to be still. Excitable Tommy relentlessly continues and asks, "Mom, it is a milk run, isn't it? Anyway, Colonel McCauley said so." Overhead, the MR-2 assumes its final trajectory toward the Moon with all systems functioning normally. "Thirty-three hours to go and I'll be the Man in the Moon," Gordon says with a grin.

After a successful landing, McCauley and his crew immediately started Phase One of their mission—the dropping of the supply pods. Each blip they see on their radar scanner represents an unmanned rocket carrying the padded supply pods. At a precisely calculated moment, the supply pods, released by remote electronic control, will drop within a concentrated target area and be recovered by McCauley and his crew.

McCauley, having piloted his ship to a safe landing, begins directing the robots pods to land nearby. All three come down within a short radius of the ship and, having allowed a few moments of playful banter, he informs the crew, "We'll make the stockpile where the nearest supply pod came down. Let's go; we've got a lot of work to do." The colonel, Gordon, and Roberts then suit up and go outside to the various pods.

McCauley and his crew had accomplished Phase One, the first supplies, critical items dropped successfully, assuring Moon pioneers their basic needs, spare parts and equipment for repairs, medical supplies, food, all of which could be stored on the surface of the Moon without shelter since its atmosphere contains no moisture.

At length, McCauley, Gordon, and Roberts continue unpacking and stacking the containers with the colonel barking gruff instructions where to position them. All the varied impedimenta is carefully disassembled and carried to its assigned areas.

McCauley and his men knew that because the Moon's gravity is one-sixths that of the Earth's, a load that would weigh 300 pounds on Earth would weigh only 50 pounds on the Moon and could be easily handled.

As the task continues, the colonel observes Gordon acting physically impaired for a moment, but the lieutenant declares he feels fine. He lumbers by, hoisting a seemingly impossible stack of boxes and, in mock surprise, mentions, "They don't weigh as much on the Moon." Roberts, however, reminds him, "There are just as many to carry." Gordon struggles while trying to lift a barrel–then staggers, clutching his chest. A few disorganized moments ensue, then he collapses completely. McCauley and Roberts race over and carry the limp figure back to the rocket. The lieutenant's plight is immediately radioed back to Earth command while a very distressed Gordon apologizes for interrupting the mission. McCauley, however, will have none of it. "Don't you worry about that, boy," he assures him. "Don't you worry." Meanwhile, Doctor Warnecke is summoned to the radio and asks McCauley to describe Gordon's symptoms. "Extreme fatigue. Short of breath. Heavy perspiration. Deep pallor. Sharp pain, exact area left chest, extending down inside left arm," comes the response. Warnecke instantly recognizes the classic symptoms of a heart attack and instructs McCauley to keep Gordon in his helmet to insure a plentiful oxygen supply. The doctor then informs Professor Grayson that, in his present condition, the lieutenant might not survive the acceleration forces generated at liftoff. Grayson instructs McCauley to compute the lowest possible acceleration force necessary for leaving the Moon. When the colonel arrives at "2 Gs," Warnecke insists that "acceleration forces would definitely prove fatal." With only two hours to departure, all hands scramble to find a solution.

Gordon again apologizes to McCauley for the trouble he has caused and realizes he doesn't have much of a chance. "Don't declare yourself obsolete just yet," the colonel responds. Back on Earth, Grayson and Warnecke weigh their few remaining options and the doctor mentions experiments using water as an "acceleration shield." This is quickly nixed as McCauley has no such device on hand. The only other alternative is to abandon him on the Moon as the men must lift off within 73 minutes. "Gordon has a choice," Grayson reasons, "but it's only how he wants to die." Back on the Moon, McCauley is alarmed at the prospect of launching as scheduled and insists, "I can't take off knowing it's going to kill him!" The order nonetheless stands and Grayson laments that McCauley lacks an "acceleration shield." Meanwhile, it falls upon General Barry to relay the bad news to Carol Gordon and she and Tommy embrace, sobbing. "But Colonel McCauley, he said it was a milk run!" he emotes. "I'll never believe anybody anymore!"

Outside MR-2, the ever-resourceful McCauley determines to construct a scratch-built acceleration shield from spare parts scattered about the pods. Assisted by Roberts, he begins welding a steel drum with water nozzles, which is manhandled back to the ship.

A man's life depended on McCauley's ability to rig a complicated piece of equipment out of makeshift material: two drums, emptied of their contents, a few couplings and valves.

Once the shield is hooked up to water hoses inside MR-2, Roberts takes one glance and half-jokes, "What is this thing, Ed, my shroud?" He ponders if it will work and McCauley sternly insists, "It will." Gordon is next sealed tightly inside, the jerry-rigged apparatus is hooked, and fluid is transferred from the rocket's cooling system. The crew hurriedly secures the drums to the floor and Roberts asks, "Will it work, Ed?" The colonel concedes, "I don't know–it's got to!"

On Earth, a man with a heart attack, rushed to the nearest hospital, may have the odds in his favor. But when that hospital is 240,000 miles away, the odds are desperately against him.

No sooner does the crew fill the water shield than McCauley declares, "Takeoff time is three minutes overdue–let's go!" The men instantly scramble up the ladder and into their cockpit to launch. Minutes later, the MR-2 departs the Moon's surface.

One factor helped Rick in speeding the blast off—the same platform used for landing becomes a launching pad for take-off. Countdown can be almost immediate.

The MR-2 departs late, but on course. Once in orbit, McCauley and the men rush down and hastily drain off the water. Happily, after removing the top drum, they are relieved that Gordon survived the lift-off dazed, but unscathed. "Hi," he groggily intones. "Anybody interested in how a sardine feels?" McCauley quips, "Sardine, nothing–you're a flying fish, boy, on your way home!" Gordon protests the fact he goes back in the drums during reentry, insisting, "I'll get water-logged!" "Oh, no," McCauley tells him. "This is one time, Rick, you ought to be awful happy to be all wet!"

Back at the Gordon residence, McCauley drops by to check on his charge and Tommy proudly displays his new model rocket. "Have you told Tommy he's going to be flying one of these things some day?" the colonel inquires. The parents discretely decline and allow McCauley to relay the good news. He informs Tommy that, when he is old enough, the Air Force has arranged a direct appointment at the Air Force Academy. "Oh, boy!" Tommy blurts out in excitement. McCauley assures him, "Just want to make sure that we always have a Gordon on our team."

"Lost Missle"

(Aired November 4, 1959)

Starring: Harry Townes (Doctor William Thyssen), Marcia Henderson (Helen Thyssen), Ken Lynch (General Thomas), Jeremy Slate (Captain Barrett), Gavin MacLeod, Jim Stockton

Script: Michael Plant

Directed by: Walter Doniger

Technical advisor: Major Charles A. Berry, U.S.A.F.

> *The story you are about to see hasn't happened yet. These are scenes from that story, a story that will happen in the near future when men such as these will harness atomic energy to aid them in Man's conquest of space. This is the story of Project Dragonfly, the first test to see whether Man can control from the ground an atomic-powered rocket.*

At Los Alamos Nuclear laboratory, Doctors Harry Townes and Dave Parsons are approached by Colonel McCauley, who regrets that the latter will not be accompanying them to the launch site. Parsons apologizes, but justifies his absence for two reasons: first, Project Dragonfly is Thyssen's brainchild. "Two, that long-awaited fishing trip in the mountains." Thyssen jests one day he may be fishing on Venus, but McCauley reminds them that the nuclear pile is en route to the airport and the two hastily depart. At the main gate, Helen Thyssen greets them, but she is anxious about current events. Casting a glance at her husband, she declares, "You know, I told him I'd divorce him if he wouldn't tell me what was going on. Like trying to get information out of a clam." McCauley smiles and says, "You know, you sound exactly like my wife–except she specializes in trying to get *classified* information out of me." Helen expresses additional concern, should the atomic engine explode on takeoff. "Isn't that just like a woman?" Thyssen asks. The colonel assures her that nothing will happen as the pile is not activated until it reaches orbit. "If the worst happens," he reasons, "there's nobody aboard." Helen figures the next test will involve putting a man inside the rocket, so McCauley smiles and exclaims, "You know, I think he'd like to be that man." Thyssen proclaims his innocence, noting he has flown uneventfully in space for two years. His wife cuts him off, insisting, "Eggheads like you ought to stay on the ground." McCauley, mindful of the time, cuts the chatter and takes the Thyssens toward their waiting aircraft.

At the launching base, McCauley and Thyssen eagerly eye the towering gantry housing the rocket and its valuable payload. Thyssen beams and, when McCauley asks how he feels, the latter anxiously responds, "Like a mother." "Well," the colonel notes, "let's hope it's the beginning of a great big family for you, *mother*." Thyssen would love to get on the rocket and fly, but the colonel cautions, "Helen knows you pretty well–eggheads should stay on the ground–where they belong." Inside the compound, McCauley, Thyssen, and General Thomas nervously watch as LX-318 lifts off. The various stages fire and drop off as planned, then the nuclear motor kicks in, but the ship begins veering off course. Events worsen as the base loses all contact and the rocket's trajectory is hastily computed. "To within the Moon's gravisphere?" McCauley anticipates. "Or maybe a low orbit around it," Thyssen assures him. When General Thomas demands to know what went wrong, the doctor explains how the failure probably originated in the equipment moving the eight cadmium rods in and out of the atomic pile, which is most likely becoming critical. Alarmed, Thomas orders McCauley to compute its exact course and the latter sends a plea to the communications center of the Worldwide Tracking Stations.

Literally within minutes, scientists in tracking stations in Singapore, Lima, and Heidelberg turned their instruments toward the renegade rocket, and swiftly the vital information on its course poured into a central computing station at Canaveral.

Once bolstered by precise information, McCauley has even more bad news to announce. The rocket will soon pass into an orbit of 18,000 feet above the Moon–and on a collision course directly into the Lunar Apennines, which tower 7,000 feet higher. "Well," Thyssen opines, "I guess we'll have to write this one off and try again." "If it were only that simply, doc," McCauley cautions. General Thomas explains that there is an expedition in the Lunar Apennines doing metallurgical research, twelve men with a rocket that only can evacuate six crewmen at a time. McCauley next alerts Moon Base Project 103 of the danger and Lieutenant Hargaves informs him it would take 32 hours to round up the six pairs of scientists for evacuation, even with a second rocket. The colonel warns that the atomic missile will strike nearby in only 27 hours–the men will never make it back in time. The general suddenly interrupts, "The clock moves forward, not backward. We're wasting minutes. Let's get that rocket on its way!" McCauley protests that only half the men will ever reach the base in time, "What about the others?" "That atomic firecracker is setting the timetable, not me," Thomas barks. "The rescue ship leaves from there with those who can make it... we've got no choice." McCauley disagrees and suggests using the rescue vehicle to intercept the renegade rocket, then board it and deactivate the pile manually. Thyssen protests, "The machine wasn't designed for manual operation... I hadn't thought about it." McCauley fires back, "Well, think about it now!" Thyssen insists two men are necessary–one to active the rods and one to monitor the dial to ensure the pile does not go critical. "If that dial goes to the left, the rods are moving in fine. If there's the slightest flicker to the right, yell–or we're *stardust!*" The general abruptly declares that neither man will be going, but Thyssen insists, feeling personally responsible for the mishap. The general, once informed that Doctor Parsons is marooned in the mountains, realizes he has no choice. "We're *talking*–you should be on your way!" Thomas insists. McCauley and Thyssen depart immediately.

Outside the Medical Building, McCauley has an impromptu encounter with Helen, still unaware her husband will undertake a dangerous mission. "I told you he never tells me things!" she protests. "Helen, none of our astronauts have the know-how to deactivate that engine and it's got to be done," he explains. "Did he ask for this job?" she inquires. McCauley nods. "That old goat. Keep an eye on him, will you?" she pleads. "He's my favorite egghead." "Mine too," the colonel confesses. Thyssen then approaches and, with discretion being the better part of valor, McCauley ambles off. The doctor attempts to comfort Helen and promises to call her at the hotel. She gathers herself together and tells him, "You do that. You know how I always like to keep in touch." Thyssen kisses his devoted mate, then makes off to join McCauley. "Will you give this to General Thomas before I take off?" he says while departing. "It's a way to reach Dave Parsons." Soon after, rocket 0915, piloted McCauley, Thyssen, and Captain Barrett, blasts off in pursuit of their quarry. Helen, now joined by Dave Parsons, nervously waits back at the launch center. "I should have gone!" he insists. "Dave," Helen reminds him, "there wasn't time!" At length, 0915 pulls alongside LX-318, and McCauley and Thyssen suit up and exit to go aboard. Thyssen, momentarily immersed in the star field before him, murmurs, "I'd almost forgotten..." McCauley interrupts his reverie with a brusque, "Let go" and the two men float over to their objective.

In the vacuum of space, McCauley and Thyssen traveled at the same speed as their space vehicle. Magnetic shoes enabled them to walk on the metallic surface of the ship and, by using their jet packs, in effect, as miniature rockets, they propel themselves across space to the nuclear rocket that had to be deactivated.

Once aboard, Thyssen instructs McCauley to watch the atomic gauge on the NR-1 pile while he attempts inserting the rods mechanically. He is appreciably alarmed to discover that the pile is already reading critical. Collision with the Moon is also computed at 33 minutes, so their movements assume renewed urgency. Back on the rocket, Captain Barrett radios that Ground Control wants them to relay their activities step-by-step. Thyssen is perplexed by the order, but McCauley conjectures, "Well, I guess if or when we make a mistake, they figure we won't be around to make a report on it." Thyssen begins dissecting various mechanisms and is ready to move the rods by hand. He positions McCauley on the opposite side at the gauge and cautions him to call out if the needle moves to the right. "I know," the colonel interjects. "Yell–or *stardust*." Thyssen resumes turning the rods when the heavy compartment door suddenly slams on his hand, crushing it. He passes out from pain, forcing McCauley to take his place. "Ed!" a panicked Barrett declares, "zero is in–!" "*I know!*" McCauley angrily cuts him off. Back on Earth, Doctor Parsons tries guiding the colonel along, but cannot figure which way to turn the control dial. With anxious moments ticking by, he informs McCauley, "You don't know how!" "Can you give me an alternative?" the colonel ponders. "I can try to guide you," the doctor gobbles, "but I am not there. I might be wrong!" The colonel dryly counters, "Then I can always blame you." McCauley struggles with the second drive, asking which way he should turn it. "Someone has got to check that reading!" he shouts. "There's no *someone* around," McCauley calmly notes. When Parsons cannot decide which way to turn the dial, McCauley suggests solving the problem "scientifically" and asks if he has a coin. "Tails, I turn it to the left, heads I turn it to the right." The doctor flips it and call out tails. "I hope it's your lucky coin," the colonel says and, after an interminable struggle, he yanks the control free. Cheers erupt at the control station and Parsons informs him that the pile is now loose and can be removed. "Are you still with me?" he ponders. "We're not exactly stardust," McCauley quips. "Let me ask you a question. Would you be willing to sell that lucky coin of yours?" Parsons gladly agrees, then McCauley and a groggy Thyssen work their way back to rocket 0915, atomic pile in hand. On board, the doctor mentions he has to call Helen as "she likes to keep in touch." His voice comes beaming over the Ground Control radio and he says, "Funny girl, she worries about eggheads!"

"Moonquake"

(Aired November 11, 1959)

Starring: Arthur Franz (Captain Tom Farrow), Denver Pyle (Doctor Peter Riber), Bek Nelson, Ross Elliott, Brit Lomond, Robert Karnes, Ann Doran, Mike Keene, Leonard Graves, Sumner Williams

Script: William Templeton

Directed by: Lee Sholem

Technical advisor: Major Charles A. Berry, U.S.A.F.

> *The story you are about to see is not true; it hasn't happened—yet. These are scenes from that story, a story that will happen soon. Just as man experienced his first earthquake, he will one day feel his first moonquake. This is the story of people—people who traveled 240,000 miles into outer space to answer the question, "What is the Moon made of?"*

Mrs. Jane Farrow startles groggily in her hospital bed, then calls the nurse. The latter approaches and asks what is wrong and Mrs. Farrow complains that the moonlight, beaming in through an open window, has woken her up. As the nurse moves over the shut the blinds, she reconsiders and asks that they be kept open. "I want to see the moon," she murmurs. The nurse, somewhat puzzled, relents and states, "I suppose a lot of people will be looking at the Moon tonight." Jane Farrow presses her by asking, "Is there any more news of the *Trailblazer?*" The nurse mentions that they will probably land tomorrow morning and ponders, "Just think, the men on her will be on the Moon for breakfast!" Jane changes the topic to her car accident and anxiously inquires if any news has appeared in the media. "No," the nurse assures her, "all the news is about the spaceship. Automobile accidents have to take second place." Curiously, Mrs. Farrow does not want word of her plight to reach her husband. "He'd worry about me," Jane insists. "You see, he's going to be one of the men breakfasting on the Moon tomorrow morning."

On *Trailblazer I*, radioman Tom Farrow listens intently to a German broadcaster discussing their flight. "Well, that's the news of the world, folks–and we're certainly it, especially you, colonel," he informs them. When pressed by crewmates to translate fully, Farrow states that the world lays awake for news of McCauley's men have landed on the Moon to examine its crust over the next seven days. "Tom Farrow, the communications officer–that's me–is known to be particularly intrepid," he declares in mock awe. A crewman responds, "Get a home station to see what they're really saying about you!" Farrow obliges him and a report comes over about Jane Farrow being injured in a car accident. McCauley, sensing their trajectory has become adrift, demands to know how far they have traveled in the past two seconds and asks for navigation tape K-22. Farrow, apparently shaken by the news, hands him the wrong tape. "What are you trying to do, get us killed?" Captain Robbins remonstrates. "That's enough of that, Robbins!" McCauley growls and corrective measures are taken. Within minutes, McCauley begins guiding *Trailblazer* toward the lunar surface. "Prepare for vertical orientation," he commands.

> For the spaceship to land on the Moon, McCauley first changed its position by using the ship's gyroscope, then fired its rocket to counteract the gravitational pull of the Moon.

No sooner does the *Trailblazer* settle than McCauley divides the six men up into pairs to work on the surface. Farrow, however, will remain in the ship to man the radio and McCauley instructs him to inform Ground Control that they have landed. The colonel then smiles and says, "Ask for a complete report on Mrs. Farrow." Farrow thanks him for his concern. "Let me ask you something," McCauley interjects. "If you had known about your wife's accident before we took off, would you have given up your place on the ship." Farrow reflects momentarily, then states, "Only if staying behind would have helped." McCauley continues, "Is there anything you can do that a good doctor can't do?" "No, if I was there I would have helped her," Farrow murmurs. "Would she have wanted you to stay?" the colonel continues. "No, I suppose not," Farrow concedes. McCauley concludes his little session with a smile. "My guess is knowing that her husband has landed on the Moon safely is going to do her more good than anything else." "Thanks again, colonel," Farrow replies, somewhat relieved. Once down in the compartment bay, McCauley lectures the men, noting, "We have a big job to do and only seven days to do it in." He informs them on the exact grid coordinates they are to examine, ordering them to report any new positions immediately.

In order to determine the composition of the Moon's crust and what might be the structure below it, McCauley and his crew went about the difficult task of boring into the surface of the Moon, setting charges, and detonating them so that a seismograph could record the shocks of the explosions. All of the information would then be carefully analyzed to give Man the answers to the mystery of the Moon's structure.

Back at the hospital, a radio reports news of the Moon expedition as highly successful and the nurse states, "Well, they'll be home in a few days, Mrs. Farrow. Time to rest now, you want to be looking your best." She smiles, then glances balefully at the nighttime sky. On the Moon, McCauley informs the men, "One more piece of pie to cut, then we head for home." However, dissent ensues when Robbins protests being assigned to work with Farrow. "Do I get extra pay for the danger involved?" he demands and asserts that yesterday Farrow set a double charge of explosives that nearly killed them both. McCauley, to quell the mutiny, assigns Robbins to work with Brugle while the colonel will work with the unpopular radioman himself. At that moment, Farrow descends the ladder, resents the change, and demands to know why it was made. "Those are my orders," is McCauley's blunt response and the teams disperse. "I don't need a chaperon!" Farrow protests, then sheepishly apologizes for his subpar performance of late. McCauley reassures him. "On a mission like this, you've got to expect a few emergencies," he declares. "Let's... try and not create them, huh?" Farrow agrees by noting, "Very well, sir."

Outside, the men detonate charges at regular intervals, which is successfully recorded and transmitted back to control headquarters. There, the commanding general informs Dr. Strauss, the project head, who opines, "Perhaps before I die, I'll be able to make the flight?" "In ten years they'll be building supermarkets on the Moon," the general cheerfully predicts.

Back on the Moon, McCauley finishes preparations to set off the final test charge, but the final blast precipitates a severe reaction on the seismograph. "Pattern irregular! Pattern irregular!" Doctor Riber screams over the radio. "Moonquake! All stations! Moonquake!" Before it subsides, Farrow is sent tumbling into a chasm and *Trailblazer* topples over on its side. The men race back to the wreckage to find Riber dazed but unhurt. "Moonquake," he murmurs. "Who would have imagined that?" However, the ship's communications gear is smashed beyond repair and Robbins concedes, "It's gonna take a radio genius to put this mess back together." However, only Farrow can fix it and he has yet to report back. McCauley quickly sets out after him before his oxygen runs out. Back on Earth, the general inquires if the expedition has checked in and the sergeant tells him no. Meanwhile, McCauley's progress is slowed by the numerous fissures that have opened, so, utilizing the Moon's one-sixth gravity, he begins jumping over them. At length, he encounters Farrow, who is injured and has a broken radio of his own. The two men struggle back to the *Trailblazer* and the colonel instructs Robbins and Brugle to meet them with spare oxygen tanks. "Fissures make it impossible to continue any farther," McCauley reports. "I estimate we each have a half-hour of oxygen. If Robbins and Brugle don't make it here with spare tanks in fifteen minutes, I'll transfer my oxygen to Farrow." Riber protests, "Colonel, what's the idea?" McCauley explains, "Farrow has got to get back. He's the only one of us who can restore communications." Brugle and Robbins, listening in, redouble their efforts and arrive with spare tanks as planned. When the fissure between them is too big to safely jump, they toss them across. Fadden is then dispatched from the ship with a 30-foot ladder. A makeshift bridge is lowered across the chasm and McCauley crosses with no difficulty. However, the limping Farrow slips through the rungs and nearly falls through before the men can pull him to safety.

At the hospital, the nurse informs Jane Farrow that scientists think explosions on the sun are interfering with radio communications between Earth and the Moon; hence *Trailblazer's* silence. "I am not worried," she murmurs. "I know Tom's still alive. I think he'll find a way to..." She gasps, fighting back tears, then asks, "Am I am being very foolish?" The nurse empathizes and tells her, "No, Mrs. Farrow, I don't think you are." "I love him so much," Jane confesses. Once back at the ship, Farrow examines the radio and estimates he needs at least 30 hours to effect repairs. "If I work straight through, the sooner I'll know–the sooner *we'll* know what they plan to do about us," he insists. Nearly a full day passes before Farrow restores communications. McCauley finally informs Ground Control of their plight. "Thank God, you're all alive!" the general exclaims. "We've been trying to reach you by radio!" The men are further heartened to learn that a rescue rocket will be launched immediately and that they should be off the Moon in 52 hours. Dr. Riber exclaims, "Tom, did you hear that!" The exhausted Farrow, however, is fast asleep. Riber wants to wake him, but McCauley cuts him short, insisting, "No, let him sleep. He's heard all the news he wants to hear." The rescue rocket eventually lifts off from the Moon, carrying McCauley and his crew back home.

At the hospital, a bed-ridden Jane Farrow is listening to the radio with her eyes closed when husband Tom sneaks in asks, "Who needs sleep?" Jane opens her eyes and darts upward to kiss and hug Tom, demanding, "How did you get here?" McCauley then steps into the room with a bouquet of flowers, direct from the crew of the *Trailblazer*. Jane tells him she supposes all the wives were on hand to greet their men and says, "I was feeling pretty sorry for myself, too!" McCauley humorously implies that "I suppose that all wives have a right to feel sorry for themselves." "You know, one thing I've learned, colonel," Jane insists. "Wives with husbands on the Moon shouldn't look up–while driving in traffic!" A smiling Farrow gives his wife another big kiss.

FLIGHT CAPSULE

STAGE 2

STAGE 1

XMP-

P512-146

"Space Trap"

(November 18, 1959)

Starring: Peter Hansen (Doctor Charles Cooper), Robert Gist (Captain Dan Freer), Russ Conway (General Devon), Dallas Mitchell (Lieutenant Pat Warren), Ronald Foster (Lieutenant Neil Templeton), Michael Chapin, Joe Haworth

Script: Marianne Mosner and Francis Rosenwald

Directed by: Charles Haas

Technical adviser: Major Charles A. Berry, U.S.A.F.

The story you are about to see hasn't happened yet. These are scenes from that story, which will happen someday as Man begins to make repeated probes to the Moon. As in other fields, there will be some mechanical failures and some human failures. This is the story of the attempted rescue of a spaceship in trouble and of her crew, sealed helplessly within her cabin.

After days on the Moon, Doctor Charles Cooper, biologist on the space research program, prepared to return to Earth, his mission accomplished: the gathering of spores which might prove the possible existence of some form of life on the Moon. Assisting Doctor Cooper in loading the invaluable data and cultures of active Moon spores, the ship's navigator, Lieutenant Neil Templeton. The commanding officer, Captain Dan Freer, approved a routine check of the Moonship for departure.

On the Moon, Captain Freer begins pre-flighting MR-127 and inquires, "How's things out there, Doc?" "Everything under control, Dan," crackles the reply. Doctor Cooper and Lieutenant Templeton finish taking soil samples, then return to their vessel. Once inside, Cooper begins storing his valuable samples and Templeton drawls out, "How's our little ol' spores doing?" "Resting comfortably, we hope," Cooper declares. When Freer jests Cooper sounds like he just finished robbing Fort Knox, the doctor assures him, "Dan, all the gold in Fort Knox couldn't buy what's in here if my theory holds up." Templeton interjects that Cooper might win a medal, to which Freer adds, "Maybe you'll get the Nobel Prize." "Never mind, fellas," a disinterested Cooper notes. "Just get me back to my lab." Freer jokingly adds that his own kids are probably checking him on their celestial map and Templeton, not to be outdone, interjects, "You know, the last time out, my wife called the base and I told her 'Honey, you don't have to worry–there's no women out there in that space!'" Laughs ensue, then Freer contacts Ground Control to confirm liftoff in 12 minutes and commences his final instrument check.

Using standard procedure of converting the landing legs of the rocket to a launching pad for takeoff, the men in the MR-127 began their 240,000-mile return trip to Earth and their families.

Back at Ground Control, General Devon inquires as to the progress of events, which Colonel McCauley assures is flawless. Devon, visibly pleased, then departs, requesting that the colonel keep him posted.

Minutes after blastoff, the MR-127 dropped its booster on schedule for its reentry pattern into Earth's atmosphere.

As MR-127 coasts closer to Earth, Lieutenant Templeton jests to Captain Freer, "Hope we hit *Terra Firma* on time, Captain. I got me a date with a redhead–my wife!" "At your service, Lieutenant," Freer beams with a smile. "Far be it from me to louse up an Air Force man's schedule." Doctor Cooper, listening intently, declares, "You guys don't sound like astronauts–more like commuters. I'm getting to feel like one myself." Freer make another routine check-in with Ground Control as he passes the halfway point and Colonel McCauley gets on the microphone to declare, "I am speaking for all of us down here, you've done a great job. Doctor Cooper, how are you feeling?" The doctor mentions that he and his spores are doing fine and states, "If they live up to my expectations, all of you fellas will go down in the history of biology." Freer cuts in to declare that he will check in again at 0800 hours. However, MR-127 fails to report at the designated time and tensions mount at Ground Control. Frantic pleas for a reply elicit no response and McCauley murmurs, "I don't like this, they're *way* overdue. Keep trying." The colonel explains the situation to General Devon; then, noting the ship is way off course, gets on the radio and declares, "MR-127–urgent–if you read me, switch to ground control so we can take over. Confirm!" Nothing but silence ensues. The controller ponders how they can guide the vessel if the crew does not respond and the colonel grimly concedes, "We can't." McCauley explains to General Devon that the ship is approaching Earth's atmosphere at 24,000 miles per hour, whereupon they will disintegrate. The general immediately orders a simulated rendezvous with another rocket computed while attempts to establish contact continue. A perplexed McCauley confesses, "I don't get it. The meta-track shows flying performance okay, the ship is handling well–" Devon cuts him short. "The only other alternative is something happened to the crew." "We can't very well tell from down here," McCauley concedes. "The only way to make sure is go up there." Worse, the estimated rendezvous time shows only an hour's window, at which time MR-127 will already be in the atmosphere. Rescue appears impossible until McCauley suggests shortening pre-flight preparations and simply lifting off. Devon reluctantly consents; McCauley will be taking Lieutenants Dobbs and Warren as crewmates. "I'll get the countdown started," Devon informs the colonel.

The MR-127 rushed on silently--a ghost ship in space. Without guidance from Earth or a pilot aboard, it would smash into Earth's atmosphere in ten short hours. A rocket on its launching pad takes six hours to prepare for takeoff. With every emergency procedure thrown into action, the MR-101, sister ship of the MR-127, with Colonel McCauley in command, began its ascent from the Earth's surface four hours and twenty-eight minutes later.

Now in orbit, McCauley continues calling out to MR-127 without effect. "I don't understand it and I still don't believe in premonitions," he declares. "You may recall a strange coincidence, Pat, but just before he took off, Doctor Cooper told me he had an odd feeling he wasn't going to make it back." Warren counters, "Stuck on the Moon–anybody would get an odd feeling." Suddenly, MR-127 appears on the radar scope and McCauley begins maneuvering to pull alongside. That done, he suits up and prepares to sortie outside. Ground Control tracking places them at only 43,000 miles from Earth, perilously coasting in at 18,000 miles per hour.

With their safety margin shrinking, both ships and their crews raced Earthward through space at ever-increasing speed—56 minutes left. McCauley, traveling at the same speed as his spaceship, could stay alongside it unless he himself exerted a force that would push him away. In order to prevent floating in this weightless condition, McCauley depended on magnetic shoes to permit him to walk almost normally on the metallic surface of the ship. To examine the hull of the MR-127, McCauley cautiously used his jet pack to propel himself through space.

The colonel alights on the MR-127 and begins examining the outer hull for any damage. He radios Ground Control that nothing is visible and he is unable to open the airlock from outside. General Devon orders him to determine if anyone is still alive and do so as quickly as possible.

Always aware of no atmosphere in space to carry sound, McCauley had to rely on touching his helmet to the hull to hear any response to his signal, if there was to be one from within the ship.

McCauley pounds on the MR-127 several times, hoping for a response. None is forthcoming and he requests further orders. General Devon, assuming the crew is dead, orders him to commence Operation Salvage: cutting into the hull and retrieving the valuable spore samples. He has only 48 minutes. "If I cut into this hull," Mc-Cauley advises, "I'll be releasing cabin pressure. If anybody in there is alive, he'll be killed instantly." Devon assures him that no other option remains.

MR-127 plunged toward flaming destruction as it approached the Earth's atmosphere.

Back on MR-101, McCauley struggles with doubts as he begins preparing a cutting torch. "I get the feeling that someone is still alive in there and will die if I cut that hull," he opines. His crewmates try dissuading him, but the colonel persists. "What could have happened? No porthole blown out, no escape hatches unsecured. What else could it be, lack of cabin pressure?" Warren curtly reminds him, "If it's oxygen, they're dead by now." McCauley, beset by a troubling flash of insight, murmurs, "No, but if it's carbon dioxide not being absorbed, they may still be alive. I want to try something." The colonel asks and receives permission to pump oxygen into the MR-127 before cutting the hull. General Devon concurs and McCauley floats back to the stricken craft. A hose is attached, air begins flowing, and he bangs on the hull once more–still no response. The colonel informs General Devon and he is about to begin cutting. Pausing one last time, McCauley knocks again and a groggy Doctor Cooper knocks back. Operation Salvage is suspended and McCauley instructs Cooper to open the airlock manually. McCauley enters and can now pilot MR-127 to safety with only seven minutes left. As both vessels safely reenter, General Devon, relieved, asks the colonel what may have caused the problem. "Well, as far as I can determine, there was a stoppage in the carbon dioxide absorbing system," he states. "It would take an emergency action. Everybody can relax." The crew is fine and already looking forward to their next trip–home.

Days later, McCauley meets up with Doctor Cooper, who has apparently forgotten the awards banquet being thrown in his honor. He hands Cooper his dress jacket and inquires if the latter has had any "strange feelings" or premonitions lately. Cooper abruptly tells him, "I don't believe in them." "I do," McCauley notes with a grin. "I had one when I was about to cut that hull open!"

P512-25

"Asteroid"

(Aired November 25, 1959)

Starring: Bill Williams (Doctor Stacy Croydon), Herbert Rudley (Doctor Waring), Joyce Meadows (Lynn Croydon), Walter Reed, Bill Crane, Lionel Ames, Richard Bull

Script: Ted Sherdeman

Directed by: Lee Sholem

Technical advisor: Major Charles A. Berry, U.S.A.F

> *The story you are about to see isn't true, it hasn't happened—yet. These are scenes from that story, which may happen soon. Scientists for years have attempted to study fragments called asteroids. One of these asteroids has recently come closer to Earth than ever previously observed. You are about to see the story of a group of men who plan to actually land a spaceship on one of these asteroids.*

Colonel McCauley, General Barker, and several scientists closely examine the photo of an asteroid christened "Skyra." Doctor Waring hypothesizes that asteroids are the remnants of a major planet that once existed between the orbits of Mars and Jupiter, but was somehow destroyed. His colleague, Doctor Stacy Croydon, disagrees, simply declaring them the "junk" of the Solar System. "I don't see that it matters," Barker declares. "The fact remains, the thing is up there at an obtainable altitude of 3,000 miles and its orbit thus far shows a barely perceptible K factor." Despite its present stability, Waring predicts that Sykra will gradually fall into the Earth's atmosphere and become a huge meteorite. Almost two miles long and a mile thick, it is too big and too close to ignore, so Barker orders McCauley to take a ship to land on the errant body to determine if a space station can be established on it. His flight will be preceded by a series of unmanned reconnaissance probes to gather data.

> *Unmanned reconnaissance rockets were sent into orbit around the asteroid to probe into Skyra's secrets, sending back to Earth the information their instruments gathered, information that was carefully analyzed and studied by scientists in order to give the answer to the question, "Should Skyra be explored in an attempt to use it as a space platform?"*

Doctor Waring subsequently informs General Barker that, based on information gathered by the probes, it may be possible to employ Astra as a space station. McCauley asks what if it should be impractical and if the asteroid becomes a meteorite. "Well, its mass is large enough so that a large portion of it may very well survive the final plunge into our atmosphere–another Arizona crater." "And if it lands in a populated area?" McCauley asks. The general states they have two choices, which the colonel summarizes as either use it or destroy it. "Which rather neatly states your mission, Colonel McCauley," Barker fires back. "You take Doctor Croydon, Major Emory, and Captain Draper with you."

At the Croydon residence, the doctor and McCauley step out into the front lawn, where wife Lynn is grooming one of their prize-winning show dogs. "He's the most conceited dog I've ever seen," she informs him. McCauley grins and quips, "You know, if I was as pretty as he is, I'd be conceited, too!" He then inquires how she feels about Stacy making the flight. Lynn puts on a good face and, after some hesitation, says he wants to go, so she supports it. Stacy jokingly assures that he will not flirt with any female Martians he encounters. "Or any other kind, mister!" she jests in mock anger. Her countenance suddenly becomes serious and she asks McCauley what it is like out in space. McCauley reflects momentarily, then emotes, "It's cold and black." Stacy also gives his take on conditions, but Lynn wants to hear from the colonel directly. "Well, it's kind of hard to explain," he waxes philosophically. "It's something to be experienced, not described. Tell you one thing, though: no man can feel very important once he's been out there." Before departing, Stacy promises to bring her back a piece of Skyra. "You'll be the only woman with a hunk of asteroid set in a ring." "Just bring yourself back," she murmurs. "Oh, that's Ed's job," Stacy counters. "He's doing the driving." The two men then drive off while Lynn anxiously watches them pass from view.

Once in orbit, McCauley asks Doctor Croydon if he is okay. "Just a slight feeling that I've left my stomach somewhere on the ground," he moans. At length, the rocket approaches Skyra and the crew begins checking the radiation levels and scouting possible landing sites. "I can't believe it," Doctor Croydon exclaims. "I'm about to actually set foot on an asteroid. Now I know how Columbus felt when he discovered a new land!" The asteroid is declared safe, but McCauley cannot find a landing zone, so he decides to hover above its surface, then moor the craft by cables. Waring chimes in that since Astra is composed mainly of iron, magnetic boots should allow them to walk around easily despite a lack of gravity. As the doctor suits up, McCauley cautions him to keep the sun shield down on his visor to filter out harmful rays. "Each time we turn into the sun, it won't be slowly," he lectures. "Sudden glare could blind us." Then he, Draper, and the doctor suit up and head into the air lock.

Since Skyra had no gravity and was orbiting in space, McCauley first tested its metallic content to determine whether it was possible to walk on Skyra without being spun off.

Colonel McCauley, Captain Draper, and Doctor Croydon make their way to the surface, carefully navigating the towering, jagged topography around them. McCauley declares, "Skyra's surface has a high metallic content, magnetic shoes should hold us." He gently jets his way from the ship, secures a tether line, and is soon joined by the other two.

McCauley and Draper secured the spaceship to Skyra because Skyra's erratic orbit might leave the men stranded on the surface if the ship and the asteroid separate.

The colonel reports the zero-gravity conditions present, but magnetic shoes appear to be functioning, plus they can use their jet packs in an emergency. With their vessel secured, the three men being exploring their surroundings. "Doctor Waring," McCauley states, "your prediction about the asteroid being unrideable might well prove to be true." The colonel and Captain Draper commence their surface exploration while Doctor Croydon ambles off to gather geologic samples.

Colonel McCauley and his crew had the rare experience of being the first men to ever set foot on a fragment of some distant star. But the awesomeness of seeing for the first time a portion of another world did not lessen the dangers.

A decent interval passes, then McCauley reports in. "We are approximately 1,500 yards from the tie-down site. We have not yet found any level surfaces sufficient in size to accommodate the building of a space station."

In order to find their way back to the spaceship, guidelines had to be carefully fastened to metal pins, as each move forward opened new and mysterious vistas.

Having an opportunity given to few men, Doctor Croydon wanted to bring back as many rare samples of the asteroid's surface as possible in order that scientists and astronomers might probe deeper into the origins of this visitor from outer space.

While examining an outcropping, Doctor Croydon suddenly begins floating and he informs McCauley of encountering a magnetic-free zone. "Keep the guideline in view at all times, Stacy," the colonel warns. "Don't wander too far away from it." Ground Control, at the behest of Doctor Waring, asks Croydon if he has evaluated the surface composition. The doctor informs them, "So far, the surface has revealed all three classes of composition we found in meteorites which have reached Earth. This area I am now on has a fused, glassy appearance and seems to contain no metals. Magnetic boots will not hold at all in this spot." He concludes by noting a very interesting outcropping and makes his way to it. McCauley also observes that gravity conditions have not improved and that stockpiling of building or construction materials on Astra is impractical. "I will activate the alternative plan and proceed to set charges and destroy it," the colonel reports. "Should be about two hours. Will inform you when ready."

Knowing that Skyra would have to be destroyed before it became a flaming meteor that might crash to Earth, McCauley and Draper were faced with the task of setting huge charges of explosives deep below the surface of Skyra that would shatter the asteroid into fragments, which would burn up as they attempted to enter the Earth's atmosphere.

McCauley orders Draper and Croydon to return to the vehicle immediately, but the doctor hesitates long enough to collect an intriguing sample. "I've got it and it's a beauty," he assures the colonel. McCauley, about to arm the detonator, summarily orders Croydon back to the ship before the asteroid explodes in 10 minutes. However, after inadvertently lifting the sun shield from his visor, Croydon is blinded by the intense sunlight and collapses. McCauley arrives back at the ship, only to discover that the doctor never returned and immediately sets out to disarm the detonator. Draper, meanwhile, retraces Croydon's step to bring him back. Back in the ship, Major Emory warns that they have four and a half minutes left. Draper asks the colonel if it is possible to disarm the detonator in time. McCauley concedes, "That's a good question!" A somber McCauley then instructs all hands, "At two minutes, Draper has to return to the vehicle. If I haven't disarmed the detonator in an additional one and a half minutes, Emory is to cast off and at full power get away from here." General Barker, alarmed at possibly losing his best astronaut, orders McCauley to abandon the rescue mission and depart immediately. "Ed, do you read me? Acknowledge!" he bellows. The colonel, feigning deafness, simply mumbles, "Can't understand you, general, too much static..." Barker angrily slams the microphone down in frustration.

The timing device on the automatic detonator ticked off the seconds towards destruction. McCauley had to find and disarm it while

Draper searched desperately for Doctor Croydon. Each man looked for a mark of the trail they had previously traveled.

Draper, floating above the crevices, luckily locates Doctor Croydon and calls in, "Colonel, he seems to be blind. His radio is smashed." Meanwhile, Colonel McCauley feverishly scouts around to find the detonator. Major Emory calls out, "Colonel-one minute and 45 seconds left before detonation. Can you get back here in time?" "No." Fortunately, Draper assists the ailing doctor aboard and McCauley peremptorily orders, "Blast off, get away from Sykra right now! Acknowledge, Henry." Emory complies, but no sooner do they depart than McCauley stumbles upon the detonator and stops it. Momentarily resting his head on his hands, he declares, "I made it... *just!*" "Ahh, you live right, colonel," Emory emotes, "We're coming back to get you." Cheers also erupt back at Ground Control and this time, McCauley does not rearm the detonator until the rocket is looming directly overhead. Once back in space, all hands watch the asteroid erupt in flame and disappear while the colonel makes his report. "This is McCauley calling launch base. We are returning home, mission accomplished-at considerable cost. Doctor Croydon has been blinded."

Outside the Croydon residence, McCauley pulls up and greets Lynn while the doctor walks down the street in heavy sunglasses, assisted by a seeing-eye dog. Surprised, the colonel exclaims, "Say, I thought the medics said that Stacy's eyes would be all right." She explains that they are fine; her husband is simply training seeing-eye dogs to help others. "I am not breeding show dogs anymore, just guide dogs," the doctor declares. Looking at the puppies running amok, McCauley states he is glad his son Pete isn't around, then Lynn insists he take home one. "But you've got to make us one promise," she intones. "Name it *Skyra*—" pointing to her new ring, fashioned from the former asteroid.

"Edge of Eternity"

(Aired December 2, 1959)

Starring: Joyce Taylor, Corey Allen, Kem Dibbs, Mary Webster, Louis Jean Heydt, Sue Carlton, Clark Howat, Hal Hamilton

Script: Kalman Phillips

Directed by: Nathan Juran

Technical advisor: Colonel Lawrence D. Ely, U.S.A.F

> *The story you are about to see has not happened yet. These are scenes from that story that will happen when men such as these travel in space and must surround themselves with an artificial atmosphere, similar to that on Earth. If this fails to function, death would be inevitable. In the story you are about to see, these men on an expedition to the Moon are brought to the very edge of eternity by just such a failure while their families await their return.*

At a gala party, Doctor Summers interrupts the revelries to call forward the crew and the spouses of a forthcoming Moon expedition. "I'll call the roll," he announces and beckons Colonel Ed McCauley and his wife Mary, Lieutenant Johnny Baker and his shy fiancée, Ellen, and Major Hardy Stockman and his bawdy, outgoing mate Pat. Summers next presents each pilot with a framed photo of his beloved, insisting, "These are just to remind you that, no matter what you find up there, the good things are back here on Earth."

A gay sendoff party, but a serious mission. McCauley and his crew spend two weeks on the Moon gathering samples of soil, rocks, and minerals that, when analyzed, might show Man how to use the Moon as a source of the elements that might enable him to live there. Their mission was accomplished except for the 240,000 mile return trip to space station Astra orbiting the Earth.

"Everybody set to go home?" McCauley asks while strapping himself in. Major Stockman, casting a baneful glance at youthful Baker, blares out, "Lover boy's been ready ever since we came!" Baker, taking the jibe in stride, counters, "I didn't see you buying any Moon rings!" The colonel shuts them both up long enough to commence their launch sequence. Lunar Expedition C-12 departs flawlessly and the ship maneuvers directly for space station Astra orbiting the Earth. "Oh, boy," Stockman murmurs. "Just two days away from Patsy's good old-fashioned home cooking..." Suddenly, the rocket shudders and begins losing control. "Switching to emergency power," McCauley barks. "Close all vents!" They have apparently been struck by a meteorite and, once things stabilize, damage is assessed and it appears minor. However, Baker notices the gauge on the cabin oxygen reserve and declares, "It's falling off–it's venting." McCauley and Baker subsequently suit up to check damage to the aft section while Stockman pilots the ship.

As feared, McCauley finds a large section of damaged pipe from which the air supply was lost. "How are we going to get back to the space station without a reserve supply of oxygen?" Baker ponders. "I wish I could answer that," the colonel concedes. "Maybe Major Briggs can." Once inside, McCauley relays his predicament to Briggs at the space station. He explains that they have enough air left for 16 hours, with another 12 hours in the suit tanks–making 28 hours altogether. Briggs observes they need twice that amount to reach the station and he offers to arrange a deep orbit rendezvous with a rescue rocket from Canaveral. "And remember," McCauley lectures, "if it isn't within 28 hours, it's too late." Back on Earth, Mary, Pat, and Ellen are enjoying coffee together and Mary notes the young bride-to-be can't take her eyes off the clock. "It's my date with Johnny," she says dreamily. "We think about each other every hour on the hour." The two wives smile approvingly. The ladies also hope that their men are getting ready to return and Ellen balefully suggests, "I'd hate to have to change the date on the wedding invitation."

Back in space, Briggs relays bad news to the crew. "We've tried everything. The best we can do is a ship that's now refueling that can reach 100,000-mile orbit when you do," he states. "Our oxygen should make it. What's the catch?" McCauley demands. "They have to orbit on the other side of the Earth. It would take you longer to rendezvous with them than with us," Briggs continues. "Sorry." Accepting his fate, McCauley fathoms that there is enough combined oxygen in their portable tanks to keep one person alive until the end. Baker and Stockman recoil at the idea of sacrificing two men to save one, but the colonel brushes off their dismay. McCauley then informs them that he is sacrificing himself up front, leaving the other men to draw lots. "Ed, this is no time to pull rank!" Baker protests. "I'm pulling rank!" the colonel barks back. Then Stockman matter-of-factly declares, "I won't do it, Ed." McCauley angrily reminds him, "This isn't a request–*it's an order*!" He then snaps a pencil in two, presents them to the men, and Baker draws the long piece. "Good luck, kid," Stockman says, greatly relieved by losing. "Get the tanks on, Johnny," McCauley insists. "Kiss the bride for me." "Me, too," Stockman chimes in. As the distressed Baker goes aft, McCauley and Stockman occupy themselves by writing a couple of final letters.

Back at the McCauley residence, Ellen shows off her first wedding presents to Mary, then the phone rings. Ellen passes it to her, noting the base is calling. "Are they on their way back?" she ponders. Mary's eyes widen as the bad news is relayed, but she struggles to hide her anxiety from ebullient Ellen. Back on the ship, air is running out and as McCauley and Stockman have trouble breathing, Baker looks on, disturbed. He then lifts his face plate, hands the men their suits and demands, "What am I to you, a mascot? Colonel, I'm sorry, I can't do it. A safe ticket home while you guys die is not for me. We started this with three and that's how we should finish." McCauley sympathetically nods, then lectures, "Look, I know how you feel, Johnny, but we're not going to throw a life away for no purpose." He snaps the lieutenant's face plate down and locks it. "How about that kid." Stockman smiles as he struggles to speak. "It's like getting a big boost for the main engine when you think the tanks are empty." "Main engine?" McCauley reflects. "It's a crazy chance, but there must be oxygen in there... 40 pounds... you know, it might work if we can connect that tank to the cabin pressure system." Baker again lifts his face plate and urges them to try. McCauley angrily orders him to lower it, but the lieutenant insists, "Colonel, there's a chance to save all of us, but you guys need this oxygen. Now it's three of us all the way!" McCauley reasons that if the valves are not damaged, it's still a long shot, and he asks young Baker, "You still want to throw away that one-way ticket home?" "I like this one better," he says with a smile. "Maybe three of us can ride on it for the price of one."

McCauley and Stockman suit up, go aft, and begin reconnecting the pipes. Spirits rise as oxygen begins flowing and Baker reports that the indicator needle is rising. Suddenly, a leak erupts and the air is lost. A few precious hours of life have been gained, but still not enough to reach the space station. McCauley relays the bad news to Briggs at Astra, who then switches to Dr. Summers at Canaveral. The doctor, who has been monitoring communication, advises McCauley that there might be a few pounds of liquid oxygen left in the fuel tank. All he has to do is orient his ship towards the sun so that the tank warms and the liquid turns to breathable gas. "Wish him luck from me," he concludes. "McCauley, it's a chance," Briggs notes. "Did you get it?" "I got it–every beautiful word," is the response. Deft maneuvering places the ship accordingly and he cautions, "We only have a few hours left in these tanks. Let's hope we'll have something to breathe when we take them off." Despite these innovations, only 10 pounds of pressure results and, worse, Dr. Summer computes that they remain two hours short of air to complete the journey. "Well," McCauley wearily concedes, "we still have a hope and a prayer." Briggs instructs him to set the vessel on automatic pilot so that it docks with the space station regardless of what happens. "We came close," Baker says. "Let's play it out to the end," the colonel remarks. Stockman then breaks in, "I wonder what the girls are doing?" "Quiet, you're wasting oxygen," McCauley bristles.

Hours later, Briggs inquires about the status of the ship and learns its trajectory is perfect for a station rendezvous. The major then radios McCauley to check on him and he groggily states that the men are still alive, if barely. "How much longer?" the colonel wearily asks. "A little more than an hour–think you can hold out?" The colonel states that if they do not, there are some letters they want sent directly down to Earth. Briggs does not respond and simply grimaces at the thought. The ship silently drifts to within docking range of Astra and Briggs hails them a final time, getting no response. "Trust McCauley to get back–dead or alive," he mutters. The vessel docks automatically and the station men rush inside with oxygen tanks to revive the crew if possible. "Well, they sure gave it a try," Briggs insists. Fortunately, the three astronauts begin stirring and McCauley's eyes flicker with life. "The colonel seems to be coming around," the major happily exclaims. "Well, *they made it!*"

Newlyweds John and Ellen Baker leave the church and fight their way to the car, bombarded by rice and best wishes. Ellen thanks the colonel for bringing her husband back, but McCauley, in faux anger, bellows, "You just better be back in two weeks because I have another assignment for you!" The couple races off, leaving the colonel to philosophize, "I supposed the wife of every spaceman has to get used to him being away so much." Turning to Mary, he empathizes, "It must get awfully dull for you." Mary simply flashes her smile and succinctly informs him, "Oh, it's many things, *but it's never dull!*"

"Burnout"

(Aired December 9, 1959)

Starring: John Sutton (Air Vice Marshal Malcolm Terry), Lance Fuller (Captain Bob Stark), Robert Clarke (Major Gibbie Gibson), Donna Martell (Molly Gibson), Barbara Bestar, Ken Drake, Tom McNamara

Script: Donald Duncan

Directed by: Alvin Ganzer

Technical advisor: Colonel Lawrence D. Ely, U.S.A.F.

> *The story you are about to see hasn't happened—yet. These are scenes from that story that will happen when Man develops newer and more highly complicated spaceships. This is the story of a test of a man and a machine, the dramatic moment to prove the ability to return to the Earth from outer space.*

In an industrial setting, Professor Emerson, British Air Vice Marshal Malcolm Terry, and Colonel McCauley observe new space materials under development. "This new metal alloy withstands temperatures high enough to permit reentry into the Earth's atmosphere approximately 4,000 miles per hour faster than before," Emerson lectures. Air Vice Marshal Malcolm informs him that the British National Space Agency has nonetheless questioned the smaller margins of safety inherent in this new approach. "Well, Sir," McCauley explains, "we feel we have an advantage in the steeper reentry pattern because of the recovery factor in the vehicle." Professor Emerson chimes in, noting that a ship would no longer have to circumnavigate the Earth to land, allowing for quicker recovery. Terry, arching his eyebrows, questions if anything going 21,000 miles per hour at temperatures of 3,700 degrees centigrade could ever be considered "routine." McCauley notes that, given the hundreds of unmanned tests that preceded it, "the first flight should be routine... relatively." Then Terry inquires what would happen in the event of an instrument malfunction and the colonel states that the crew is equipped with an escape capsule if necessary. "But colonel," the Air Vice Marshal insists, "instruments are not infallible." "In that case, Major Gibson can use his own judgment," McCauley informs him. "As we know, the first rule in space flying is fly on instruments."

Later, at a hotel poolside, Captain Bob Stark and Major Gibbie Gibson kill time by racing in the pool while McCauley suns himself. They are distracted by Nan, a pretty but wisecracking waitress, who brings them drinks and informs the major there is still no answer to his long-distance call. She also mentions that their laundry will be delivered by evening and says, "You needn't give me that 'top security' look. When all three of you place calls for your wives, it adds up to just one thing. There's going to be a launching!" Suddenly, McCauley alerts Gibson that his fiancée, Molly, just entered the gate, apparently looking for him. "No wonder she didn't answer the telephone!" he exclaims and bounds over to greet her. The waitress looks at the two men, smiles, and declares, "That's the occupational hazard of space–happy marriages!" Stark jokingly asks her not to rap the service and she insists, "I'm not rapping it. I'm trying to get in on it!" Meanwhile, as Stark and Molly joyfully claw at each other, McCauley walks up and yells, "Hey!" insisting on a kiss. Molly obligingly greets the colonel and Stark, inviting them to dinner. "Oh, no-no," he moans. "We've seen enough of him for the last three months. Tonight it's your turn." Shooting a hard look at Stark, McCauley mumbles, "Come on, Daddy-O."

Years of research, the work of many men, fused into a rocket waiting to find out if the new reentry vehicle can reenter the earth's atmosphere without burning up.

At Ground Control, Professor Emory explains to Air Vice Marshal Terry that the test flight will be conducted in daylight and over the ocean to avoid populated areas. "It's a short flight," he assures the colonel. "There are no *short* flights in space," McCauley corrects him. Within minutes, Stark and Gibson blast into high orbit, then they commence the intricate business of steep-angle reentry. With all instruments reading normal, they nose the ship over into the atmosphere and enter a period of radio blackout. "Well, that's the last we hear from them until they complete reentry," McCauley states. "These are the tough minutes to sweat out." Air Vice Marshal Terry seconds him, declaring, "I'd imagine we'd all prefer being up there." Meanwhile, no sooner does the rocket start descending than it begins to buffet violently. "I don't like the action of the ship," Gibson declares. "I don't either," Stark fires back. "Instruments check out okay."

The reentry vehicle plunged towards Earth at a speed and an angle never before attempted. The friction of the Earth's atmosphere caused the metal to glow with intense heat. The men attempted to control the ship's reentry path by skipping it out of its downward pattern.

Gibson and Stark briefly fire their retro-rockets for three seconds and the bucking momentarily stops, then resumes with renewed fury. The hull also begins emitting a strange grinding noise, further heightening the crew's anxiety.

Once again, the ship headed Earthward and encountered terrific buffeting and heating as it hit the barrier of the Earth's atmosphere.

Gibson, at this juncture, begins panicking and orders, "Prepare to eject!" Stark pleads with him to relent as his gauges still read normal. "Instruments okay!" he yells. "Don't!" At that precise moment, Gibson hits the switch, a drag shoot emerges, and the capsule separates from the ship. Stark responds to his superior with an angry glare. Back at Canaveral, a message from the radar station declares that they are tracking both the spaceship and its capsule. "They've ejected!" an incredulous McCauley announces, then orders all downrange vessels to rescue them. He slams the microphone down, extremely distressed. Nevertheless, the colonel, Professor Emerson, and Air Vice Marshal Terry are relieved when Gibson and Stark have been rescued unharmed. Later, the two officers duly report to McCauley's office and he grimly inquires, "What happened?" Gibson confesses that he ejected. The colonel then asks Stark for his version and he replies, "The instruments were reading normal and didn't warrant ejection." McCauley, flustered, claps his hands and informs them that an investigation will be scheduled. "Don't talk to anyone," he growls. "You're dismissed." The two officers no sooner depart than Air Vice Marshal Terry arrives and, noting McCauley's discomfort over the matter, inquires, "Tell me, will you try again?" "Well... we may have to go back to unmanned tests in the labs, but we'll try again," he reasons. "We'll have to change crews."

On the day the investigation opens, McCauley runs headlong into a pensive Molly, quite concerned for the fate of her fiancé. "Colonel McCauley, I think Gibbie saved Bob's life," she insists. "Well," he assures her, "Gibby did what he thought was best. Excuse me." The colonel takes his seat and the grilling begins. Emerson begins by pointing out his is a fact-finding panel, not a punitive one. "We are not here to establish guilt, but to determine cause," he insists. As it unfolds, neither Gibson nor Stark agree with the course of action taken, but both pilots concur their ship acted radically different and unexpectedly. Nonetheless, Stark insists his instruments indicated no danger. Gibson, however, maintains he did the right thing by abandoning ship, pointing to his extensive flying experience. Turning to McCauley, Emerson asks if manned missions represent too much inherent risk. "There's always risk flying in space," he lectures. "We've learned to face that fact when we joined the Air Force. I think this particular test is a well-calculated risk." Emerson congratulates McCauley on such a sanguine response and inquires if the tests should continue. "Oh, yes, I do," he states. "I think the steeper reentry pattern will be a great safety factor. The tests should continue." The hearing concludes and Gibson encounters Molly outside. She is disheartened to learn that test flights will resume and she hopes that they fail. The major rebukes her for feeling that way, seeing that Ed and Bob will fly it. "You know, darling," he continues, "for the first time in my life, I hope I am wrong."

After another series of successful unmanned tests, Colonel McCauley and Captain Stark prepared for another manned flight to prove the effectiveness of the new metal alloy and the reentry vehicle.

A rocket blazes upward, piloted by McCauley and Stark. Back at Canaveral, Air Vice Marshal Terry smiles and confides in Emerson. "You know something, Professor? I must be getting old. I'll be blasted if I can do what McCauley's doing all the time–relying on his instruments. Although I know he's right, I'm afraid that the instruments would... *lose out.*" Overhead, the colonel maneuvers to begin the reentry ritual, murmuring, "Well, here we go." Immediately, the ship begins shaking violently. Retro-rockets at 225,000 feet temporarily ameliorate the problems, then the colonel begin fearing for their safety.

McCauley and Stark face the exact conditions that were encountered in the ill-fated attempt made by Major Gibson, the extreme heating of the vehicle as it attempted to cut through the Earth's atmosphere and the pounding of the ship as it tried to change its reentry pattern. As the strain on the men and the ship increased, McCauley faced the decision whether to rely on instruments or on human judgment.

Struggling for composure, McCauley radios that instrument readings are normal but, with the ship bucking wildly, his hand hovers over the eject button. Before he can push it, the gyrations stop and the rocket assumes a smooth flight during reentry. "McCauley to Ground Control," he radios. "Reentry accomplished." Back at McCauley's office, Air Vice Marshal Terry drops by to say farewell to the colonel and Captain Stark. He lauds the test program and is keen to mention the contributions of Major Gibson. McCauley declares that he and Stark are on their way over to Gibson's house now, noting, "If he didn't eject, I would have!" The colonel explains, "He prepared us for what happened. Bob and I would like to tell him that." The Air Vice Marshal graciously asks to accompany them and the two officers happily oblige him.

Courtesy Landov Media.

"First Woman On the Moon"

(Aired December 16, 1959)

Starring: Nancy Gates (Renza Hale), Tyler McVey (Major General Norgrath), Harry Jackson   (Major Markey), H. M. Wynant (Major Hale), Norman Leavitt, Denny Niles, Max Huber

Script: James Clavell

Directed by: Herman Hoffman

Technical advisor: Colonel Lawrence D. Ely, U.S.A.F.

> *Today, the first man will go to the Moon and, just as surely, there will come a day when the first woman lands on the Moon. This is the story of that woman, Renza Hale, first woman to land on the Moon.*

Inside General Norgrath's office, Colonel McCauley and Captain Joseph Hale listen intently as their superior outlines their next Moon mission, which includes Moon Watch Experiment 667/8. "I think you'll be interested in the first and last paragraphs," he chortles. McCauley's and Markey's jaws drop as the general explains, in the interest of advancing science, a woman should be sent up for 90 days as a test subject. "In other words, we're ready to colonize the Moon. It's up to you to find out." McCauley cautiously nods and declares his approval. Norgrath continues reading his dossier regarding candidate selection. "But there is no way to forecast how a woman will react. If we test one, there is no reason to presuppose that her behavior pattern will be a guide for others. It is our observation on Earth that they, women, are merely a law onto themselves and there's nothing to suggest that they will be any different on the Moon." Closing the document with a smile, the general tells McCauley, "It's all yours, colonel. Use your own judgment." McCauley, somewhat bemused, pauses momentarily, then sputters, "Thank you, sir."

Back at the Hale residence, McCauley and Hale are greeted by Renza, the captain's attentive spouse. The two men sit silently, pondering their circumstance, and she intuitively deduces that something is afoot. Some hemming and hawing ensues, at which point Hale finally asks Renza if she would like to go to the Moon. Taking the joke in stride, she fires back, "All right, I can take a hint. You guys go ahead and talk." "No, I mean it," her husband insists. "Would you like to come?" McCauley also chimes in, "Really... would you like to spend 90 days on the Moon with Joe?" "Before or after dinner, darling?" she blurts, still in disbelief, then declares, "You're out of your mind!" Joe shrugs and says, "I told you it won't work." McCauley smilingly assures her, "There's always a first time for everything. We'll take you for three months." Renza asks what she will do on the Moon for three months. The colonel smiles and says, "Same things you do down here... housekeep, cook, take care of Joe..." She protests her lack of knowledge about science and astrophysics, to which McCauley mentions that is one reason why they selected her. "Sort of a guinea pig?" she asks. More haggling ensues, but finally Renza succumbs to their combined assault and agrees to join the expedition. "So you mean you'll go?" Joe ponders incredulously. "What, you mean the *Moon thing*?" she asks. "Why, of course–I thought it was all settled!" The three drink a toast and McCauley, basking in victory, says, "Cheers!"

For three weeks, Renza submits to the usual battery of tests and examinations for space flight, passing them with flying colors. However, she objects strenuously when informed that her luggage allotment is only ten pounds and she cannot imagine living without her favorite blouse and lipstick. "If you think I'm going to the Moon for three months with only ten pounds of luggage, you're out of your mind!" she snaps. "Ten pounds–that's the limit," Joe insists. Renza, knowing she's beaten, simply mutters, "All right." Joe, unconvinced, bristles, "What do you mean all right?" "Just all right," she states and slips out the door. "She's up to something," Joe warns. "They always are," McCauley cautions. That evening, the couple entwines under a starlit sky and Joe confesses he opposed the whole idea at first, but is glad she agreed. "No man wants to put his wife in danger," he assures her. The next day, the rocket lifts off with a roar and Renza Hale is on her way to the Moon.

Each time Man ventures into space, he faces many unknowns. On this journey, a woman's first time into space, there would be many more unknowns and Colonel McCauley watched every reaction Renza Hale made, for his reports would substantially influence future colonization of the Moon.

After a safe landing, the suited-up crew debarks and slowly threads their way to Moon Base.

Phase One of Experiment 677/8 successfully accomplished. Now started Phase Two, to determine Woman's adjustment to living on the Moon.

The Moon Base crew greets the newly-arriving astronauts and Renza is formally introduced to them. "Well, Renza, welcome to your new home," McCauley states. Looking askance at the threadbare surroundings, she becomes upset and cries on Joe's shoulder. "It's alright, Mac," he assures the colonel and takes his wife off to their quarters. The men are somewhat taken aback until Major Markey declares, "Those intriguers are pretty smart–they forecast those tears just like *that*."

Even for the men who lived in the confined quarters of the Moon base, adjustment was a problem. But what would it be to a woman, the only woman living in the world where the sky is always dark, whether it was day or night.

Renza spends her first few hours getting acquainted with the automated kitchenware, which sometimes snaps open and jolts her. Her anxiety mounts by the minute.

*Thirty-third day of Project First Woman. While Colonel McCauley
and the crew continue their projects on research and exploration of
the planet's surface, Renza Hale continued to try to adapt herself to
her strange environment.*

McCauley enters the cabin after returning from research, greets
Renza, and orders everyone to sit down at the table she has prepared for them. When the colonel asks how she is doing, she sarcastically reports all her statistics to date, concluding with a clinically
dry "667/8 Renza Hale." "Very good report, madam!" McCauley
jests. "We'll put it in the log." Joe then asks what they are having for
dinner, to which she responds, "Roast beef and Yorkshire pudding.
I think, gentlemen, I have at last mastered atomic cooking." The
food, however, is unpalatable in Renza's inexperienced hands, but
McCauley and the men feign enjoyment. "It tastes good, it's just a
little tough," Joe explains as Renza storms off to her quarters. Mc-
Cauley diplomatically leans over, taps him on the arm, and motions
him to follow.

*Day Fifty—Renza Hale showed signs of irritation. Contributing
factors, isolation, no telephone, no shops, no female companionship,
and the extremely small quarters of Moon Base.*

Renza, faced with the prospect of filling out yet another dreary
report, suddenly rebels by donning her space suit and ambling outside for a stroll–alone. She is at once relieved of her cramped confine-
ment and enjoys wandering about the rugged terrain immensely.

*Renza's personal exploration of the Moon was purely feminine and
not at all scientific. Fascinated by the Moon's one-sixth gravity,
she found that a slight move enabled her to leap as if she were
weightless.*

At length, the Moon crew slogs back to base and Major Markey declares that having Renza aboard now is probably a mistake.
McCauley begs to differ, smiles, and admits, "She's doing pretty
well, too." Suddenly, Joe discovers that Renza is not in the building.
When she fails to respond to a radio call, McCauley immediately

organizes a relief effort to find her. The astronauts pile back into their suits and begin walking about.

McCauley and Joe Hale searched for Renza in one direction while the other members of the crew covered other areas. Each man had uppermost in his mind the maze of bottomless craters and crevices that dotted the Moon's surface.

Hale and McCauley eventually stumble upon Renza lying down on a rock. She is okay, only resting, and her radio is off, which explains why she never answered. Once her radio is turned on, the couple begins bickering until McCauley barks out, "Quiet, both of you!" and orders all hands back to base. The contest renews once inside, with Joe insisting that Renza depart on the next rocket. McCauley disagrees and reminds him, "I'm making the decisions, major." Surprisingly, she agrees to return "because I don't belong here!" McCauley insists she does belong, then apologizes for not appreciating how she felt cooped up inside the whole period. "From now on," he explains, "You can go out anytime you want, Renza." Joe protests, "She's my wife–I forbid it!" McCauley, casting a stern eye at the captain, announces, "Tomorrow morning, Joe, you will take Renza to the North section." Hale, however, continues objecting, so Renza strides up to him and declares, "What do you think I do all day–sit and twiddle my thumbs!" The slugfest continues until McCauley warns, "That's *enough*, both of you." The two part and Renza requests separate sleeping quarters for the evening. As she storms off, Major Markey warns his superior, "You're taking quite a chance, Mac, that girl has a mind of her own!" "Well," the colonel reasons, "it's a calculated risk... and the stakes are pretty high."

The following morning at breakfast, Renza summarily declares she will not take her hike. When asked why, she responds, "I just don't want to go, that's all." Moreover, she wants to depart on the next available ship, not wishing to be in the way any longer. Joe bristles and bellows, "Put on your suit! You're going if I have to drag you!" "Make up your mind!" she hisses back. "One minute you don't want me to go and the next you're screaming at me!" The two storm off into the airlock, at which point Major Markey wearily intones, "Women..." McCauley nods in agreement.

Captain Hale and Renza begin their stroll under the starlit sky and the couple gradually makes up. Some sweet talk ensues, which is inadvertently broadcasted over the radio. McCauley listens briefly, smiles, then orders everybody off that frequency for the next five minutes.

By day's end, the base crew returns to find their table a lavishly adorned banquet with candles and a very elaborate meal. "It's real!" Markey exclaims. "How did all this stuff get up here?" A well-coiffed Renza Hale makes her entrance and tells them, "Hi, fellas, dinner will be ready in a minute. No time to change, so sit down, huh?" The bewildered astronauts oblige her and when Joe asks, "Where did all this come from?" she smiles and purrs, "Manna from Heaven." After a few more moments, Joe repeats his question. Renza simply smiles and he blurts, "Don't give me *that* look–I want to know!" She then brings out a cake honoring the fourth anniversary of McCauley's landing on the Moon and they all drink a toast. Joe, however, keeps pressing her for an answer, but she insists, "You won't catch me that easily, darling!" McCauley simply smiles and concedes, "No matter *how* you did it, Renza, it was pretty slick." Not knowing any better, Joe again insists on learning how she obtained everything and she pleads the Fifth Amendment to avoid incriminating herself. McCauley happily lauds her with "Bravo!" and the festivities begin.

Day Ninety–Project First Woman successfully concluded. Future colonization of Moon possible and practical–with certain minor corrections.

Back in General Norgrath's office, Renza Hale continues citing the Fifth Amendment to remain silent. The general pauses to take a phone call, at which point McCauley leans over and whispers, "Don't let up or they'll hand me my head!" "I promise I won't tell on you!" she says. "Can I go on the next trip?" "Sure," the colonel insists. Renza departs after Norgrath returns and the general asks McCauley if he thinks the project was successful. Too successful, apparently. Renza left a list of 65 recommendations for future Moon assignments. "I'm afraid we've let ourselves in for something," the colonel warns. "From now on, we'll have no peace." Norgrath simply grins and informs him, "Mac, there's nothing like a dame, even in space–even if we *both* had to break a couple rules!"

"Christmas On the Moon"

(Aired December 23, 1959)

Starring: Joyce Taylor, Keith Larsen (Jim Nichols), Whit Bissell (Oliver Farrar), Patricia Manning, Paul Langton, Del Russell, Sean Bartlett, Charles Herbert

Script: David Duncan, Lawrence Louis Goldman

Directed by: Richard Carlson

Technical advisor: Colonel Lawrence D. Ely, U.S.A.F.

> *It is every man's dream to be home with his family. Sometimes, for reasons beyond control, men are not able to get home. In this story, which hasn't happened yet, these men will not be able to get home for Christmas—because they spent Man's first Christmas on the Moon.*

Outside their home, Johnny and Peter McCauley gaze up at the nighttime sky, watching comets, wondering what they are–and why they "whiz." Tension mounts as Mom and Dad pull up in the driveway and the two duck inside the closet, knowing full well what is in store for them. Mary McCauley enters with an armful of wrapped gifts, calls out to her sons, and when they do not answer, she places her burden in the closet. The colonel steps in bearing a very long package and she informs him of their missing sons. He artfully makes his way over to the closet, reaches in, and pulls them out. "How'd you know we were there!" they protest. "It was a matter of deep concentration," their father assures them. He also warns that company is coming tonight and peeking around corners is not allowed. "If you want to peek at anything, peek at that," he says, pointing to the very long box. He encourages them to open it, over Mary's protests, and advises, "I'd kinda like them to open it now." Much to the boys' delight, inside is a large telescope. "It's just what I've always wanted," young Johnny declares, then turns to Peter and whispers, "What is it...?" Dad explains it's a refractor and admonishes them in advance with, "No arguments–you're going to share it peacefully!" They troop off to the bedroom porch to set it up and Mary advises her husband to decorate the Christmas tree before company arrives.

Holiday festivities ensue as Professor Oliver Farrar plays the piano and Edith, the very pregnant wife of astronomer Jim Nichols, asks why he never told them he could play a musical instrument. "Because I'm an honest man!" he declares, drawing a laugh. Nichols himself is a protégée of Farrar and extremely attached to his mentor. The professor then tactfully expresses admiration for Mary's handiwork and she asks if he likes it. "Of course I do," he exclaims. "It's a real old-fashioned, overloaded Christmas tree!" McCauley goes looking for Jim and finds him at the telescope with the children. Jim is explaining to them that comets are probably made up of ice and some scattered rocks and dust. "Don't you ever take time out from business, Jim," the colonel asks and offers him a drink. "*This* business is my pleasure," he insists. Downstairs, the adults gather as Professor Farrar explains that the comet they will study while on the Moon will not visit the neighborhood again for another 2,400 years. When Edith suggests it may have been seen 2,000 years ago, Farrar guesses she is equating it to the Christmas star. "Well, the idea is so beautiful that I'd like to believe it," he says with a smile. Nicholas, however, dismisses the entire notion of religion, much to the distress of his guests, and he declares Christmas "just a hangover from the Middle Ages." Moreover, he feels that the holiday should be abolished altogether. Edith protests his bluntness and he apologizes, but continues, "As far as I'm concerned the most beautiful thing on earth is knowledge–knowledge based on science, not *faith*. I don't believe in miracles!" Farrar, pointing to Edith's condition, counters, "As for miracles, you're soon going to experience one." Nichols further upsets the ladies by inadvertently stating he's grateful for spending Christmas on the Moon. "Jim," McCauley corrects him, "I thought we decided not to discuss that tonight." Nichols, unapologetic, admits to Edith that the only miracle he is looking forward to happens next month.

December 21st, the Comet Expedition left Earth en route to the Moon. Soon man would be able to scan the Heavens to study a comet at closer range than ever before possible.

McCauley, Farrar, and Nichols enter the Moon base and get acquainted with the crew. The colonel then ambles over to crusty Doctor Warnecke, who has made his latest move in a long-delayed chess game, and chortles, "Let see you get out of *this* one." McCauley, undaunted, nonchalantly moves a piece, announces "Check!" and leaves the doctor to exclaim, "Why you son of a gun!" Eager to begin working, the colonel orders Warnecke to give Farrar and Nichols a last-minute physical before they begin their 50-mile hike to the comet observation post. Events grind on and the crewmen arrive with Farrar complaining how the exertion has left him aching. Inside, the radio operator informs Ground Control that the guests are having a rough time and demands, "When are they going to get paved roads up here?" His counterpart on Earth, not losing a beat, responds, "I hear Washington is working on it now." "Tell them to hurry up!" Nichols exclaims. Farrar, meanwhile, compliments the base crew for their accomplishments and begins explaining the nature of his own labors. "What is a comet made of? Rock? Metals? Dust? Or perhaps some primitive form of ice? And what mysterious forces drive the tails of comets outward from the sun–radiation? Light Pressure? What?" Farrar suddenly winces in pain. McCauley rushes over, but the doctor assures him it is nothing–then collapses. McCauley radios Doctor Warnecke at the main base and describes Farrar's symptoms, and both men suspect it might be appendicitis. "If there was any inflammation to begin with, that 50-mile hike would aggravate it," Warnecke informs the colonel.

Farrar protests having to lie down and wants to return to work, but Nichols and the colonel insist he remain still. "Even stubbing your toe on the Moon is serious," McCauley informs him. Nichols pulls the colonel aside and whispers that Farrar would never quit his job unless he was seriously ill. Worse still, the Moon has begun passing through the comet's tail, which unleashes a prolonged micro-meteorite bombardment. McCauley curtly informs Nichols that he cannot have Doctor Warnecke walk through a meteorite shower unless it was vitally necessary. Their fears are confirmed when Farrar's temperature is found rising and McCauley has no choice but order Warnecke to the observation post immediately. "Be prepared for an emergency operation," he warns. "Stay in radio contact at all times." "We read you, Mac," Warnecke states, then reads his a message from Earth. "We are praying for the success of your mission and wish each of you a very merry Christmas. Signed, Mary McCauley." "Prayers... merry, merry Christmas..." Nichols mutters. "Sure, tell it to Professor Farrar and then maybe you won't need a doctor."

Back on Earth, Edith and Mary bemoan the fact their husbands are AWOL for the holidays and they'll miss their Christmas party. The boys then ask them to join them at the telescope and watch all the shooting stars. "Aren't they pretty, Mom?" they excitedly ask. After a moment's reflection, Mary says she is sure their husbands are safe where they are, asking Edith why she is so solemn. "I'm an astronomer's wife," she states. "On the Moon, there's no atmosphere to burn them up. They'll be *hitting* the surface." Edith then looks a bit startled and announces, "Mary, I feel *funny*." Mary assists her pregnant friend to the living room and calls a doctor. Back at the observation base, the men watch meteorites pelting their vicinity with increasing violence. An impatient Nichols fumes as he wonders where the rescue team is.

Knowing the man's life depended on them, Major Warnecke and Lieutenant Teal raced to Advanced Base in spite of the hazards of the meteor shower, which bombarded them.

A concerned McCauley raises Warnecke on the radio, who states he has to cross a plain with projectiles crashing all around him. "I read you, Mac," he explains. "We're still coming, but the meteor shower is getting heavier." McCauley advises him that Farrar's condition is deteriorating and Warnecke insists that he has no choice but to get there and operate. McCauley realizes this is impossible across an open plain, so he questions Nichols as to the comet's direction and angle of approach. Once informed, he divines that a nearby chain of mountains affords some cover and instructs Warnecke to take an alternate route. Nichols protests that the change will result in delays while Farrar's condition is deteriorating. "They can't help Farrar if they're *dead!*" McCauley barks and the order stands. The rescuers will lose radio contact for most of the journey, but McCauley instructs them to follow the series of flags staked about so as to not get lost. Before signing off, Warnecke advises the base crew to keep Farrar's temperature down with alcohol rubs, wet towels, anything. "He can't stand much more," he warns. "You can pray."

Farrar, growing delirious on the table, recites English poet John Dunn as McCauley and Nichols fail to reduce his fever. Meanwhile, as the rescue team threads toward the advance base, a meteor knocks down one of the markers. Several hours lapse before Warnecke radios that he is lost. McCauley promptly suits up and departs amidst a hail of meteorites to lead them back and positively orders Colonel Adams not to let anyone out until the shower passes. "If I can get through this flak, I should be back with Warnecke in an hour," he declares. Nichols, watching Farrar perish before him, says, "An hour? If his temperature keeps rising, that will be too late." The colonel, looking Nichols straight in the eye, growls, "As Warnecke said—*we can pray*." McCauley departs, running and dodging furiously, while the crewmen ponder what to do. Adams radios the main base to check on the team's progress and a message is relayed to Nichols: "Edith was taken to the hospital Christmas morning, two weeks earlier than expected. Stand by, there's more–both mother and son are fine. Signed, Mary McCauley. " "A son!" the doctor murmurs. Nichols, suddenly overwhelmed by his own insignificance, turns to the widow and pleads for divine intervention. *"Oh, God, if you are out there... you know that I have denied you. If you have the power, I ask nothing for myself. I pray only for the life of a wonderful man. For the life of a man who loves thee. It's no use letting him die..."*

Suddenly, a large meteorite strikes near the building. An incredulous flash of intuition strikes Nichols and, while muttering, "Go and catch a falling star..." he heads for the airlock. Colonel Adams stops him cold. Nichols states he can save Farrar and begs Colonel Adams to let him outside. "30 seconds, that's all I need," he pleads.

"My prayer was answered." Adams, against his better judgment, relents and Nichols bounds outside to retrieve a large chunk of meteoric ice. Once inside, the two men break in into pieces, wrap it in towels, and place them around the dying Farrar. McCauley radios in that the shower has stopped and the rescue team will arrive shortly. Adams relays welcome news that Farrar's fever seems to be subsiding. Adams and Nichols, standing by the observation port, watch the three men approach the base. Adams smiles and asks, "Remind you of something?" "Yeah," Nichols reflects. "Three men bearing gifts–this time, it's the gift of life." Shortly afterwards, the operation succeeds and Warnecke confesses, "It was a close call, but there's no reason now why he won't do fine. It was the ice that did it." McCauley strolls up to Nichols and asks, "Where'd it come from, Jim?" Nichols beams and says, "I think it came from God on Christmas day–the gift of life." Grasping Nichols' arm, the colonel squeezes slightly, smiles, and quietly murmurs, "Amen..."

Back at the McCauley residence, Mary is unhappy over taking down the Christmas tree so soon. "Do we have to cut it up, branch by branch, then burn it?" she emotes. "It always makes me sad to do that." The doorbell rings and the Nichols drop by with the infant son, whom Mary immediately coddles. A smiling Jim declares, "Thank goodness we're not too late!" "Why?" McCauley asks. "To rescue your Christmas tree." "What for?" the colonel demands. "*Our* Christmas party," the doctor responds. "On the 11th of January!" Edith adds. McCauley, pulling Mary close, looks up obligingly and assures them, "We'll be there."

"Quarantine"

(Aired December 30, 1959)

Starring: Warren Stevens (Doctor Randolph), Simon Oakland (Doctor Horton), John Milford (Doctor Hamilton), Guy Stockwell (Lieutenant Murphy), Ray Yeal, Donald Freed

Script by: Stuart James Byrne

Directed by: Walter Doniger

Technical advisor: Major Charles A. Berry, U.S.A.F.

> *The story you are about to see has not happened—yet. These are scenes from that story, a story that will happen when Man has built a space station orbiting above the Earth, a station that will be a research center in which dedicated people such as these will conduct experiments in many sciences for the benefit of mankind. This is the story of an experiment plunging out of control, endangering the lives of those aboard the space station.*

General Warren gazes wistfully at a nearby rocket gantry, momentarily oblivious to Colonel McCauley standing nearby. "Excuse me, Ed," he confesses. "For a few minutes I was a kid with his nose pressed against a plate glass window of a store, looking at a hot rod in every drive." McCauley smiles and states, "It's all yours, Sam, even that space station orbiting out there." The colonel asks why General Warren simply doesn't suit up and join them above. The general smiles, insisting that his only task is to find men who can serve a useful function "up there." McCauley advises him that he just received the scheduling assignment only to find that Doctor Horton, an outstanding physicist, and Doctor Randolph, a brilliant biologist, will spend 15 days on the cramped station together. The two men exude a most virulent loathing for each other, however, and McCauley questions the wisdom of having them aboard concurrently for so long. "The committee felt that their projects deserved that priority ahead of the other scientists," Warren reasons. "I'm sure that the disagreement that they had in the past—" The colonel cuts him off with, "Sam, I am sorry to disagree with you, but when those two cool, detached scientific minds get within radar distance of each other, it makes the Hatfield-McCoy feud seem more friendly than Damon and Pythias." He therefore seeks permission to ask one of the scientists to forego this flight and attend the next one. General Warren, obviously sympathetic, declares, "If you can work that out with Damon and Pythias, you've got a deal!"

McCauley shows up at the laboratory of Doctor Horton, who explains that conditions in space will not be right for his experiment for another two years, so he must go now. When the colonel asks if Doctor Randolph's work is equally important, Horton sneers, "Oh, I'm sure he thinks so." McCauley then reminds him that, in the confined quarters of the station, the light, gravity, and water are all artificial. "Something we can't fake is the ability for one man to get along with another," he lectures. "Aboard a space station we all tie our shoes' laces in the morning so that we don't trip over each other all day long." The colonel then states that both Horton and Doctor Randolph will be playing musical chairs over the next few days to see who goes. McCauley next pays a similar call on Horton's counterpart and salutes him with, "Doctor Randolph, I am not going to mince words!" "That's not your reputation," Randolph acknowledges with a smile. The colonel explains their mutual predicament, yet the doctor graciously offers to postpone his trip owing to the late shipment of specimens from India. "Do I thank you or do you thank me?" McCauley inquires. "I'm not sure," Randolph opines. "But do you mind if I *don't* thank Doctor Horton?"

McCauley's destination, the space station Astra—1,075 miles above the Earth—making a complete orbit every two hours, designed to house the laboratories and research centers that would enable scientists to probe for dramatic advancements in all fields of science. McCauley, along with Doctor Horton, approaches the space station in the rocket ship. The crew in the space station waited to moor the ship in the airlock located in the hub of the orbiting station, an airlock that enabled personnel to proceed from rocket ship to space station.

Once aboard Astra, McCauley and Horton are greeted by Lieutenant Murphy, the executive officer. The doctor brushes him off, insisting that he be allowed to set up his equipment immediately. Horton relents, however, when offered a cup of coffee and Murphy jocularly exclaims, "Right this way, gentlemen, the cub car is in operation!" McCauley next runs into Doctor Hamilton, the resident astronomer, and pleasantries are exchanged, but again Horton insists that he begin work immediately. "Top man, Horton," Hamilton notes. "Does some really outstanding work in high frequencies. Yet an odd one, too–gets terribly wrapped up in his work." McCauley shrugs in agreement, noting, "Yes, he does indeed..." In time, the routine on Astra is disrupted once Horton's experiments begin playing havoc with communications to Earth. McCauley walks into the command section just as Hamilton informs ground control that Horton is again requesting conformation that his equipment is being sent up. Snatching the microphone, the colonel bellows, "Cancel the confirmation request!" and storms off to confront the doctor. He finds him deeply engrossed in his work, whereupon McCauley diplomatically requests him not to seek confirmation on requisitions–all his orders receive prompt attention as a matter of course. Horton blithely ignores him, then, looking up, asks what he wants. McCauley backtracks and says he was just checking on the latter's progress and departs. Meanwhile, Doctor Hamilton exults over the latest batch of space photos he has taken and informs McCauley, "We are going to learn things about the universe that we never even imagined." Their reverie is broken when Ground Control dispatches a message from General Warren indicating that Doctor Randolph is on the next rocket with his equipment. "Please extend fullest cooperation in all available facilities," it continues. McCauley, believing that Randolph would not make his appearance for another five days, angrily demands to learn why the scheduling was changed, but the operator cannot say. The doctor climbs down the airlock ladder and runs headlong into Doctor Hamilton. The two joke about artificial gravity for a few seconds before McCauley steps up. Randolph mentions that his specimens from India arrived sooner than he thought, but the colonel lectures him on the necessity of courtesy and cooperation. Horton unexpectedly steps up, demanding to know why two of his items were omitted from this latest shipment. The two old adversaries warily eye each other and when Horton insinuates his equipment was omitted to make room for Randolph and his, McCauley erupts, declaring, "The confines of a space station leave no room for personal animosities." Both men nod in agreement, then stalk off.

Hours later, Murphy brings McCauley a message to be sent by Doctor Horton, which he peruses, then angrily says, "Send it!" Hamilton asks what is wrong and the colonel notes that Horton is seeking additional time on the station "on the theory that if it worked for Doctor Randolph, it's going to work for him." McCauley takes some unmitigated delight informing Horton that his request for an extension is denied. Randolph, meanwhile, begins working at his own furious pace, but he becomes inexplicably ill while handling some viruses. Contacting Colonel McCauley by TV monitor, he quarantines himself to keep the infection from spreading. McCauley immediately shuts down the ventilation to Randolph's laboratory and orders decontamination equipment deployed. Randolph speculates that the virus has mutated while exposed to radiation aboard the station and warns, "It could destroy us all." However, after this is found not to be the case, McCauley suspects that Horton's work may be implicated and he confronts the doctor about it. "Colonel, I'm not a biologist," he angrily informs McCauley, "but I am a physicist and your idea is quite extraordinary!" Upon further reflection, he states that certain high frequencies have been known to affect strains of virus, so perhaps he can help find a cure. "Is there anything I can do?" Doctor Hamilton innocently asks. McCauley nods and states, "In that great big star-filled universe of yours, see if you can find a couple of angels. We're going to need all the help we can get."

Back in his lab, Doctor Randolph stumbles around, getting weaker. He is subsequently paged by Horton, who alerts him that his high frequencies may be behind the infection. "Doctor, I can't bring my equipment to you," Horton reasons, "so you must come to my lab with your cultures. We can expose them and you to my high frequency magnetic fields." Randolph agrees, but ponders how he can get to Horton's laboratory without infecting the entire station. It falls upon Colonel McCauley to suggest that they both suit up, depart the airlock in his lab, then transit across the station wheel to the airlock on Horton's lab.

McCauley, weightless in the vacuum of space, traveled at the same speed as the space station. His jet pack, acting like a miniature rocket, would enable him to move about and change his direction.

Outside the space station, McCauley guides the ailing Randolph from his airlock to Doctor Horton's laboratory. Several days lapse before Horton announces Randolph is cured. "We found a magnetic frequency that will make the virus dormant until we can develop or find a more permanent remedy," he informs McCauley, then asks for some hot soup. The two adversaries are finally on better terms. "I'm glad that's finished," Hamilton admits. "Yes," McCauley opines, "and maybe something good is beginning." Back on Earth, Horton shows Randolph a piece of electronic equipment and asks, "Incredible, isn't it?" McCauley steps up and says, "Yes it is–you two." Horton informs the colonel that he and Randolph may have stumbled upon a whole new manner of controlling disease and the latter declares, "Our next trip to your space station should prove that out." Smiling, the colonel mockingly asks, "Would you gentleman like me to arrange for you to go separately?" The two former adversaries sheepishly eye each other for a second, then Randolph breaks the impasse. "Together," he assures McCauley. "Together."

"Tankers In Space"

(Aired January 6, 1960)

Starring: James Drury (Major Nick Alborg), Murray Hamilton (Lieutenant Colonel Bill Alborg), Phillip Terry (Colonel Stoner), Robert Brubaker, Mary Newton, Helen Mowery, Jennifer Lea, Jack Emrek

Script: Arthur Weiss

Directed by: Alvin Ganzer

Technical advisor: Lieutenant Colonel Frank P. Ball

> *The story you are about to see has not happened yet. These are scenes from that story that will happen, for it is the story of the first attempt to refuel a rocket in outer space, a story that men such as these will one day experience as Mankind reaches for the stars.*
>
> *One of the most demanding elements of refueling is precision, precision that comes from the teamwork of men working together over a long period of time. Colonel McCauley located and made part of his crew two brothers, both pilots, both astronauts, both skilled in the procedures of refueling, but most of all, two men who work together as if though they were cast from the same mold.*

Colonel McCauley's car pulls alongside the spacious house of Air Force officers Bill and Nick Alborg. Bill greets McCauley and introduces his mother and his wife, Dorothy. Younger brother Nick, however, is late, being preoccupied with his lovely fiancée, Helen, in a nearby field. The two make their belated appearance, then the colonel compliments Mrs. Alborg and her family and lovely home. "No mother could ask for more," she beams. "Two fine boys, their families, and this place to work when... when they get through flying around up there." Readying to depart, Bill teases his younger sibling, "You ready, kid?" "I'm way ahead of you," Nick responds. But Mrs. Alborg protests about letting Colonel McCauley depart before feeding him and the colonel politely consents. Some time later, Mrs. Alborg asks if McCauley has had enough and he jests, "I don't think I can move out of this chair!" She readily invites him back sometime. The colonel graciously accepts, once the three men have finished the latest test. Mrs. Alborg stops smiling and murmurs, "Well, now that you've been fed, colonel, I'd better send you and the boys off before somebody accuses me of stopping progress." Bill and his wife are about to enter the house when he shoots his commander a sympathetic glance and says, "Be back in a minute, colonel?" McCauley, taking the cue, smiles and slowly says, "Take your time, Bill." A pensive Mrs. Alborg asks if the colonel has any children and he states he has two sons, including one that just turned nine. "Then you understand," she emotes. McCauley nods his head in sympathy, saying, "Yes..."

The scene switches over to the rocket motor test site, where technicians are making final preparations to load RP-10, a new and very explosive mixture, into the tanker rocket.

> An important item on McCauley's briefing program was to make sure that every member of the crew was fully aware of the tremendous force of rocket propellant and the full reason why these propellants had to be handled at every stage of the operation with maximum perfection.

McCauley and the two brothers approach Colonel Stoner, a propellant expert, who is preparing a demonstration for General Warren and some civilian visitors. "First you take about 500 gallons of hydrazine," Nick says in a mockingly authoritative tone. "And about 500 gallons of nitrogen petroxide," Bill mimics. "Make sure you keep them well apart..." Nick adds. "Cause when they get together," Bill chimes in. "There's fireworks!" they state in unison. "Hey, McCauley," Stoner jokingly asks, "don't you guys ever finish a sentence without each other's help?" Colonel McCauley, rolling his eyes, blurts out, "Brothers–but with just one brain!" General Warren subsequently explains to his guests that the tanker will make orbit once, then be intercepted by a second rocket, the R-101, under McCauley, whereupon refueling in orbit will be attempted. To underscore the hazards involved, Colonel Stoner pours some of the ingredients into a dish on the ground and they ignite with great fury. "Gentleman," Warren lectures, "that's the potential of the propellant we are going to be transferring in large quantities from a tanker to a rocket ship, a thousand miles out, 14,500 miles per hour." Turning to McCauley and his crew, the general informs them they have an hour for pre-flight. The three men salute and depart.

The first rocket to take off was the tanker manned by Colonel Stoner and Major Nick Alborg, whose assignment was to follow a program placing the tanker in a planned orbit. On another launching pad, Colonel McCauley's ship, the R-101, awaited its takeoff signal, which would be timed to the split second in order to effect a rendezvous with the tanker in outer space. The rendezvous problem was simple on paper: the tanker was comparable to a bullet fired around the Earth–McCauley's ship, the R-101, another bullet fired to intercept the first one. Early procedures were completed without incident. Tanker Able settled into the prescribed orbit and awaited the rendezvous with McCauley's R-101.

Once in orbit, Ground Control orders McCauley to home in on Tanker Able's radar beam. The R-101, locating the vessel on its scope, gradually slides into position alongside. "Easy, boy," Stoner advises them. "We got very impatient cargo aboard. No nudges!" Once positioned, McCauley and Stoner suit up and reel out the refueling line to commence the procedure.

Outside the spaceship, McCauley would travel at exactly the same speed and through the same vacuum as the spaceship itself and, therefore, unless he exerted some other type of motion, he would remain alongside the ship. To avoid unnecessary floating in a field of weightlessness, magnetic shoes allowed him to walk almost normally on the surface of the ship. His jet pack, in effect a miniature rocket, gave him sufficient thrust to move about in any direction.

McCauley and Stoner carefully hook the fuel nozzle into R-101's receptacle and liquid propellant begins flowing. Trouble ensues immediately as the hose flexes and begins drawing the two ships together. The transfer is halted, but both vessels continue careening into each other and more trouble ensues when the hose release mechanism fails. "Straining the hose has jammed the coupling!" McCauley declares. The device must be removed manually to separate the vessels.

The first collision of the ships served as a crisis warning to McCauley and his crew. Each successive contact would bring disaster closer until finally the hydrazine and tetroxide tanks would burst.

At length, the rockets graze each other again, and this time the R-101's fin punctures Tanker Able's hull. McCauley, still struggling to release the nozzle, orders Bill to put the impact wrench in the decompression chamber and radio his brother in the tanker, which has suddenly grown silent. "Nick? Nick, this is McCauley. Tanker Able acknowledge!" he exclaims. Suspenseful moments pass before Nick responds, "Keep your shirt on, I'm all right," then explains he was aft examining the fuel bay for damage. Ground Control also frantically calls in and Nick informs them, "We have stopped the transfer due to oscillation of ships. Inspection of tank bay shows breakage in one liquid oxygen tank. We are still connected by the hose and we are colliding fore and aft." General Warren declares, "It's like two ships tied together in a high sea pounding each other. Why don't they cut loose?" Meanwhile, McCauley retrieves the impact wrench for the airlock and begins tediously removing all bolts from the nozzle assembly. The collisions continue and at one point, Nick radios, "Bill, I'm sure one of the RP tanks went." The colonel then comes on: "Nick, this is McCauley. Transmit a detailed report to control. This doesn't have to happen again." Nick explains his predicament to General Warren: "Situation as follows: oxygen and RP tanks damaged, with contents escaping. Stand by." The general anxiously notes, "With that potential building up, if the hydrazine and Tetroxide let go, they've had it." Another collision results in further damage while, back on Earth, Mrs. Alborg, Dorothy, and Helen cast anxious glances upward. Nick then radios, "Colonel, the gauges are dropping on the hydrazine tanks." McCauley announces he will float over and take a look, dodging another collision en route. Taking a brief glance, he states, "One of the ribs is bent across the hydrazine flow pipe. They've both been sheared. How much longer, Stoner?" Stoner states only two more bolts to go, then Bill warns him to get out of the way, the ships are swinging back. "I'd like to," McCauley says. "My pack is hung up." Instantly, Bill orders Nick to hit forward thrust for one second and the ships lurch away. With McCauley in the clear, Bill asks his brother, "You ready, kid?" "I'm way ahead of you," comes the reply and Nick departs the tanker to help free the colonel. He does so just as the ships impact again and they jet pack themselves to safety.

By now, the buildup of gases in the tanker renders an explosion inevitable, so McCauley and Nick float back to R-101. Stoner also unloosens the last bolt and disconnects the fuel line. A frantic Ground Control keeps demanding, "R-101, are you there?" "We'll know in about 60 seconds," McCauley mutters as all eyes train on the tanker. The tanker erupts in a fireball not far off and, relieved, the colonel informs Ground Control, "Modification of transfer procedure indicated. Recommend use of solid pipeline instead of pliable hose. This will keep ships in fixed position." R-101 safely returns to Earth.

Later, during a barbecue at the Alborg residence, Bill declares, "You know, that kid's got plenty of guts. He stayed perfectly calm and I don't mind telling you I was plenty nervous. How about you, colonel?" McCauley reflectively states, "Well, that's putting it mildly." It suddenly dawns on Bill that Nick and Helen are not present and he asks where they are. Suddenly, a car pulls up, toots its horn, and the couple enters the yard. Bill demands to know why he is so late. Nick apologizes and says, "Well, you won't believe this, but we ran out of gas!"

"Sea of Stars"

(Aired January 13, 1960)

Starring: Fred Beir (Lieutenant Art Frey), Jack Ging (Lieutenant Jerry Rutledge), Nan Peterson, Tom Brown, Audrey Clark, Angus Duncan, Jim Cody

Script: Marianne Mosner and Francis Rosenwald, Kalman Phillips

Directed by: Lee Sholem

Technical advisor: Colonel Lawrence D. Ely

> *The story you are about to see has not happened yet. These are scenes from that story that will happen when Man will have a space station orbiting miles above the Earth, its crews and scientists doing advanced research in astronomy, weather observation, biology, and medicine for the benefit of Mankind. But there will be many unknown complications for the men who live and work aboard this orbiting satellite. This is the story of one such complication.*

At the rocket launching area, Lieutenant Jerry Rutledge approaches Colonel McCauley, handing him his flight plan for the upcoming launch. The colonel does not like the modest safety parameters involved, but compliments it as a good compromise overall. Rutledge says it would have been easier to achieve on the computer and McCauley quickly corrects him. "Learning to do these problems without the help of a computer may save your life one of these days." The colonel then growls, "Where is Lieutenant Frey? He should have worked out that navigation problem I gave him a long time ago!" Rutledge tries explaining that Frey had to work out some details with his fiancée, Anne–and who should enter at that precise moment but the tardy lieutenant himself. "Navigation papers, sir!" he gasps. "You're late with it!" McCauley reminds him. Scanning the paper, he declares it unsatisfactory with a glaring two-second error. "Do you realize that, at 16,000 miles per hour, how far we'll miss that space station in two seconds?" he asks. Frey suggests that they could correct the error with directional controls, but McCauley vetoes the idea, asking what he would do if they were non-functional. "In space, we plan on disaster in order to avoid it," the colonel lectures. "Rework that problem and get it to me tonight. We report for duty on the space station tomorrow morning. That's all." No sooner does McCauley depart than Frey grouses about how hard the colonel has leaned on him lately. "He never gets off his perfection kick, does he?" "Maybe that's the secret of his long life," Rutledge suggests. Frey happily mentions they have time for one tennis game that evening, whereupon–flashing a ring box–he plans to propose to Anne.

At the tennis court, the belles and beaus enjoy a good game, with Frey and Anne getting trounced. Rutledge brags they hardly gave them a workout and Jasmine suggests there must be "something else" on their minds. Anne declares she has none, but that her date has nothing but space on his mind. Frey, judging the time right, waves the little box in her face. Anne mockingly protests, "Don't jump to conclusions just because a girl likes to look inside ring boxes!" Their sweet reveries sour when Colonel McCauley arrives unexpectedly in a staff car and marches over. "Oh, boy," Frey moans. The colonel abruptly states that the launch has been moved up and that he needs the new navigation plan immediately. Frey protests, but McCauley matter-of-factly states, "Lieutenant, your alternate for this mission is standing by in case you are scrubbed for any reason at all." As McCauley departs, he orders the men to appear for a briefing in two hours. "He's practically invited you out of the mission, so why couldn't you accept?" Anne demands. Frey sheepishly explains that he has to keep up his hours on the space station, then kisses her goodbye.

Space Station Astra, orbiting over 1,000 miles above our Earth, isolated except for its communication systems and approached only by rocket ships from Earth.

On the station, Frey bemoans that he still has another week in space and worries about Anne. "You know, I don't have any lease on that girl and there are a lot of characters around that can offer her more than I," he whines. Rutledge tells him not to worry, then Frey bitterly remonstrates that McCauley has been unfairly leaning on him. The colonel enters at that precise moment, furious that Frey is 30 seconds late in relieving the navigational control officer. The lieutenant storms out of the room and Rutledge asks for permission to speak. "I might be a little out of line, but it's about Art–aren't you being a little tough on him?" he inquires. "He'd make a fine astronaut," McCauley concedes. "He has all the qualities, courage, loyalty, intelligence." Rutledge nonetheless pushes the envelope and again asks why he keeps badgering his friend, so the colonel declares, "Because in space, there is no margin for error. Accuracy must become a habit. Your life may depend upon it." Suddenly, the observation officer summons McCauley over the intercom, stating that an unidentified object is approaching the space station at high speed. The colonel notes that its tracking computes at 16,240 miles per hour, apparently on a collision course. Further computations predict a direct hit on the space station in two hours and twenty-five minutes. Ground Control subsequently identifies the object as S-16, an old satellite. To avert a disaster, McCauley, Rutledge, and Frey board rocket S-107 to intercept and destroy the interloper with a "sand missile," which, Major Franklin explains, shoots a corrosive curtain of particles in its path.

McCauley and his crew aboard the S-107 started for the target. Behind her, the space station on red alert; ahead, a satellite out of control, roaring destruction.

Rutledge and Frey expertly pilot S-107 to within firing range of the errant satellite. The missile launch is successful and the target disintegrates, but their own vessel is damaged in the process and loses two directional control rockets. "We've reached escape velocity–going close to 27,000 miles per hour in the wrong direction," McCauley states, then asks Frey for their present trajectory. "If I am correct, sir," he states, "it's straight for the sun and this time, I'm afraid I am dead accurate." The colonel concedes, "It's a long way from home."

The S-107 hurtles through space, time and distance her enemies. Unless Colonel McCauley could correct the ship's direction, the S-107 would continue unchecked into the sun.

McCauley relays his predicament back to Major Franklin on Astra, who states he cannot get a rescue rocket to reach them in time. McCauley then contacts Ground Control to acquire his precise location from radar sets on Earth.

Minitrac stations all over the world went into action, checking the path of McCauley's ship as it sped towards the sun.

Earth stations confirm S-107's trajectory toward the Sun and things appear hopeless, but McCauley insists, "We may have a chance to turn this ship back." He explains a dicey expedient whereby the last remaining directional rocket will be used to cause the ship to tumble "like a rowboat with one oar, it would just keep turning around." Then, at a precise moment, the main engines will fire once S-107 points itself towards Earth. "How can that help us, sir?" Frey ponders. "It's *better* than heading into the sun," McCauley curtly reminds him. The gambit works and the rocket begins settling into orbit. Asked if they should plot a course back to Astra, the colonel notes, "No, with our directional rockets all fouled up, we'd never make it. We're going to have to head out towards a bigger target. Compute a course for Earth." Major Franklin advises McCauley that he has assumed a pretty steep entry. "The skin of your ship better be in perfect condition to keep from burning up–better check it," he warns. As McCauley departs the cabin to suit up, he orders Frey to check the release mechanism on the escape capsule. "We may need it," he remarks.

McCauley, wearing magnetic shoes, was able to leave the spaceship and walk on its metallic surface in order to examine and estimate the damage the corrosive sand had done to the S-107.

Back inside, the colonel informs Rutledge and Frey that the outer hull is badly pitted and warns them, "Reentry stress and heat may finish the job that the sand started." When Frey mentions that at least the escape capsule appears to be in working order, the colonel says, "This ship cost the taxpayers about nine million dollars. I think we ought to try and save her." Rutledge adds that steering is impossible with the directional rockets out and McCauley assures him, "Oh, yes there is." The colonel explains, "You know, releasing the capsule will create a drag pressure that would slow the ship down as well as change its direction." However, calculations would have to be "right on the button," as he assures a jittery Frey. "In this business, we don't expect mistakes. And besides," he says, smiling, "Don't forget your date with Anne." The crew tries the desperate maneuver, but the directional rocket fails to fire, so McCauley suits up and goes aft to investigate the relay control box. He corrects the problem and remains at the control box once the rocket is fired despite warnings of a tremendous jolt. The maneuver succeeds and stabilizes S-107, but the colonel is knocked out cold. Frey goes aft to retrieve him as Rutledge prepares for reentry by firing the escape capsule. Back on Astra, one crew member observes that the tough part is coming up, but Major Franklin beams, "It may be tough, all right, but I'll bet on McCauley!" Back on S-107, Frey continues whining about doing computations on the button, but Rutledge reminds him they have no choice. "Now let's see if his working on you paid off," he states, patting Frey's shoulder. "Start figuring."

With McCauley injured, the fate of the S-107 was in the hands of Frey and Rutledge. They attempted to execute a reentry to Earth under procedures reserved for absolute emergency.

The ensuing reentry works flawlessly and Rutledge exclaims, "Art, I think you did it." "Not me," Frey objects, "McCauley–all that stuff he drummed into my thick head. Anne, baby, here I come!" Rutledge pilots the S-107 a safe landing on Muroc Dry Lake just as the groggy colonel starts coming to. "You really brought us in, colonel," Frey informs his superior.

Back on the tennis court, the two couples are enjoying themselves and Frey is happily nuzzling Anne, promising her sweet lights and soft music that evening. "I'm not so sure," she says as a staff car pulls up and the ominous figure of Colonel McCauley steps out and approaches. "Here we go again!" Frey moans. Grimaces quickly turn to grins as the colonel announces to Frey that his request for a 30-day leave to get married has been granted. "However, if a certain young lady should turn you down, I have another mission for you tomorrow morning." Anne protests to Frey that he had no right to assume she would accept his proposal, then has second thoughts after espying her engagement ring. "Colonel McCauley," she asks, "Where do you astronauts get all this confidence that you exude?" McCauley awkwardly reflects for a moment, then states, "It's practice, Miss Handlin, practice... I mean in our professional careers." Once he departs, Frey slips the ring on Anne's waiting finger.

"A Handful of Hours"

(Aired January 20, 1960)

Starring: William Schallert (Doctor Orrin), Mark Dana (Doctor Prescott), Peter Baldwin (Lieutenant Bob Kelly), Robert O'Connor, Logan Field, William Lundmark, Del Russel, Scott Davey, Wade Cagle

Script: Michael Plant

Directed by: Alvin Ganzer

Technical advisor: Colonel Lawrence D. Ely, U.S.A.F.

The story you are about to see hasn't happened yet. It will happen when men such as these leave their families and journey to the stars. They will use the most complex equipment science has yet devised, yet their success or failure may depend on the simplest tool or the simplest emotion. This is the story of an expedition to outer space-- and the drama of the men who made it.

At a junior speed track, Colonel McCauley coaches son Johnny as he drives his miniature race car against Jerry, an equally young opponent. In a mock announcement, he declares, "*Today, racing history is being made in a match race between those Devil-may-care drivers, Speed McCauley and Slip Stream Kelly. Tension is rising in the grandstand as these two great drivers come down to the finish line, head and head!*" Johnny ekes out a win and the colonel congratulates him, noting, "Wait till Pete finds out that you've won!" Johnny gasps and says, "Gee, Dad, don't tell him. He'll make me give his car back!" Young Kelly also complains to his father, astronaut Bob Kelly, that his car "conked out" before the finish line and he wants him to fix it. With a Moon mission scheduled that evening, he tells his son to wait until he gets back.

Jerry, crestfallen, promises not to ride in the car until it is fixed. He then confronts his adversary, declaring, "Okay, Johnny, you're the champ till my Dad gets back from the Moon."

After a successful flight from Earth, Colonel McCauley neared the Moon with his important passengers, Doctor Prescott and Doctor Orrin, whose projects held top priority in the space program.

As the rocket races to its lunar objective, McCauley radios Moon Base to commence landing procedures. A bout of static interferes initially, but contact is made and he jokingly alerts Colonel Adams he expects dinner for four–"roast chicken, baked potato, sour cream with chives, please." Adams responds, "Coming right up, colonel!" McCauley quickly corrects him, "Coming right *down*, colonel!" Suddenly, another burst of static knocks McCauley's off the air and the base cannot guide him in. Worse, the vessel's automatic landing pattern has already engaged and the ship rotates backwards and descends. "Crash landing, colonel?" Prescott anxiously inquires. "No, doctor," the colonel assures him, "routine procedure." Back at the Moon Base, the Solar Observatory informs Colonel Adams that a solar disturbance is responsible for the radio disturbance and will continue for some time. Adams quickly orders Lieutenant Denny to organize a rescue party as soon as possible. "Dinner for four..." he mutters.

McCauley's rocket alights safely, then hits a soft spot and topples over. Meanwhile, Colonel Adams spends anxious moments scanning the sky for signs of McCauley's ship, which still cannot be raised by radio. Lieutenant Denny reminds him, "Sir, if they came down behind those mountains, it would break our radio contact anyway." The radio operator announces that the radio interference has cleared up, but McCauley's frequency is completely dead. "Maybe their transmitter's been damaged," he suggests. "Keep trying," Adams commands.

At the crash site, the four occupants, dazed but unhurt, scramble out and assess their situation. "Bob," the colonel lectures, "The spare oxygen tank. We'll need it. Catch!" The big tank floats into the lieutenant's arms almost effortlessly. Doctor Orrin protests that he wants to take some of his equipment, but McCauley cuts him off. "Sorry, Doc, we carry only survival equipment. Let's move!" Kelly informs the colonel that the ship's fuel tanks are ripped and might explode. The four men race to a nearby outcropping for cover, but Doctor Orrin suddenly turns and runs towards the ship. McCauley, reacting instantly, tackles him to the ground. "Are you out of your mind?" Orrin protests. "If you tore my space suit, I'd be dead now!" The rocket wreckage erupts in flame and Orrin, sporting a change of heart, mumbles, "Thank you, colonel. Next time I'll listen." The light from the explosion alerts Moon Base where the ship went down–48 miles from the base and in rough terrain. Adams barks, "We better get that search party out there, quick." "Who's to be in charge?" Lieutenant Denny innocently asks. "You!" is the curt response.

> *The surface of the Moon is a treacherous one. Its craters and crevices made the attempt to reach Moon Base a journey of terror for McCauley and his men. Two ranges of mountains had to be crossed before they would be able to make contact—if the men could survive the journey itself.*

The four men struggle through the rugged lunar landscape and eventually, McCauley orders a rest period to replenish their oxygen tanks. "How far would you say we've come, colonel?" Prescott asks. "I'd say a little more than halfway," he replies. "This will get us there." Still unsatisfied, Prescott asks why they don't radio the base from where they are. McCauley informs him that they are out of line of sight until they get to the mountaintop. "Radio waves travel in a straight line, Doctor Prescott," Kelly chimes in. "I know *that*," he haughtily remarks. Tragically, when the lieutenant turns the tank's air valve, it breaks off. Their fates are almost certainly sealed, but Kelly inadvertently mentions he always carries a wrench. A moment of horrified reflection ensues once the lieutenant realizes it is *inside* his space suit. "Well, colonel," Prescott sarcastically comments, "How long do you think the oxygen we have in our tanks now will

last us?" McCauley confesses he does not know. "Ironic," Doctor
Orrin mutters. "Our survival depends on an elementary tool like a
wrench."

> *The wrench inside Kelly's space suit was the key to life and death—*
> *life for the three men but death in seconds for Kelly if he opened his*
> *space suit.*

Back at Moon Base, Colonel Adams informs Earth Control that
his rescue team is out of radio range and he will not know what
they found until they reacquire a line-of-sight position. McCauley's
team, now saddled with an incapacitated Doctor Orrin, continues
groping towards their objective. He orders another pause and asks
the doctor if he is all right. Orrin responds that he and his wife used
to deliberately go to Austria or Switzerland to climb mountains, so
"I guess I'll have to say I'm enjoying this." "You're all right," the
colonel assures him. "We're all doing fine." Lieutenant Kelly begins
speculating that sooner or later they are going to need that spare
oxygen. "Are we going to make it?" he asks. "Sure we will," Mc-
Cauley responds. Kelly presses the issue, but the colonel mentions
that a rescue team should reach them long before that eventuality.
"C'mon, Mac, be straight with me—you need it?" Kelly pleads. Doctor Prescott then mentions how weak his companion is. "If we do
not open that suit, I'd say that Doctor Orrin will be dead within two
hours," he snarls. "Isn't it time you dispense with sentimentality?
Three lives depend on our getting that oxygen!" "I'll be the judge of
that," McCauley firmly replies. "But Doctor Orrin is invaluable in the
space project!" he protests. "Let him sleep," the colonel counters.
"You're wasting a lot of oxygen arguing," Orrin feebly states. Kelly,
meanwhile, begins looks skyward, nervously rubbing the wrench beneath his suit.

Once at the rocket wreckage, Lieutenant Denny is informed that
there are no survivors. "We've covered the whole area," the sergeant
informs him. "I don't think anybody could have lived through this."
Denny, dejected, orders the men back to base. McCauley also prods
his team back into motion and Prescott sharply reminds Lieutenant
Kelly that he forgot "something." The lieutenant walks back a few
paces and picks up the spare oxygen tank, at which point Prescott

spitefully insinuates, "If you're too tired, maybe I ought to carry that." Kelly spitefully slams the tank into Prescott's chest and keeps walking. "Maybe you better," he murmurs.

Each step McCauley and the crew made called for endurance beyond any that Man had ever needed. Desperately, they carried the one thing that stood between life and death, the cylinder of life-saving oxygen, but with no means of opening it and using it.

The colonel's team limps on, fatigued and needing air, while Doctor Orrin has to be assisted by two men. They stop again to rest with Orrin becoming delirious and mumbling incoherently. "Doc, try and get some sleep, would you please?" McCauley tells him. Prescott bristles, leans over to the colonel, and declares, "I don't think you've met each other. This is Doctor David Orrin, Nobel Prize winner, or maybe you don't recognize him. Maybe you just don't know that lack of oxygen can permanently damage a man's brain cells." "So does tearing a hole in a man's space suit," is the colonel's riposte. A good and moral man, Kelly looks pained, realizing the burden he carries. He offers to open his suit and McCauley summarily orders everyone to shut off their transmitters and save power. "When we get to the top of the mountain, we'll need power to contact Moon Base–I said all of you." Back on Earth, sons Johnny and Jerry are working on their race buggies when the latter declares he would like to take it for a test run, but had promised his father that he would not. "Not till he gets back," Jerry murmurs, then, casting a glance at the moon, continues, "But gee, Pop, you'd sure better hurry."

Each step McCauley and the crew made called for endurance beyond any that Man had ever needed. Desperately, they carried the one thing that stood between life and death, the cylinder of life-saving oxygen, but with no means of opening it and using it—unless one man would sacrifice his own life to save three.

The four astronauts stagger along as best they can until Kelly stumbles and falls into a crevice. With his radio turned off, he cannot call for help as the arrogant Prescott watches him dangle helplessly and simply smiles. A revived Doctor Orrin suddenly pushes him aside and, extending his hand, rescues the lieutenant. The exertion proves too much and Orrin suddenly faints. McCauley rushes back, has Prescott turn on his radio, and demands to know what happened. "Is he asleep now? You call that sleep?" the doctor harshly intones. "Listen, colonel, if anything happens to Doctor Orrin because you won't get that wrench, I will hold you responsible! It's three lives against one!" McCauley, fed up with Prescott, shoots him an icy glare and mutters, "Turn off your transmitter." Meanwhile, the radio operator at Moon Base begins receiving Lieutenant Denny on the crater rim and he informs Colonel Adams, "I regret to report there are no survivors."

Having survived the hazards of their journey of terror, McCauley and the men saw their goal—Moon Base—was just a short distance below them, but beyond the limits of their oxygen supply.

From the mountaintop, McCauley tries contacting Moon Base, but elicits no response. "Why don't they hear us?" Prescott angrily demands. The colonel summarizes that the batteries are too weak and that they can only receive, not transmit. "Everybody stand up. Maybe they can see us," he orders. The colonel then notices that Bob is missing, calls for him, then retraces his steps. He finds the lieutenant lying on the ground, a wrench clutched in hand, apparently having sacrificed himself for the others. The colonel pries the tool from the lieutenant's hand, contemplates it slowly, then casts his eyes skyward.

To McCauley, the wrench would always be a symbol of Man's devotion—one man sacrificed his life that three men could live.

The three survivors, bolstered by fresh air, arrive back at Moon Base, whereupon Colonel Adams pleads with McCauley to eat something. He wearily obliges and sits down at the table with Doctors Orrin and Prescott. Back on Earth, the colonel again supervises a miniature car race between Johnny and Jerry. The latter asks the colonel if his late father said that he'd better win. In a paternal tone, the colonel informs the child, "He told me to tell you that what counts is how you play it along the way. And even if you don't finish, you still haven't lost." McCauley pauses mournfully for a second, then pats young Jerry and raises the flag. As the cars tear off, he looks intently at him, yelling, "Go, boy!"

"Earthbound"

(Aired January 27, 1960)

Starring: Joyce Taylor, Robert Reed (Russell Smith), Annie Benton (Julie Wills), Bryon Morrow (Glen Stillwell), John Garrett (Captain Williams), Don Edmonds (Lieutenant Eden)

Script: Robert Hecker, David Duncan

Directed by: Nathan Juran

Technical director: Colonel Lawrence D. Ely, U.S.A.F.

> *The story you are about to see hasn't happened yet. It will happen one day during the conquest of space, for no matter how far men expand their capabilities, there will always be one man who seeks to go beyond—too far, too fast, too soon.*

The scene opens at a bustling rocket factory with men and equipment industriously darting about. Colonel McCauley, adorned in his hard hat, steps up near the entry ladder, apparently waiting for somebody. Inside the ship, Russ Smith, a young technician, makes final adjustments to a panel, then ventures outside. Observing McCauley, he anxiously introduces himself and babbles about the wonders of space flight. "I see you've been reading the newspapers," the colonel notes. Smith continues his excited rant, whereby McCauley discreetly reminds him of how important his own work is and that he better get back to it. Crestfallen, Smith sheepishly reenters the ship and begins soldering again. Outside, McCauley is accosted by Mr. Stillwell, the company chief, bearing blueprints for final modifications to the guidance control system. McCauley is impressed, noting, "Much more compact. Gives us more space, enables us to increase our payload." Stillwell says he'll put his electronics men to work at once and both men enter the spaceship.

Smith, meanwhile, is attaching a harness to the main instrument frame when Stillwell espies him working and angrily demands what he is doing here. "Just shifting these components, Sir!" The boss continues, "I gave orders to hold this work until approval of the new design!" Stillwell then introduces McCauley to Smith, whom he describes as "one of our younger, more eager electronics men." The colonel admits they have met previously and Smith informs them he was only following the new plans. "How did you get a copy without advance approval?" McCauley asks. "From memory, sir, or didn't the project engineer tell you? This new design was sort of my own idea," Smith beams. "What do you think, colonel?" "Well," McCauley hesitates, "you could be fired for installing modifications without approval, but your design is excellent." The colonel asks why he did not take this bright idea through official channels and Smith explains that it would take too long. "Why waste time?" he asks. McCauley and Stillwell glance at each other, smile, and Smith is told to get back to work. The boss also hands him the blueprints, "in case your memory fails you." The young man goes chasing after Stillwell, but McCauley halts him in his tracks, then Smith asks him how he can get into space. Noting his youth and good health, the colonel suggests joining the U.S. Air Force and the space program. When Smith protests it would take four years to get a commission, McCauley states, "Well, we always have a shortage of trained men on the ground. Perhaps you'd be happier where you are. Let me know."

Back at the McCauley residence, the colonel rehearses the dinner speech he will be giving and wife Mary interjects that he cannot even tie his bow tie correctly, doing it for him. McCauley protests that he will never memorize his speech if she keeps interrupting. "Oh, you'll remember," she advises. "When you get up there, just talk to me." "That's one way to get the last word," he mutters as the doorbell rings. Mary marches off to let the babysitter in, declaring, "Just for that, you won't get any prompting!" "All right," McCauley drawls in mock resignation, "I may end up talking about... babysitters." At the door, Julie Wills pops in and apologizes for being late, then McCauley asks if she's set the date for her marriage yet. She is still thinking about it, but they will finally meet her fiancé once he comes over to pick her up. The McCauleys depart and, later, the bell rings. Russ Smith excitedly approaches, unaware of whose house he just entered. They kiss and cute banter ensues, then Smith starts bragging about all his responsibilities at work. "It burns me up," he protests. "Always *waiting* for things to happen." Smith also claims to be Colonel McCauley's chief consultant and mentions, "It's true, Julie. You'd think a lot more of me if I were one of the men in the sky." Julie emotes that the only reason she has not married him is his inability to settle down. Things take a sudden turn for the worse when the McCauleys return and the colonel, introduced to Smith by Julie, feigns delight at "meeting him." He also pretends to have "invited" Smith to accompany him in space on his next mission. As the couple leaves, Smith thanks the colonel for covering him and the colonel asks if he's playing with fire. "Well, maybe," he ponders. "But by that time, we'll be married and it won't matter!" Smith races out and McCauley, muttering under his breath, says, "Brother, you've got a lot to learn about women."

Back at the factory, preparations continue, readying McCauley's rocket for launching, and the colonel introduces Captain Williams to their navigator, Lieutenant Eden. Meanwhile, Smith is inside, working furiously on the control panel. McCauley explains to his crew that the components have been substantially modified and, tapping Smith on the shoulder, notes, "One of our bright young men in the electronics division came up with this brilliant idea." Williams comments that there is now more space for a man to work in case of emergencies, at which point Smith, listening intently, burns his hand slightly. When the officers leave, he makes preparations to stowaway in the assigned space by laying a cushion over an electronic panel. The spaceship launches as scheduled with Russ in the back. Unfortunately, his weight, aggravated by Gs produced during liftoff, crushes the power panel. As they orbit, Williams tries to start the new guidance system and the system shorts out. The crew switches to emergency power and McCauley goes aft to check on the control panels—only to find Smith lying unconscious on the floor. The colonel is livid, telling the groggy Smith, "Come out of it! Only long enough for me to tell you that you're the darndest fool I've ever had the misfortune to know!" Smith comes to, exclaims he is in space, and McCauley corrects him, bellowing, "You'd better enjoy it right now. It may be the last thing you'll ever see!" He informs the wayward electrician that, due to his stupidity, the engines are dead and they've lost power and guidance. "It must have shorted out," Smith reasons. "Must be how I burned my shoulder." "I wouldn't worry about a scorched shoulder right now," McCauley angrily lectures. "If that unit isn't fixed in an hour, we'll all be cinders!" Smith volunteers to repair the damage he did, but McCauley angrily slams him back into his seat, roaring, "You stay put!"

Lieutenant Eden attempts to fix the control panel, but he is all fumble fingers, so the colonel says, "All right, lieutenant, get out of here. Our lives seems to depend on the man who got us into this mess!" Smith, always glad to be useful, begins repairing to the panel. The lights return, but when McCauley hits the engine button, they fire briefly–then go silent. The colonel deduces the problem is the outboard actuators and they have maybe fifteen minutes to repair it before the hitting the critical air density. "Russ, you wanted to go into space and you're going into space!" McCauley tells him. "Out there, falling?" he asks. "We're falling right now," McCauley yells. "If you chicken out, we're all cooked!" Smith dons a space suit and, accompanied by McCauley, he works his way towards the motors. He is completely dazzled by the sight of Earth and the stars, but the colonel snaps him back with, "Remember, look at nothing but your work!" Minutes race by, but the two men work to somehow fix the actuator. "We have approximately five minutes," the colonel warns him. "Watch out for sharp angles–you tear that suit, you're dead." The repairs are completed, but strain is too much for Smith and he passes out. McCauley begins lugging him back inside. "Hey, we're getting frictional heat already!" William notes in alarm. "How much longer?" "Three minutes," Eden reminds him. The colonel enters the cabin, ties Smith to his seat, then takes control. "It better work this time or we're dead," he declares. "Here we go!" As hoped for, the motors cough to life and the ship safely reenters the atmosphere. Smith, having awakened, cheers in approval, only to sink back down after hearing that the Air Police will arrest him upon landing.

Back at the McCauley residence, the colonel pensively explains his course of action to Mary. "Well, what else could I do? He almost killed four men, destroyed a multi-million dollar spaceship." Pausing a second, he reasons, "You know, they sent him to Atlanta today. Under the circumstances, I think he came out pretty lucky. I pointed out that a team of elephants couldn't get him back into a spaceship!" The colonel feels that a young genius like Smith should not be wasted and is pleased they are starting him at the bottom of the Electronics Design Division. The door rings and the colonel ambles over to answer. "You know, Mary, no matter how foolish the kid was, he still showed a lot of courage when the chips were down," he reflects, walking to the door. Julie then enters and excitedly tells the McCauleys she can no longer babysit as she and Russ are getting married in Atlanta. "He's finally settled down," she beams. "That's great news," McCauley mutters as he continues out the door and Mary inquires where he is going. "To find a new babysitter!" is the reply.

"Caves of the Moon"

(Aired February 3, 1960)

Starring: John Howard (Doctor Rowland Kennedy), Donald May (Captain Doug Bowers), Paul Comi (Major John Arnold), Lillian Hamilton (Mrs. Bennett)

Script: Meyer Dolinsky

Directed by: Lee Sholem

Technical advisor: Major Charles A. Berry, U.S.A.F.

> *The story you are about to see hasn't happened yet. These are scenes from that story, that will happen one day after man has made many probes and landings on the Moon and then seeks to establish a permanent base there. But he must first find the key to his existence—a source of water. The story you are about to see is a story of people, people whose mission is to search for primitive ice in the caves of the Moon.*

> *Colonel Edward McCauley was placed in command of the Air Force's project to search for primitive ice in the caves of the Moon in an effort to overcome the one obstacle that could keep men from living on the Moon: water. Dr. Roland Kennedy, the scientist who conceived and so ardently fought for this exploration, was granted his request to join the mission. Three months after the project was started, the entire crew assembled for a final briefing.*

Colonel McCauley lectures the mission crew how their path will take them over the Lunar Apennines. Dr. Kennedy sardonically chimes in, "I remember as a kid looking up at the face of the Man in the Moon. If anybody had told me that his nose was called the Lunar Apennines, I might never had taken up science." McCauley smiles and asks if there are any other "urgent" matters he needs to discuss and Kennedy mentions that his teenage son Paul wants to join the space corps and asked him to ask the colonel if he "could use a junior astronaut, aged 13." Taking the challenge in stride, McCauley assures the doctor that he also has a young one "that gives me the same sort of static" and that he will give Paul "every possible consideration." Captain Bowers suggests they all return to business and Kennedy lectures that they are making an educated guess how ice formed in caves eons ago while the Moon was accreting and may still exist. "We don't really know," he concedes. Major John Arnold mentions that the lunar cycle of two weeks of daylight and two weeks of night will press them for time. McCauley further declares that they have to explore all the caves and be off the Moon before the night cycle, when temperatures hit 250 degrees below zero. The colonel also mentions that a portable solar panel will provide the main source of power and that the "igloo," replete with an air lock, will be erected at the mouth of the cave to protect it from micro-meteorite bombardments.

That evening, Doctor Kennedy returns home and is upbraided by Mrs. Bennett, his maid, for being so late. She also hands him a telegram informing him that son Paul has been killed in a boating accident and the doctor is staggered by the loss. "I kept going because Barbara left him behind to take care of," he emotes, "and now... why is it that everything that comes close to me dies?" Mrs. Bennett advises the doctor to call Colonel McCauley and tell him that he is cancelling his trip. "But I am going," Kennedy insists. "It's the one thing I want to do right now."

No sooner does the expedition rocket land on the Moon than McCauley barks orders to unload and deploy all the necessary equipment. Foremost among these is the solar reflector, which Major Arnold will construct by himself. Moreover, once operations commence, "I want anybody who's doing duty in here to keep an eye on the power out meter and the signal lights. If there's a meteorite bombardment, switch to batteries immediately!" Some time later, Doctor Kennedy returns inside the igloo and declares, "We're in trouble. I took a quick look down the main passage. I've never laid eyes on anything as complex as that cave network. We'll never cover it in 14 days." He suggests cutting their rest periods to four hours of sleep per night and cover as much ground as possible. McCauley does not like that route and Kennedy angrily blurts out, "We have no choice!" The colonel, taken aback, calms the doctor, then agrees to his suggestion.

More dithering ensues and an impatient Kennedy confronts McCauley, insisting, "We ought to get started in those caves, Ed. This is the chance of a million lifetimes and if we find ice, we find water! If we have water, we have hydrogen and oxygen. Now we've got to find it!"

McCauley calms the raging scientist with, "We will, Doc, we will," then reminds him they have routine tasks to perform first. Major Arnold enters an hour late, Kennedy instantly pounces on him, and the two bicker. McCauley angrily bellows, "Break it up! Now, gentlemen, there is no need for this, we are on a very rigid timetable, and it *will* be adhered to." He calmly instructs both men back to work. Through it all, Kennedy is becoming angrier, more impatient, and uncooperative. Back on the ship, Major Bowers informs Major Arnold, "I'd thought you never get here." Arnold, very tired, confesses, "I can't operate under this kind of pressure, what with McCauley operating on a split-second basis and that Kennedy pushing us to find the ice." Bowers states, "Well, I've known Kennedy for a few years and I can't figure out what's eating him." Arnold complains that he hasn't slept in 20 hours and has four hours to go, but an unsympathetic Bowers departs the ship and tells him, "It's all yours—have yourself a ball."

> *McCauley and his crew slept peacefully, unaware of any danger—and then it happened, one of the hazards of conquering the Moon: a meteorite shower bombarding them like a deadly hailstorm!*

Within hours, lights begin blinking inside the igloo, which awakens McCauley and he frantically hails Major Arnold on the radio. Arnold, who fell asleep, mentions that a micro-meteorite storm has been going on for some time and that he is switching over to batteries.

With the mission just getting underway, the pressures of working against a deadline began to show in increasing tensions. Major Arnold's error almost cost the lives of the other men.

McCauley orders the standby reflector set up, then sternly states on the radio, "Arnold, you're relieved. Report back here immediately." A contrite Arnold receives a thorough dressing down from McCauley, who then asks, "Now the next few hours are going to be even worse—you think you can make it?" Arnold, pulling himself together, says yes. Matters suddenly worsen when Kennedy returns, trades more angry words with Arnold, and a shouting match ensues. "Hold it!" McCauley yells, then tells Arnold, "Get back to the ship!" Hackles raised, McCauley confronts Kennedy and lectures him, "Doctor, let's get one thing straight. You handle the scientific end of this expedition, I'll take care of the rest. If you have anything to say to anybody, say it to me!" Kennedy, feeling sheepish, mumbles, "I'll try and remember that." McCauley reflects momentarily, then reminds the Doctor all hands have been under stress. To break the ice, he inquires how his son Paul is doing and Kennedy, momentarily choked up, tells him he is just fine. The colonel then departs, intuitively sensing that something is wrong.

As McCauley, Doctor Kennedy, and Major Arnold started into the maze of caves deep below the Moon's surface in search of primitive ice, each man realized their efforts might solve the problem of conquering the Moon. Each move forward, each turn, took them further from their base.

With time running out and temperatures falling, exploring the cave proves to be tedious and time-consuming with hints of water in the form of stalagmites and stalactites everywhere, but no ice. The weary men keep looking.

In order to find their way back and make certain they would not explore the same cave twice, McCauley placed markers at strategic points along their line of search. Also, to further aid future expeditions in the caves of the Moon, an accurate photographic record was kept of the various rock surfaces the men discovered.

The exploration team continues tramping on. At one point, McCauley orders Kennedy to check the temperature. The doctor reports six degrees below zero. "No change," he states. The colonel motions them on.

The strain of each day's searching with rest periods as short as possible began to takes its toll and gave McCauley another dangerous problem to cope with—explosions between the men.

As the team rests, Kennedy agitates to rouse the men and continue exploring. "Hey, I thought this was supposed to be a ten-minute break!" Major Arnold protests. "If I can take it, so can you!" Kennedy growls back. McCauley intervenes and reminds Kennedy, "I'll give the orders here, doctor," then motions for Arnold to rise. The major wearily obliges and they continue onward.

As each day's exploration was completed, Doctor Kennedy recorded the progress of the search, hoping that the next day might prove his theory correct—that there was ice deep within the Moon.

Back inside the caves, Kennedy mentions a new route to check, which draws an immediate protest from Major Arnold. "Today? You're out of your head! I'm dragging! We haven't had four hours sleep in the last 48 hours!" McCauley sharply snaps him back in place with, "We're moving out, John, and you're going with us!"

McCauley, knowing the importance of their mission, on which the future of Moon colonization rested, pushed the search for the ice almost beyond human endurance. The rigid timetable and the unknown hazards of the endless caverns deep below the surface of the Moon added to the growing strain on all of the crew, but placed an even greater burden on Colonel McCauley, who had to constantly weigh the question of the safety of his men against the completion of the mission.

On the final day of the mission, McCauley announces that they have two more caves to explore for ice. The team groggily moves off, but, en route, a partial cave-in injures the colonel and he is evacuated back to the igloo. Kennedy wishes to go on exploring on his own, but Major Arnold bluntly reminds him that he is now in charge. "You're going to help me carry him back, and that's an order!"

This added catastrophe made it impossible to continue the search for the ice and stopped all hope for the completion of the mission.

Once inside the igloo, Kennedy and Arnold continue bickering until McCauley finally silences them both. Rising painfully from his bunk, he mutters, "Listen, in a little while the temperature is going to drop to 250 degrees below zero. We're going to have to write this whole trip off as a complete failure." He orders them to begin packing and Kennedy announces that he dropped his camera at the cave-in and wants to retrieve it.

Doctor Kennedy, obsessed with a desire to prove his theory, plunges heedlessly through the endless caverns, not realizing that he might be jeopardizing the lives of the other members of the party. Almost at the point of complete exhaustion, he continued his desperate search with just a few hours remaining before the expedition would have to leave the Moon for the return to Earth.

Back at the cave, the groggy Kennedy carelessly slips, falls, and is knocked unconscious. McCauley and Arnold begin wondering why the doctor has not returned and they uncover both his camera and the note announcing Paul's death. Instantly, they see why the doctor has been so unreasonable. "Let's check those caves," McCauley orders. The two go looking for him while Major Bowers curtly reminds them that liftoff time approaches in only three hours. "Ed, let's turn back," Arnold protests. "We've got a right to live, too." McCauley agrees to a further 10 minutes, then they will retire.

Driven by his desire to save Doctor Kennedy, McCauley and Arnold took a desperate chance with their remaining time and continued the search. Fortunately, they found a tunnel they had never explored and picked up Doctor Kennedy's trail.

McCauley and Arnold finally concede the doctor is lost and they are about to give up. The colonel takes one final temperature reading, then observes, "It's dropped to 40 degrees below zero. Something's changing this temperature awfully fast." Fortunately, the colonel glimpses Kennedy's limp figure in a nearby crevice. While rescuing him, he also beholds a large patch of ice on a rock, proving the doctor's theory. Once back in the igloo, McCauley informs Kennedy that they found the tragic telegram and asks why he did not inform them. "What for?" Kennedy dejectedly insists. "You wouldn't have let me make the trip." Major Bowers suddenly cuts in, declares there is only 14 minutes to liftoff, and demands to know what is keeping them. "It wasn't just the ice I was looking for," Kennedy concedes. "I needed this mission." McCauley assures Major Bowers all hands are on their way. The rocket lifts off as planned and begins its fiery return to Earth.

"Dateline: Moon"

(Aired February 10, 1960)

Starring: Harry Lauter (Jimmy Manx), Lisa Gayne (Joyce Lynn), Ray Montgomery (Paul Carlson), King Calder, Patrick Waltz, Rand Brooks, Dennis Moore, Dana Enlow, Brad Forrest

Script: Mike Adams

Directed by: Alan Crosland, Jr.

Technical advisor: Captain M. C. Spaulding, U.S.A.F.

The next step that Man takes as he leaves the Earth in his attempt to land on and explore some of the distant planets of the Solar System is of utmost importance to those who remain Earth-bound. The day will come when each of these voyages will take men along to report the findings and experiences of those who venture into these strange new worlds. This is the story of two such men who will be able to file their copy with the dateline: "Moon."

Colonel McCauley tries calming a group of impatient journalists, all eager to win a drawing that will enable one to visit and report from the Moon for two weeks. He shakes hands with chief editor Mr. Morrison, who apologizes that his lead reporter, Jimmy Manx, is late for the occasion. Morrison asks if there is any way the drawing can be postponed until Manx arrives, but the colonel smiles and says he is only there to pick the two winners, then excuses himself.

Lisa Gayne, Manx's secretary, then bursts into the room and tells Morrison that she looked all over for the elusive reporter, but cannot find him. He sends her back and Lisa says, "All right, there may be a couple of spots I missed." She finds Manx casually concluding a poker game and issuing blank checks to collect the money owed him. "Honestly, Jimmy, you promised Mr. Morrison you'd be there!" Lisa protests. "I didn't say I'd be on time," he assures her smilingly. One of the game's losers wagers, double or nothing, that Manx will not be going to the Moon and he readily accepts the challenge. Manx and Lisa finally debut at the drawing and Morrison upbraids her for not getting him there on time. "Mr. Morrison, I'm his secretary," she protests, "not his keeper!" The point is moot, seeing that Manx was one of two reporters chosen, and he slides over to get acquainted with the colonel. At this time, McCauley is explaining to the press that his next mission involves automatic relay transmitters to facilitate exploration, or RVBN, "Radio Survival Beacon Network." Manx tries his usual smooth approach on the colonel, who remains unimpressed. "Will I have to salute you, too?" he jests. "No," McCauley counters, "but you will have to sign an agreement placing yourself under military rules and regulations." Manx also encounters the other winner, Paul Carlson, declaring, "Well, we ought to get some great interviews from the natives, eh?" McCauley smiles and quips, "That will be the story of the century." Carlson asks the colonel if he ever felt that the Moon was inhabited and he states no. "Of course, there are many, many theories about the Moon," he states. "But I personally believe that it is just as lifeless as it appears to be and always has been." "But what a story," Carlson beams. "The discovery that at one time or another, in the dim past, there had been an intelligent being on the Moon! Maybe from another planet!" The meeting adjourns and Lisa confronts McCauley, warning him that Jimmy will do anything to get a story. "I think you should know that." "Are you warning me?" he asks. "I suppose so," she concedes, "but more for his sake. I don't want him to get in trouble up there." McCauley assures her that Jimmy Manx and the Air Force will get along just fine, then departs. "I hope you know what you're saying," she mutters.

A rocket blasts off for the Moon, carrying the two journalists, and they arrive at Moon Base as work on the relay network is continuing. They are singularly unimpressed by the Spartan accommodations and, when Carlson steps out, Manx opens his travel kit and nervously fingers a curiously engraved stone. Later, Manx protests that he will not be allowed to visit any of the beacon crews and must accompany McCauley on guided tours of the nearby vicinity only. "We've all been checked out in the use of space suits," he insists. "Checked out, yes–experienced, no," the colonel politely informs them. "What's the matter, colonel, are you afraid we might see something out there we're not supposed to?" he goads McCauley. "We have no secrets on the Moon," the colonel assures him and takes the reporters on their first conducted tour.

> *The crews under Colonel McCauley's command worked against a tight and carefully planned schedule on the installation of radio survival beacon relays which, when completed, would enable future expeditions on the Moon to explore new and unknown areas of the planet's desolate surface with a greater degree of safety.*

Within days, McCauley informs the reporters that the work is nearly completed and they will be returning to Earth soon afterward. Manx begins pushing McCauley for permission to broadcast his show live from the Moon over the combined worldwide network. "Should work out that way," the colonel states. However, when Manx keeps pressing him for permission to go on exploring alone, McCauley refuses, owing to the lack of time, to take him. Manx further makes his presence grating when McCauley catches him running an illicit poker game. He summarily disbands it, noting that gambling for money on the Moon creates morale problems, then informs Manx he has permission to make his broadcast on Sunday night. Once the colonel leaves, Manx propositions an officer by offering to forgive his gambling debt if he will look the other way as he slips off the base unobserved. The officer glares contemptuously at the reporter, then dutifully informs McCauley of the stunt. The colonel wants to avoid making an incident of it, but hereafter the reporter is restricted to the base. Manx, however, has already slipped outside and McCauley orders the work details to begin searching for him. Meanwhile, Manx surreptitiously plants his engraved stone near the "D-2" marker. McCauley catches up with him just as he is about to run out of oxygen and takes him back to base. "You won't be taking any more pictures or anything else on the Moon," he angrily lectures him. "From now on, you'll do your reporting from right here on the Moon Base." Manx does not understand why he is so angry and blithely asks, "You don't think you can make this stick, do you McCauley?" The colonel shoots him a look that could freeze water, orders the men back to work, then walks away.

Back on Earth, Mr. Morrison does not think McCauley would ground their star reporter for nothing. "But you know Jimmy." Lisa is just grateful he was not killed. Back on the Moon, the crew working near "D-2" happen upon a mysterious carved rock in the sand and Lieutenant Gorman frantically asks the colonel for permission to return to base. Manx, listening intently nearby, has a smug look on his face. McCauley closely examines the object, not knowing what to make of it, but it was apparently fashioned by some kind of intelligence. Manx and Carlson excitedly want to send off the story, the biggest in recorded history, but McCauley demurs. "I don't think there are any implications involving national interest here," he reasons, "but I prefer to thinking on a higher level on this." No story will be sent–yet. "Are you forbidding me from filing a story?" Carlson indignantly inquires. "No," McCauley calmly replies, "I am just asking for your cooperation." The colonel then locks the mysterious object in his safe box. That evening, Manx goes on the air from the Moon and begins interviewing the few men still willing to talk him, beginning with Colonel McCauley. When asked if his work is ever routine, the colonel declares, "The awesome and terrible beauty of the Moon is just as overpowering as it was the first time." Suddenly, Manx produces the mysterious artifact from his pocket with the inevitable suggestion that it was made by an intelligence other than Man's. "We are not alone," Manx beams. On Earth, Mr. Morrison nearly falls out of his chair, declaring, "That lucky fool has just come up with the news break of all time!" McCauley, clearly angered, insists there is no scientific verification for any of this and Manx dismisses him. Lisa nervously notes, "Jimmy seems to be making the colonel look bad on purpose." Morrison nonetheless orders his entire staff to get on the story. "We're going to ride this for all it's worth," he insists, "and believe me, it's worth plenty!"

Back on the Moon, Carlson angrily berates Manx for his duplicitous stunt and tells him, "I hope I'm around when you finally fall on your head!" McCauley then enters and demands the object, which he is placing in storage until scientists can examine it. "When they get through with it, they'll have all kinds of information on it–its age, tools used to make it," the colonel notes. "Maybe even deduce something about the being that made it," Carlson conjectures. Manx squirms in his seat, lost in thought. Sometime later, the devious reporter again steals the object from McCauley's locker, dons a suit, and goes back to the site to re-bury it. Who should tap him on the shoulder from behind but McCauley himself, who beckons for the "mystery" object. "All right, Manx, burying that once was enough," he tells him. "You can't bury what you've already done." Back at Moon Base, Manx continues denying his role in the farce, which only draws the colonel's ire. "I feel sorry for you, Manx," he declares. "It's a pity you weren't satisfied just to observe and report one of the greatest adventures ever undertaken by Man." Carlson bitterly asks McCauley when he can file a 1,000-word story, then, looking angrily at Manx, "The 1,000 words of the kind of story that a newspaperman hates to write." McCauley tells him whenever he's ready.

Back on Earth, McCauley is in the office of a contrite Mr. Morrison and the colonel confesses that, despite his doubts about Manx from the onset, "somehow I wanted to believe it." Morrison again tells McCauley what they have already told the world–his organization apologizes for the actions of Jimmy Manx, who, he confidently predicts, will never again find work in journalism. "Yeah, he tried to fake life on the Moon," McCauley reasons. "Now he's going to have to try and find a new life here on Earth."

"Mooncloud"

(Aired February 17, 1960)

Starring: Robert Vaughn (Perry Holcomb), Allison Hayes (Mandy Holcomb), Douglas Dick (Harold Carter), John Cliff, Bill Masters

Script: Michael Plant, Sidney Kalchiem

Directed by: Otto Lang

Technical advisor: Captain M. C. Spaulding, U.S.A.F

If Man could harness even a small part of the natural nuclear power of the universe, the colonization of distant worlds will someday be possible. But as science progresses, the unknown factors become more hazardous and the greatest unknown is often Man himself. This is the story of these men, who sought the source of nuclear power on the Moon, and the unknowns they faced.

On a military base, an officer flags down Colonel McCauley in his car and informs him that Doctor Perry Holcomb has passed his physical exam and is waiting for him in the conference room with Doctor Harold Carter. Turning a corner, the colonel finds his parking space is occupied by a lovely woman, Mandy Holcomb, who wants very much to talk with him. "Perry would be furious if he knew about this," she warns. Apparently, she fears that a lifelong rivalry with Harold Carter might explode dangerously, as "he hates Perry." "That's impossible, Mrs. Holcomb," McCauley insists. "Doctor

Carter made a special request to have your husband come along as his assistant." She explains that despite surface appearances, their "buddy-buddy" bit is just an act and Carter, out of professional jealousy, requested Perry to come along for the satisfaction of "having him under his thumb." "What does that mean to me?" the colonel inquires. She explains that Perry will not stay in his place; he has to stay on top, even if it costs Carter his cherished Harkness Award. "I think Harold would rather see him dead first," she states. "Does your machine know more about him than his wife?" McCauley dismisses the notion and mentions that even his own wife used to fret every time he flew with a new copilot. "Bring him back," Mandy says as she leaves. "They don't make them any better." McCauley reports to the conference room, only to find the two doctors shooting a game of craps on the table. He declines to join them when invited and Carter comically declares, "The colonel is not amused." McCauley promptly informs them, "The colonel is going to get fired if General Tunney walks in and finds you shooting dice." Holcomb states he just wanted to disprove the old cliché that eggheads are all squares. McCauley reminds them that the Pentagon requires a pair of geochemists, not vaudeville artists, and somberly warns them, "Seriously, the old man is not too good at jokes." Who should walk in that moment but Tunney himself, who begins briefing the men on Operation Deep Rock. Apparently, an earlier expedition detected a belt of nuclear radiation at the Alphonsus Crater, and that from beneath a layer of lead 25 feet thick. This indicates a potential amount of raw nuclear material near the Moon's surface. "Now if Doctor Carter's theory is proved true," General Tunney lectures, "the ramifications are enormous. A local source of atomic energy on the Moon could realize our dream of a self-supporting Lunar colony and it might also provide the power for Man's next step into space."

The expedition rocket approaches the Moon and begins landing procedures to touch down at an advanced post near the rim of Alphonsus Crater. "Couldn't we land at the Moon Base?" Captain Van Fleet asks. "The hike out here would have done you fellows good." McCauley, smiling, says, "We thought it would be better if you made the hike back to Moon Base." The ship lands and the men take up residence in their advanced base. Van Fleet is getting ready to walk off, although he wants a cup of coffee first. "Okay,"

McCauley tells him, "but if you stay here any longer I'll put you to work." Doctor Holcomb then mentions that something happened in the Alphonsus Crater back in 1958, when a cloud of gas was observed floating in it from observatories on Earth. He mutters, "Mooncloud…" Later, Holcomb returns from a field trip and declares things are not proceeding as planned. Carter gets on the radio and demands that he return with the detonators, but Holcomb insists on finishing his coffee first. Holcomb also informs McCauley that, unfortunately, the radiation levels are diminishing the further down they go, which spells the end of Carter's dream. "We should have had positive results by now," he states. "I think we're on the wrong track." The colonel asks him why he has not informed Carter and Holcomb explains, "You don't hand out a death sentence until you're certain–and I mean just that. If Hal fails in this, I think it will just about kill him." McCauley reminds him that the expedition must conclude within two days, then Holcomb asks for permission to go to the Alphonsus Crater alone and set off explosives there. He justifies this based on observations of nuclear activity there dating back to 1958. The colonel refuses, citing the danger. "I know Hal is wrong about this," Holcomb insists. "All he's going to get out of this is a couple of tons of lead ore." The colonel shrugs. "If he says no, there's nothing I can do. He's still your boss."

That evening, Holcomb waits until McCauley and Carter are fast asleep, then he tip-toes to the airlock, suits up, and makes for the Alphonsus Crater. There he sets explosive charges and detonates them before returning to the advanced base. Carter is livid by this insubordination and accuses his subordinate of being unable to allow anyone else to have some success. "He has to go one better," the doctor remonstrates. "Always one better!" The two bitterly exchange words and Holcomb insists he was only trying to help. "Anyway you can forget it," he explains. "It didn't work. Nothing happened." McCauley also dresses down the errant doctor for breaking every conceivable regulation and, when Holcomb sarcastically asks if he's going to be clapped in irons, the colonel assures him, "No, but I can make sure that this is your last trip to the Moon!" Carter again explodes, accusing Holcomb of muscling in on his other projects, to which the latter strenuously denies. McCauley looks at the feuding men in disbelief until General Tunney comes on with incredulous news that activity has been observed in the crater–McCauley and his team must investigate at once. "You have top priority orders for an immediate investigation. I hear one of your men set the thing off," he chortles. "Congratulate him!" The colonel and Holcomb suit up and prepare to depart while an embittered Carter remains behind at the radio. "I swore you'd never do that to me again, but you have," Carter informs Holcomb, "and I'm going to kill you for it." The colonel immediately orders him to calm down and stay on communications.

McCauley and Holcomb work their way to the crater rim and observe the moon cloud forming there. As they take separate paths, they turn their tape recorders on, quite unaware that Doctor Carter trails closely behind. McCauley begins sampling the gas floating around him, informing Ground Control that it is definitely radioactive. Holcomb does the same at his end with identical results. Carter, meanwhile, picks up one of the flag markers, apparently intending to stab Holcomb with it. However, as Holcomb explores the rim, he falls down and becomes stuck, his foot lodged in a crevice. He is initially relieved to see Carter hovering at the ledge and tells him to contact McCauley, but Carter mocks him. "Plead," he sneers, "I want to hear you plead!" Holcomb continues asking for help and Carter continues reciting all the slights–real or imagined–he suffered at his hands. "I am going to let you just lay there. This is going to be my project," he hisses. "Nobody is going to steal it from me." "I never stole anything from you, Hal," Holcomb reasons. Growing unhinged, Carter continues ranting. "But you know what I resented the most? Not even that you got Mandy, but that you never had to work for anything! You just reached up into the stars and took it!" Holcomb denies ever complicating his career, insisting, "You set your sights too high and you missed!" He urges Carter to take a good look at himself and not overlook what he is doing. The despondent doctor lumbers off, declaring, "Lay there and die! Because your oxygen will run out before McCauley can find you." The colonel, meanwhile, continues taking gas samples from the crater floor when Carter, experiencing a change of heart, informs him of Holcomb's predicament. A contrite Carter subsequently tells his colleague, "I couldn't do it, Perry. I'm coming down to help." McCauley also arrives and helps lift the injured astronaut up, after which the rocket blasts off for Earth.

Back at the Holcomb residence, McCauley, the doctor, and Sandy are having dinner when she lifts the old Harkness Award trophy from the floor and places it on the mantle. "Somehow I feel it won't embarrass Hal anymore," she reasons. Mandy also mentions meeting with Hal and actually liking him for the first time. Holcomb also informs McCauley that Carter has applied for a transfer to conduct independent research. The colonel simply adds that, "You know, it's amazing how competition stimulates some people and destroys others." Mandy confesses, "I don't know what happened out there; apparently Hal found himself." McCauley then mentions that Holcomb's tape recorder came back with no tape in it. The doctor hands it over, admitting that he had erased it. When McCauley asks why, Holcomb explains, "Well, everything considered, I felt I was advancing the cause of science."

"Contraband"

(Aired March 2, 1960)

Starring: James Coburn (Doctor Narry), Robert Osterloh (Doctor Rice), Robert Christopher (Doctor Bromfield), Don Ross (Doctor Orr), Pat McCaffrie, John Close

Script: David Duncan, Stuart James Byrne

Directed by: Alvin Ganzer

Technical advisor: Captain M. C. Spaulding, U.S.A.F.

> *New technology will enable Man to travel to more distant planets. But no matter where he travels, one thing will always be the same: Man himself. Human nature will not change in the strange outposts of space. There will always be love and hate, courage and fear—and even greed. This is the story of an expedition to a distant world that was brought to the brink of disaster by one man's greed.*

In a military office setting, Colonel Foretti displays an expensive Moon crystal to Colonel McCauley and asks where it came from. McCauley recognizes the item: it originated in a mission he commanded the previous June and it was turned over to the Bureau of Standards. Foretti then produces out a much larger sample of the same stone, which neatly fits onto the original rock. He then mentions how this item was illegally sold to an industrialist for $70,000 and, logically, the heist can be traced back to one of the four scientists accompanying the mission that retrieved it. Or even McCauley himself. "Why not a ship of another nation?" he asks. "Then it could have been smuggled into this country." There is too much corroborating evidence suggesting that the item originated from McCauley's earlier mission. The colonel inquires why the stone is so valuable and the officer informs him, "Well, it can slice diamonds like butter, has very valuable optical properties, and retains them at 3,000 degrees centigrade." McCauley still cannot bring himself to believe one of the scientists stole it, but the officer reminds him, "Greed does funny things to men, colonel." McCauley reasons that greed is only part of the problem, that there has to be a bigger deposit near the Moon Base. "Then somebody is keeping a secret," Foretti assures him. "Now you understand why we haven't questioned any of the other suspects." The colonel next summarizes that he is to take the four men back and simply watch them. At this juncture, a highly irritated Doctor Narry, the chief mineralogist, bursts in the room, protesting that he will have to fly another mission with Doctor Bromfield, whom he loathes. "I can't stand a man who laughs all the time," he insists. The colonel informs him, "I am not the final authority, Doctor Narry, but you can always refuse to go yourself." The doctor is upset, but insists on going. "Just try and keep me away," he snarls while leaving.

In the conference room, the four scientists are waiting for McCauley and Doctor Bromfield makes his presence unwelcome through his nervous, persistent laughter. He had been taunting Narry over his role in the mystery and the latter protests his innocence. "I stated that I cataloged every sample or specimen I had taken from the Moon without ever seeing that particular sample." "Maybe the little sample has been growing!" Bromfield blurts in mock surprise. Doctor Rice also expresses his skepticism, but Broomfield mentions that since he received an honorary doctorate from his university, he has never been bothered by the lack of money. "Not for myself," he insists, although he wishes he could endow some worthy scientific research program. "Philanthropy," Narry sneers. "Only a form of ostentatious luxury. I just wish I knew how that sample got by me without my knowing it." Bromfield goads him further, at which point Narry grabs him by the collar. McCauley fortunately enters and orders the two to break it up. The colonel begins discussing their upcoming mission and tells them a special effort will be made to locate the deposit of "Specimen 9" somewhere near the Moon Base. "With the cooperation of all," he declares, "I trust we'll find it."

A rocket approaches and lands on the Moon and McCauley lectures his passengers about the rules. He also notes that Major Stubblefield will remain on the vessel at all times, manning the radio. The team ensconces itself in the shelter and the men immediately begin bickering during breakfast. When Doctor Bromfield talks laughingly about the light gravity, Doctor Rice informs him that it should not interfere with swallowing, "it only makes me feel lightheaded." Doctor Orr, unable to resist a jab, comments, "Last time we were here, it apparently made somebody light-fingered." McCauley, seeking to expedite the matter, inquires, "Do you prefer this out in the open?" The scientists shrug. "Certainly," Narry smugly states. "It would give Bromfield something more to laugh about." "It just might," Bromfield assures him. McCauley then admits that, as commander of the last mission, he would be in the best position to smuggle "Sample 9" aboard, then sell it. He also mentions that the gemstone was worth at least $200,000, yet only sold for one-third that. "The seller got cheated!" Bromfield asserts. "And so did the government," the colonel insists. "If anybody knows where it is, it will go a lot easier for you if you say so right now." The appeal solicits no response, so McCauley emotes, "Don't you realize I am just trying to give the guilty man a way out? It doesn't prove anything. All the government wants is the deposit." With no takers, the colonel has little choice but to announce that the group will split up and search for the deposit in teams.

Tensions mounted as McCauley and the scientists searched for the deposit of Specimen 9, each man realizing that McCauley watched every move he made. Each man knew he was suspected, but only one man knew he was guilty.

Doctors Rice and Bromfield go exploring and the latter stops to cut and pick up a few rock samples. Rice confesses that this is the most distressing situation he has ever been in and, if he realized he was going be accused of theft and defrauding the government, he would have never come. "Yeah," Bromfield assures him, "but if you had refused to come, you would have been suspected all along. So would any of us." McCauley is excavating with Narry, who tells him, "Very interesting rocks around here, colonel." "Forget about that for now. We're running low on oxygen. Let's get back to the base," comes the dry response. En route, Orr points outs something to McCauley, half-buried in the sand, which the colonel recognizes as some kind of marker. "It might be something one of the other missions used. We'll check it when we get back to the base. Let's go." Once back inside, the men review their various samples as Bromfield sardonically quips, "But not one trace of Specimen 9."

McCauley, meanwhile, cannot identify the marker and speculates that men from some other nation might have placed it there. No matter, Bromfield asserts. "Meanwhile, the fungus is still among us." Doctor Rice protests, "I can't stand this much longer, colonel. It's like being on trial." Then Doctor Orr asks McCauley what Major Stubblefield doing all this time. Narry slyly inquires if the colonel is shielding him, upon which the colonel laughs. "Shielding him? I hate to say this about my co-pilot, but he couldn't tell a diamond from a glass bead. He knows nothing about minerals." Unconvinced, Narry insists that the colonel call him on the radio. McCauley's demeanor stiffens and he curtly informs him, "Doctor, on this base I don't take orders. However, I'll accept your suggestion." McCauley demonstrates by radioing Stubblefield, upon which the latter informs him the astronomers on Earth conclude from photographs that some other nation is visiting the Moon whenever the Americans are absent. The colonel shrugs and says, "Well, gentlemen, my apologies." Bromfield speculates that is why he could not find the marker in the code book. "Someone else has been here." Rice chimes in, "Then it wasn't necessarily one of us at all. What a relief!" McCauley advises them that they all get some rest. Narry suddenly lunges at Bromfield and the colonel separates them, declaring, "That will be enough of that!"

That evening, a mysterious visitor appears outside the shelter, approaches the window, and gently taps. McCauley is awakened and initially dismisses it as a micrometeorite, then suits up and goes outside to investigate. The colonel apparently reopens the hatch and returns to bed. Subsequently, a figure tip-toes out of the shelter in his own space suit, walks up to a rock formation, and begins chipping away. McCauley suddenly appears behind him and the figure runs, only to be tackled by the colonel. "What are you trying to do, kill yourself?" he berates the suspect. "There's no place to run to on the Moon." The culprit is Doctor Rice. Back at the base, McCauley declares that Major Stubblefield was sleeping in his bunk while he was out nabbing Rice. He then explains how Rice was suspected all along, especially after he had recently endowed his university's chair of geology with large sums of money, which confirmed Air Force suspicions. McCauley is puzzled that, after giving Rice two chances to either confess or reveal the deposit's location, he took advantage of neither. "Because of the disgrace," Rice mutters. "I'd never be able to hold my head up again." The colonel then mentions that Major Stubblefield planted the marker and made the bogus news announcement to lure Rice into revealing the location. "I had to make you feel that you were completely removed from all suspicion so that you'd take me to 'Specimen 9.'"

Back in the commander's office, McCauley produces the few examples of the coveted ore that could be retrieved. "Just enough to buy a few islands and stock them with yachts," Foretti blurts. Doctor Narry inquires what is going to happen to the fallen colleague Rice. McCauley states that no decision has been reached and "I don't think he really cares, he has a lifetime to try and find his own integrity again." Narry then presses for when the men can resume their work and Foretti insists just as soon as they return the newly-missing piece of Specimen 9. McCauley, noting the sample is stuck to his superior's sleeve, plucks it off for him, declaring, "Nice try, Colonel Foretti! Would you please lock this stuff up before we all have to go back to the Moon–including you!"

"Dark of the Sun"

(Aired March 9, 1960)

Starring: Carol Ohmart (Muriel Gallagher), Dennis McCarthy (Doctor Caleb Fiske), Manning Ross (Doctor Torrance Alexander), William Lechner (Major Paul Ellis), John McNamara, Robert Darin

Script: David Duncan

Directed by: Alvin Ganzer

Technical advisor: Captain M. C. Spaulding, U.S.A.F.

In ancient times, Man was terrified when the Moon passed in front of the Sun, plunging Earth into darkness. Today, men use an eclipse to aid in studying the Sun's secrets. The day will come when Man will attempt to probe even deeper into these secrets. This is the story of a group of men—and a woman—who ventured into outer space to explore the source of power of our solar system.

In an Air Force office, General A. W. Withers, Colonel McCauley, and Major Ellis fret over how to pick three candidates from a stack of volunteer scientists who will participate in a special solar research mission. Withers bemoans the fact he has applications from astronomers he has never even heard of and Major Ellis, a medical doctor, states that the general's own staff will have to select three for training. When Withers asks Ellis if he would like to pick them instead, the latter declines, noting, "My job is to make sure the three winners stay healthy!" Glancing over to McCauley for sympathy, the general inquires if he might be interested, which elicits a long, low, "Not me... not me." Pressing the issue, Withers opines, "You've got command of this mission–now what do you suggest?" McCauley shrugs and confesses, "Nothing right now. It will take the wisdom of Solomon to get us out of this!" The general suddenly takes inspiration and suggests that their new computer, "Ol' Solomon," analyze and pick the best three candidates. "There's only one thing we have to remember, General," McCauley observes. "Ol' Solomon here is just a machine. He'll give us the right answers as long as we ask the right questions." Within minutes, three names are generated and submitted: Doctors M. C. Gallagher, Caleb Fisk, and Torrance Alexander. The three scholars are then notified for interview purposes, of which only two will actually accompany the experiment. The following Monday morning, when McCauley reports to General Withers for duty, the general has him read Gallagher's physical description for the dossier: "Height 5 feet, 5 ½ inches, weight 117 pounds–he's a little fellow, isn't he? Chest 36, waist 23, hips 38..." the colonel pauses, disbelieving. "What do the initials 'M. C.' stand for?" "Muriel Catherine," General Withers informs him. "Ol' Solomon doesn't have any concept of sex, you see?" The colonel, smiling ear-to-ear, feigns innocence and ponders, "What do we do now?"

Flabbergasted, the general commences a tirade about not letting a woman near the spaceship. "I am not going to see the Air Force playing nursemaid to some dried-up, sexless spinster, who was probably born with a slide rule in one hand and a table of logarithms in the other." Colonel McCauley diplomatically indicates that the comely Doctor Gallagher is standing right behind him and the general snorts, "McCauley, don't interrupt me. Space is man's last refuge from the female sex and I don't intend to see it invaded!" Doctor Gallagher suddenly introduces herself, along with Doctors Fisk and Alexander; then, to compound the general's embarrassment, she feigns disinterest and says, "But I don't want to interrupt the general. You were saying something extremely... interesting." Withers shoots a panicked look to McCauley, who instantly suggests he continue with his ongoing "story" about an old spinster. The ensuing joke falls flat, so Gallagher simply smiles and confesses, "I thought you were talking about me." "Of course not!" McCauley gobbles. "We're delighted to see you!" Whereupon Major Ellis bursts in, demanding to know if Ol' Solomon selected "some dizzy female for this mission?!" The colonel motions him to cork it, at which point Gallagher slides up behind him and demands to know, "What did the dizzy female say to the major?" McCauley, speechless, hands the question off to a hapless General Withers.

Later, in the conference room, a film by McCauley explains the finer points of the impending mission, which entails flying into the apex of the Earth's shadow to photograph the Sun's corona. Divested of the planet's atmosphere, much greater detail is anticipated and "our ultimate purpose is to find out if there are other forms of solar energy, which might be used by ships in space." Doctor Alexander reminds McCauley that only two scientists will accompany him and the colonel confesses he hopes that, following weeks of strenuous training, "One of you might prefer not to go." Doctor Gallagher bristles at the thought and angrily asks, "Why do you look at *me* when you say that?" After a few seconds of stunned silence, the colonel assures her, "It was purely coincidence, Doctor Gallagher. The final decision will be made at the space station." Once McCauley departs, Fisk comments that the Air Force seems to be bearing down hard on his female colleague, but she simply shrugs and confesses, "If I want the job, I have to qualify–it's the attitude I object to." Doctor Alexander comments such harassment might not happen if she were married, as "A husband and wife team of astronomers would be completely acceptable." Doctor Fisk angrily comments that Alexander sounds like he's proposing to Gallagher, which he strenuously denies. "Oh, stop it, both of you!" she remonstrates. "Some men–even scientists–make their proposals in private!" Once Gallagher storms out of the room, Alexander and Fisk trade more angry barbs before departing themselves.

Doctor Alexander successfully passes the physical exam given by Major Ellis and inquires if Doctor Fisk also passed. Ellis informs him that such information is strictly confidential, then asserts, "Five minutes ago, Doctor Fisk asked me the same question about you."

However, Ellis starts losing his composure when Gallagher enters the room behind him and asks, "Are you going to examine the dizzy female or not?" Struggling to contain his feelings, Ellis examines her and says, "You know, you amaze me–you've come through these tests quite as good as the men!" "Forget the distinctions; just examine me, please," comes the cool response. Ellis takes his stethoscope and repeatedly asks her to breathe deeply, enjoying every second of it.

> *With their tests and examinations on Earth completed, the scientists, under McCauley's command, entered Phase 2 of their training.*

As the rocket bears down on the space station, McCauley casually observes to his passengers, "Well, your first taste of space travel. Do you like it?" The scientists adjust well to the new experience, but Doctor Alexander notes life in their new abode lacks privacy. "Very few refinements," the colonel adds. Sensing an insult, Doctor Gallagher shoots him a cold look.

> *At a space station orbiting over one thousand miles outside of Earth, decisive tests would determine who would undertake the difficult mission into deep space to observe the Sun totally eclipsed by Earth.*

After the rocket docks, McCauley instructs his passengers to relax and take time to adjust themselves to their new environment. He also assures Doctor Gallagher that she will have her own special quarters. "Can't we stop emphasizing this special treatment?" she asks, somewhat annoyed. Ellis then informs them that while they are in the station's hub, they will feel like they are in a falling elevator. "But remember, it's only an illusion–and don't faint." "Would it please you if I did?" Gallagher sarcastically quips. "Sorry," Ellis concedes. No sooner do the three debark than Fisk and Alexander resume bickering over who should marry their lady compatriot. The squabble concludes just as McCauley returns, at which point Gallagher asks for those private quarters she was originally assigned. Alexander then presses the colonel, as commander of the station, to pronounce him and Doctor Gallagher "man and wife." Fisk chimes in, "That's his little plot to make sure he goes on the mission." When the colonel asks if Gallagher is in favor of the scheme, Alexander sneers, "Why not? Obviously, she needs the protection of a husband." The colonel confesses he does not know if he has the authority to unite a couple in matrimony and will inquire about it to Earth. Later, McCauley assures General Withers on the radio, "No, no, general, there's nothing wrong with your ears. I just want to know if I have the authority to marry people." Withers is as perplexed as his subordinate and promises to telephone authorities in Washington for an answer. McCauley smiles with silly satisfaction as he gets up—then runs smack headlong into Doctor Gallagher. "Forget the whole thing, colonel," she snarls. "I don't need protection and I'm not going to marry anybody!"

Soon the mission ship *Eclipse* rendezvouses with space station *Astra*. "That's us!" McCauley beams, watching the monitor. "Those are the wheels that are going to take us to the apex of the Earth's shadow." Pausing, he notes that Doctor Gallagher is not among them and he dispatches Major Ellis to find her. The major finds Gallagher in her compartment and asks what is wrong now. "When I applied for this job, I was an astronomer!" she protests. "What are you now?" Ellis asks. A smile breaks across Gallagher's face as she realizes the answer. "A woman..." Approaching the good doctor, who instinctively backs off, she purrs, "So from now on I'm going to start acting like a woman." Reaching into her locker, she pulls out a lovely dress, then shoots poor Ellis another cold look. Meanwhile, McCauley, Fisk, and Alexander suit up and drift over to the waiting *Eclipse*.

Colonel McCauley started the final phase of indoctrination for the three scientists—a flight through space to the unmanned rocket ship, which would be the laboratory for observations of solar flares during a man-made eclipse.

McCauley, Fisk, and Alexander successfully transfer to their new vessel, but Doctor Gallagher is nowhere in sight. "Stay here," he orders the scientists. "Close the airlock after me." McCauley drifts back to the space station only to find Gallagher floating by the airlock, apparently unconscious. The colonel takes her back to her quarters for Major Ellis to examine. "I don't get it," he admits. "The trip up here didn't bother her at all." Pausing a second, he mumbles, "Hey, wait a minute..." checks her temperature, and correctly deduces that she is faking her illness. "Your temperature is normal," he informs her. "You didn't give it enough time," she murmurs. McCauley asks why she deliberately disqualified herself from the mission and she replies, "Because it was the only graceful way out. Since I started this training, I've been the cause of dissension simply because I am a woman." She dejectedly concedes that space belongs to men. The colonel quickly corrects her. "No doctor, space belongs to the men *and* women who have the courage to conquer it." She is amazed they still want her to accompany the mission, for, as the colonel declares, "The dissension is caused by the men, *not* the woman." Gallagher then suggests she can solve the problem by *being* a woman. McCauley, eyeing her shapely form from head to toe, smiles and says, "Yes... I think you can."

Back on the *Eclipse*, Fisk and Alexander continue their childish tirade when McCauley arrives and orders everybody to the station. Back in Gallagher's quarters, Ellis admiringly states that she is such a magnificent specimen. Gallagher, seizing her initiative, retorts, "Not very romantic, Paul. Sounds like you're talking about a prize cow." Rising from her chair and drawing close, she says in a low voice, "Besides, don't you think you should call me Muriel?" A slow kiss follows. Then, on cue, McCauley and the two feuding scientists enter, only to find Ellis and Gallagher completely immersed in each other. Breathless, she inquires, "Why did you take so long to let me know?" The two doctors storm off and Gallagher thanks Ellis for cooperating. McCauley then switches on the intercom to hear Fisk and Alexander draw cards over who accompanies the mission. The colonel joins them in the other room, only to receive an urgent message from headquarters, and Ellis congratulates Gallagher for putting on such a good act. "You should know something, Dr. Ellis," she informs him. "I wasn't acting." More kisses follow. McCauley interrupts the festivities to announce, "I just found out I have the authority to marry people. Any takers?" He smiles and diplomatically leaves the room.

Back on Earth, General Withers congratulates Doctor Gallagher on her excellent photographs. "Mrs. Ellis," the major corrects him, whereupon McCauley presents them with a two-week leave of absence. The happy couple departs, then Withers asks the colonel why he married them on Earth after all the trouble he went to for securing his authority for doing so in space. "Don't tell my wife," McCauley pleads. "I couldn't remember the wedding ceremony!"

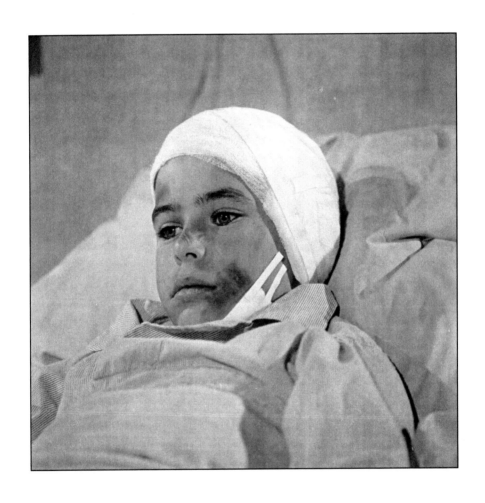

"Verdict In Orbit"

(Aired March 16, 1960)

Starring: Joyce Taylor, Peter Adams (Doctor Arnold Rawdin), Tod Andrews (Lieutenant Colonel Vern Driscoll), Norman DuPont, John McCann, Robert Dornan, Charles Herbert

Script: Michael Plant, Sidney Kalcheim

Directed by: Nathan Juran

Technical advisor: Captain M. C. Spaulding, U.S.A.F.

Colonel McCauley is seated in his office when the orderly sergeant informs him he has a visitor who "wouldn't give his name." The colonel quizzically has the sergeant send in the stranger and young Peter McCauley springs past the door. "Hi, Pop!" he exclaims, to which McCauley smiles and declares, "Some V.I.P.!" Pete excitedly exclaims that he heard his father's launching was cancelled and that Sergeant Wilson took him all over the base. "Not bad," he authoritatively opines. McCauley states, "I'm glad you approve," then explains that his launching was not postponed after all, only delayed until 7:30. "Can I stay and watch?" Pete innocently asks. "Not a chance," his father insists. "Your bike cruises at three knots–if you leave right now, you'll be home before dark and that's exactly what we promised your mother. Now march." Pete dejectedly tramps toward the door, but the colonel reminds him, "You take good care of Mommy and Johnny for me while I'm gone, huh?" The sergeant in-

185

forms McCauley that all flight personnel are in the briefing room except for Doctor Rawdin, who is on the phone. The colonel answers and reminds Rawdin that he should be present and inquires why he is late. The doctor responds that the press has hounded him since they learned the flight was initially cancelled, but he is leaving now. "We're ready to begin pre-flight briefing now," McCauley sternly states. "You should be on the base." Rawdin pleads ignorance, believing that the briefings only pertained to flight crew members. "I'll be there in fifteen minutes," he assures the colonel. A half hour passes and McCauley, visibly annoyed, informs the sergeant that the pre-flight will commence even though the doctor is still absent. The sergeant confirms that Rawdin has left his house, but the colonel orders Doctor Baskin on standby status in case Rawdin proves unavailable. Meanwhile, a pensive Rawdin gets out of his car, phones the operator, and reports that a boy on a bicycle has been struck by a car. He declines to contact the police and only gives the location of the accident before hanging up. The doctor comes charging into McCauley's office just as the briefing ends and the colonel sternly informs him that they depart in 45 minutes.

The team's rocket lifts off and rendezvouses with the space station. Once aboard, McCauley greets Lieutenant Colonel Vern Driscoll, who complains that Doctor Rawdin is getting all the press coverage—even the wife and kids want his autograph. "You know, I feel kind of sorry for the guy," McCauley reasons. "All that movie star publicity must be kind of embarrassing for a scientist in his position." Driscoll mentions he wants to hear more about the breathing device Rawdin is working on for the Venus mission. Rawdin enters and is introduced, whereupon friendly chatter ensues. The doctor congratulates Driscoll for the plans of the upcoming Venus probe and the latter confidently asserts, "I think you'll find that we're fairly efficient up here!" McCauley then escorts the doctor to his quarters.

The men who take up duty on space station Astra lead a life far removed from Earth and home. They are like Antarctic explorers at Little America, but with a difference: in Little America, except for radio contact and supply ships, the isolation is complete. Here on Astra, every few hours, the men pass over their home towns. This breeds a different kind of loneliness.

McCauley and Rawdin pass the time playing chess while Lieutenant Colonel Driscoll bemoans hovering over Miami Beach. "Night clubs! Girls! What are they?" he jokes. McCauley counters, "Your wife will refresh your memory in about ten days." The colonel also informs Doctor Rawdin that the Venus probe will have atmospheric samples for analysis in a few hours, then checkmates him. Driscoll joins them at the table and asks what the actual principle is behind his new mask. Rawdin explains it is basically a "reverse photosynthesis," which breaks down carbon dioxide into breathable oxygen indefinitely. It should work well on Venus, whose atmosphere is believed to consist of carbon dioxide and water vapor. The doctor cuts himself short to hear the news when the reporter announces that police in the Redondo-Canaveral area are looking for the hit-and-run driver who injured a young boy. The reporter continues, "An anonymous telephone call was received, now thought to be from the hit-and-run driver himself, giving the exact whereabouts of the accident." Driscoll exclaims, "How about that? Leaving a kid like that? What's the rap for a hit-and-run, manslaughter?" McCauley sullenly declares, "I don't know... it's more like murder to me." Doctor Rawdin, growing pale, speaks up in defense of the driver and says, "You never know. There could have been extenuating circumstances." "Yeah," Driscoll grumbles, "like being yellow." Rawdin repeats his assertion and Mc-Cauley drawls out, "More important than saving a kid's life?" Rather than dig himself any deeper, the doctor switches back to discussing his breathing system, which, both officers agree, could eliminate the need for unwieldy space suits. An airman suddenly enters and hands the colonel a message, but he continues talking. "Now that's quite something to think about. No wonder they pulled out the red carpet treatment for you," McCauley exclaims. "It makes all the difference between exploring and colonizing the planet." The colonel then reads the message, his pallor changes, and he orders the airman to raise Mrs. McCauley on the emergency frequency. Driscoll asks if something is wrong, but the colonel angrily stalks off into the adjoining compartment. "Did you see his face?" Driscoll asks Rawdin. "It's like we've fallen out of orbit or something..." Driscoll picks up the telegram, then informs Rawdin that the kid mentioned in the accident is McCauley's son. "Report condition critical." Instantly, Rawdin exudes an anxious, yet detached, mien.

In the control room, Colonel McCauley attempts to calm an appreciably frantic Mary, but she begs for him to come home. He insists it will be three days before a rocket is available. "Three days may be too late to see your son alive!" she wails. McCauley again tries calming her and asks if the police got the driver yet. She responds that the police are taking tire tracks and he growls, "If they do get him, they'd better keep him away from me." Mary, however, simply breaks down. "Ed, I can't cope with this for three days... I can't... I can't! Ed, I *need* you! Oh, Ed, come home!" she sobs. McCauley, livid from the toll on his family, retreats to his quarters. Driscoll visits to report that they have a new problem–Doctor Rawdin is acting erratically and neglecting his work. McCauley angrily asks, "Can't you handle it?" Driscoll insists, "Colonel, he's ruining the experiment." The colonel agrees to talk with the doctor and finds him nervously twittering about his lab. McCauley places a reassuring hand on his shoulder, insisting that adjustment to space takes time and to be patient. "Do you think the experiment is important?" Rawdin asks the colonel. "Worth sacrificing a lot?" The colonel agrees and pledges to help as much as possible. Suddenly, Driscoll bursts in and informs McCauley that Ground Control is calling. The colonel leaves and Rawdin nervously asks if the news is about the boy. Driscoll says no, but the police have identified the hit-and-run driver and, "Since they know who it is, it won't take long. I can't help but feeling kind of sorry for the stupid slob, especially if Mac ever gets his hands on him." Driscoll departs, then Rawdin, ashen-faced, realizes his fate and begins blurting out. "I was right," he insists, "I was right to go on! The progress of science and Mankind..." Pausing long enough to hold a container of test tubes, he slams them down, sneering, "Progress!" The shaken doctor quickly exits the lab.

In the communications room, McCauley finds himself talking to the Air Provost Marshal, who wants to keep matters confidential. Rawdin is positively fingered as the hit-and-run driver, to which an incredulous McCauley growls, "Yes... yes, I agree it is a *very* tricky situation." The colonel charges back into the lab, pushing Driscoll aside. He angrily calls for Rawdin and informs his subordinate, "They found the driver: Arnold Rawdin!" McCauley again shoves Driscoll out of the way as he departs. The hunt for the missing scientist begins and, when all leads turn up negative, he slams his fist down. "Well, check again! A space station is one place a man can't disappear!" Driscoll informs him that a space suit is missing–Rawdin has apparently donned it and slipped outside. McCauley orders him to contact the fugitive by radio and order him to come in. When Rawdin fails to respond, McCauley refuses to risk the lives of any of his men outside. Driscoll reminds the colonel that the doctor is too important to ignore and he angrily bellows, "My kid is important, too!" McCauley again refuses to send someone outside and Driscoll reluctantly informs him that he is taking charge. "I'll tell command you are emotionally unfit for duty." McCauley dutifully informs him that this is mutiny, but Driscoll is willing to take that risk and believes that a court-martial would see it as such. Regaining his composure, the colonel mumbles, "Yeah, you're right, Vern." Driscoll glumly concedes, "That was the hardest thing I ever had to do, Mac. I know how you must feel." Driscoll also insists that the colonel not go outside in his present state and McCauley barks, "You've just told me that already I've slipped up as an officer, don't make it any more difficult now." Suddenly, McCauley, realizing Driscoll is right, stands down and his subordinate suits up. At length, Driscoll finds Rawdin on the catwalk near the rocket housing and when he approaches, the doctor pulls a knife and threatens to puncture his own suit. He is nonetheless contrite and says, "I'm sorry about everything." Driscoll withdraws and McCauley decides to try his luck before the doctor runs out of oxygen, noting, "It's *me* he's concerned with. I have a feeling I am the only one who can get him back alive." Once inside, a wary Driscoll asks if the colonel really wants Rawdin back alive. "Yeah, "McCauley mumbles, "I want him in alive…"

At length, McCauley confronts Rawdin outside the airlock and invites him back for his own safety. He notes that a meteorite could puncture his space suit, to which the doctor fatalistically replies, "Yeah, a few seconds of agony. Isn't that what you'd like to see? I am serious, colonel, right now my life seems worth very little to me." McCauley steps out of the airlock, approaches Rawdin, and insists he means a lot to the Venus expedition. Rawdin, tormented by remorse, begins questioning if Mankind is ready to reach for the stars, that in always advancing, perhaps he hasn't paused long enough. "Why'd you come out here?" he demands. "I don't know… my conscience, probably," McCauley reasons. "I *wanted* to leave you, but I was putting personal feelings over duty." Reflecting, Rawdin confesses, "Just the exact opposite of what I did." He goes on, "I made myself go on because I felt that my job was more important than your boy's life. Where's the humanity in that?" "Maybe that isn't why you left him at all," McCauley reasons. "Maybe there's a different, simple answer, one with all the humanity in the world–you were frightened of being punished." Rawdin, stung by the realization that he was "just plain frightened," hands over his knife and accompanies the colonel inside.

Back on Earth, Colonel McCauley enters Pete's hospital room, where he is busily reciting the over-laden ice cream sundae he wants to his mother. "Holy smoke!" the colonel tells him. "Do you want to stay in the hospital for the rest of your life? You know, you had your mom and I kind of worried there for a while." Pete mentions that his heavily bandaged head still hurts, to which Mary whispers, "We're lucky it's still there." Pete then asks his father what will happen to Doctor Rawdin and suggests that they let him go, as "I'm all right." The colonel informs him that Rawdin broke the law and he will have to suffer the consequences. He then asks Pete to recite the ice cream sundae he wanted and Pete goes on, "Caramel, two bananas, half an apricot, strawberry sauce, chopped walnuts, and pecans," then winks at his parents.

"Is There Another Civilization?"

(Aired March 23, 1960)

Starring: Joyce Taylor, John Bryant (Major Bowyers), Paul Carr (Captain Swanson), Tyler McVey (General Norgrath), Joe Flynn (Carey Stoddart), John Compton, Mike Rayhill, David Bedell, Howard Vann

Script: Jerome Bixby, William Templeton, Robert W. Leach

Directed by: Nathan Juran

Technical advisor: Captain M. C. Spaulding, U.S.A.F.

Man has always gazed at the stars and wondered whether there might be life on one of those distant worlds. Someday, when Man travels across the vast oceans of space, he may discover an answer to his question: "Is there another civilization?"

Spaceship M-13 is headed home on the last leg of another of Man's successful penetrations of deep space.

Major Summers, commanding the M-13, radios Colonel McCauley back on earth that he is 40 minutes to reentry. "I'm going fishing the minute we land," Captain Lewsham jokingly announces. "No, you're not," the colonel warns. "There's a press conference scheduled right after debriefing and you'll be there. I'll see you in a couple of hours." Suddenly, Captain Farrow announces a contact on the

radar scope, apparently a swarm of meteorites heading on a collision course. Summers orders evasive action, which clears most of
the projectiles, but a loud thud indicates that M-13 was struck by
something. Their radar is down, but damage appears minimal and
McCauley informs them they are off course and not to attempt reentry until new computations can be made. Summers acknowledges
his orders and awaits the new data.

A safe landing ensues and the three men report to Major General Norgrath's office for a debriefing. Norgrath concedes, "It could
have been a disaster," but McCauley assures him it was a one-in-
a-million accident. "Whatever hit us is still lodged in the meteor
shield," Summers adds. An officer enters the room and hands the
general what they found on the ship–a bright piece of metal. "That's
no meteorite," McCauley notes. Norgrath observes that the specimen has obviously been machined and the colonel speculates that
M-13 may have stumbled onto the wreck of another nation's unannounced failure. "We've had a couple, too," Norgrath admits, who
informs Major Summers that their press conference is cancelled
until the mystery object has been scrutinized. Turning to McCauley, he says, "Ed, I want you to get a computer team busy. Analyze
the course and speed tapes of the M-13. See if we can't establish
an orbit for this pile of floating junk. And I want this thing examined, analyzed, and poked into until we know everything there is to
know about it." The general demands a thorough investigation of
the mystery object. As McCauley leaves his office, Carey Stoddart, a
decidedly snoopy journalist, approaches and asks what is going on
with this "slight accident." Pressing hard, he gets the colonel to deny
that anything was wrong with either the ship or crew, although an
investigation is ongoing. "I'm going to stay on top of this, colonel,"
Stoddart warns. "I hope you're not playing footsie with me."

Back at home, McCauley is greeted by Mary, whom, after a kiss,
conducts her own interrogation about the M-13. The colonel hedg-
es his bets, so she takes the mail he is examining from his hands and
insists, "I am *not* prying!" Pulling her close, he sweet talks her with,
"I think, without any shadow of a doubt, that you are the pretti-
est subversive agent I know." "Mmmmmmmmmmm," she goes, "then
something *did* happen to the M-13!" Repeated denials get him nowhere, so he informs her the crew landed in perfect health and are

now resting after a tough mission. "Thank you," she says in mock seriousness, "I shall file that information with my superiors immediately." The two meet in a big kiss when the phone rings and the colonel answers. Somewhat stunned, he informs Mary to change her report to "Johnny Farrow was killed in an auto accident."

The scene switches to General Norgrath's office, where test results on the mysterious chunk of metal have arrived. "This metal or alloy has many properties of pyrographite," an officer announces, "which we have been trying to get for a long time." McCauley, examining the report, continues, "This alloy conducts heat better along its surfaces than through its interior. It keeps its strength up to temperatures of 6700 degrees Fahrenheit... it's ideal nosecone material!" Major Summers states, "I'd sure like to mine some of this stuff. It would be better than gold." The colonel informs him that is exactly what they intend to do, with Captain Swanson taking the place of the late Captain Farrow. The men depart for their belated press interview and McCauley cautions them not to engage in errant speculation about other nations' space programs. "That's strictly out of our department," he lectures. Opening the door, he again runs headlong into Carey Stoddard, who hands him a newly-received telegraph announcing the drowning death of Captain Lewsham in a boating accident. Stoddard, his antenna now fully extended, presses the colonel for additional facts about the mysterious deaths of two M-13 crewmen. "I think it's tragic!" McCauley snorts, "and I think you're trying very hard to work up a story by tying together incidents that have absolutely no relationship." The three officers begin suspiciously eyeing the metal object. "Will this press conference reveal what happened to the M-13?" Stoddard probes further. "It will," McCauley snarls back. "All right," the reporter opines, "we'll see..."

Back at the McCauley house, the colonel holds up a newspaper with headlines in bold print asking, IS SPACESHIP JINXED? The colonel swears he cannot believe Stoddard stooped so low for a sensational story. "He's pretty smart," Captain Swanson notes. "That story should sell a lot of papers." McCauley would like nothing better than to make a fool of Stoddard by bringing a piece of the derelict back and having it properly identified. However, Mary pops up and insists, "I hope you won't have too much difficulty identifying my dinner." She passes the covered plate around and the youthful

Swanson exclaims, "Roast beef!" and he lopes off into the dining room in pursuit. "Well," McCauley grins to Summers, "shall we con-firm the identification?" In the bedroom that evening, Mary nervous-ly asks her husband about jinxes in the deaths of the two officers. The colonel says no and wants to go to sleep. She confesses she is superstitious and McCauley informs her, "I am going to be one very tired Air Force colonel in the morning unless we get some sleep. Goodnight, honey." Mary cannot close her eyes for some time.

The next morning, General Norgrath begins instructing McCau-ley and his crew on their mission. Major Summers, however, is ab-sent. "We'll go ahead without him," Norgrath quips. "You can fill him in later." The men learn that the derelict will reach its optimum orbit in 72 hours and, this time, the M-13 will pull alongside to take samples, not collide with them. Suddenly, a note is delivered to the general, who declares "Major Summers" and hands it off to the colonel.

An anxious Captain Swanson predicts, "Major Summers is dead, isn't he, sir." McCauley confirms that he was accidentally electrocuted in his bathroom. Hours later, Carey Stoddart appears at McCauley's office, regrets the death of Major Summers, and pon-ders why he has to go to cemeteries to get a story. "You didn't have to come in here to make that speech," McCauley growls. Kicking the reporter out, Captain Swanson enters and nervously asks, "Would you rather not have me go on this mission, sir?" "Would you rather not go on it?" McCauley asks back. The captain informs him that he was ordered for a complete psychological examination beforehand and "I had a hunch you ordered it." "I did," McCauley assures him. "We're both going to take the test."

Unlike the previous flight, Colonel McCauley and the crew of the M-13 took off on a course designed to bring them into rendezvous orbit with the remains of the derelict.

McCauley expertly nurses his vessel alongside the debris field and Swanson exclaims, "There it is... it looks like a floating junk-yard." The two men then suit up to retrieve some additional re-mains. After McCauley screens the pieces for residue radiation, they begin collecting samples, including a piece so large that it has to be secured to a bulkhead. Later, as they descend back to Earth, Major Bowers begins reading off the outer hull temperature as it rises. However, the large piece breaks loose and forces the reentry process to abort. "It's loose," Swanson exclaims. "That thing is loose!" McCauley orders him aft to re-secure it and, when the remains will not budge, the colonel comes back to assist. Nothing seems to work, so McCauley orders Bowyers to point the ship back into the atmosphere and let gravity move the piece into place. "Take her down, Johnny. Hold her until I give you the word," he insists. As the two men struggle with the piece, Bowyers continues announcing the rising temperatures outside and, once the critical zone is reached, he aborts. Meanwhile, Swanson failed to secure the clamp, so McCauley orders another try. "Better secure it this time," he informs Swanson. "We won't have another chance!" Bowyers holds his course until the skin temperature exceeds 4,000 degrees–way past the safety limits–before the wreckage is secured. "Are you going to try anything else before you get down?" Swanson says to the wreckage. "What's the matter with you?" McCauley snaps. "You talk as though that thing were alive." "I'm beginning to wonder," Swanson confesses. M-13 proceeds to make a safe landing. That evening, Mary frets that her dinner will be ruined if Captain Swanson arrives any later and she worries something may have happened to him. "I know Swanson. He loves to eat!" he assures her. "You're getting the jitters." The errant captain shows up at the door and announces, "Sorry I'm late, I decided to walk over." "It's all right," the colonel shrugs. "It's *not* all right," Mary protests. "You scared me half to death!" McCauley reminds her they are here for a pleasant evening together. She nonetheless storms off, exclaiming, "All right, I'll go see if my dinner is still fit to serve." Swanson then asks the colonel if he has seen Major Bowyers and is told he took the next two weeks off to go mountain climbing. "Oh no!" Swanson declares in a panic. McCauley smiles and tells him he is actually in town and will be at tomorrow's press conference.

The next day, General Norgrath announces to the gathered press and officers that the results of the wreckage examination are so provocative that the Pentagon has imposed a complete news blackout. However, McCauley will provide them with some details. He tells them that remains of micro-meteorites found in the surface of the debris indicate that it has been in its present orbit for at least 500 years. Captain Swanson excitedly declares that places it in the 15th century and McCauley announces, "That's right, captain, you point out an inescapable conclusion." The colonel informs them that the fragments recovered once belonged to a rocket ship that was probably destroyed when it collided with a large meteor. "From a different world in the universe," he cautions them. "Where is this other world?" Stoddart asks. "We don't know," McCauley concedes, then mentions that a sealed bearing they found contained microscopic bubbles of chlorine gas, apparently trapped there during manufacture. They conjecture whether the designers actually breathed chlorine gas and again McCauley demurs, suggesting that such gas might serve as the basis for other forms of life. Finally, Stoddart asks if they have any ideas of what the vessel looked like. McCauley presents a model based on the reconfigured remains and the audience gapes in awe. "Somewhere, a race of intelligent beings built this ship 500 years ago," the colonel ponders. "How far have they advanced now?"

That evening, the colonel reposes at home and Mary anxiously asks him if he is feeling all right. "That is the sixty-fourth time you have asked me that in the last 20 minutes. I feel fine!" he insists. The doorbell rings, Mary answers, and a somber-faced Carey Stoddart enters. "What are you doing out at this hour of the night?" McCauley demands to know. "Did you hear about Swanson?" he asks. "It came in on the wire." The colonel and Mary go stone-faced in anticipation of bad news, but Stoddert, breaking into a grin, informs them, "He got married today." McCauley smiles and tells Mary, "Maybe this is more of the jinx." She breathlessly exclaims, "Oh, I've never been so happy about a marriage since my own!"

"Shadows On the Moon"

(Aired March 30, 1960)

Starring: Gerald Mohr (Doctor Bernard Bush), Harry Carey, Jr. (Major Blythe), Mort Mills (Doctor George Coldwell)

Script: David Duncan

Directed by: Alvin Ganzer

Technical advisor: Captain M. C. Spaulding, U.S.A.F.

No matter how well planned missions into space will be, no one can predict the unknowns Man will meet and have to overcome. What he may see on some distant star will be different from anything here on Earth, and the terror far beyond the wildest nightmare. This is the story of an expedition that ventured a quarter of a million miles from Earth and where two men fought the unknowns in the shadows on the Moon.

Colonel McCauley and Major Blythe are exploring on the Moon's surface when Blythe espies a rock formation with an uncanny resemblance to a human profile. "If I saw a formation like that on Earth, I'd swear it was created by man," he exclaims. "Well," McCauley continues, "since we're on the Moon, we can eliminate that possibility." The major insists on taking some sample pictures and the colonel, growing annoyed, tells him to hurry up.

Colonel McCauley and Major Blythe survey and map an unexplored region of the Moon's surface. Their discovery of a source of radioactive ore would be of great value in Man's conquest of the Moon's hostile environment.

"Jim," McCauley announces, "here's something interesting: this rock shows traces of some radioactive elements." "You sure it's not too hot to handle?" Blythe inquires, but McCauley shrugs it off as relatively harmless. Moreover, he speculates that they may be standing on the site of a future nuclear power plant that could provide lunar colonies for millions of years. "I'm talking about a breeder reactor," he explains, "the kind of a power plant that breeds more fuel than it uses." Blythe nonetheless remains transfixed by the "face formation" and the colonel instructs him to forget it and return to base. "Don't let your imagination run away with you, will you?" he lectures. To expedite matters, the men deposit much of their equipment on the ground near the base of a rock and tramp onward. "Natural erosion," Blythe mutters to himself as they depart. "I just can't believe it."

Their assignment completed, McCauley and Blythe launch their rocket from the Moon's surface for the return to Earth. They carried with them ore samples and maps that would be evaluated for use by future missions—and a photograph of an outcropping of rock that bore a strange resemblance to a grinning face.

Back in his office, McCauley explains to Doctors Bernard Bush and George Caldwell the importance of their upcoming return flight to the Moon. "Just think of the results," Bush exults. "A breeder reactor on the Moon, a reactor capable of producing more atomic fuel than it consumes. Why, the entire Moon may be available to us as a source of energy!" McCauley agrees and informs them that the sample they hold contains twice as much Uranium and Thorium as any rocks on earth. "Our job is to discover the extent of the layer," he notes. Coldwell speculates that, on Earth, such formations sometimes cover hundreds of square miles and similar conditions might prevail on the Moon. "Maybe not," McCauley reasons. "The same natural laws on the Moon bring about different conditions on Earth." Coldwell then congratulates Major Blythe on a good picture of the stone face, but Blythe's imagination runs amuck. "You know, it's still hard to believe that that was made by Nature," the major reasons. "How could it be–no wind, no rain, nothing to erode the rock." McCauley chimes in that Blythe is determined to prove the object is man-made despite the fact that extreme temperature variations on the Moon make the rocks expand, contract, and shatter regularly. Bush further speculates that the Moon might have had an atmosphere in the distant past and maybe that is where mankind originated. "That may account for our instinctive longing to go back," he declares. "I've heard wilder theories. There's pitifully little we know about the Moon–and that includes you, colonel." "Well," McCauley says with a smile, "let's consider this expedition an opportunity to expand that knowledge. Remember, gentleman, our only enemy is the Moon itself."

Colonel McCauley headed up a new expedition, whose mission was to explore the feasibility of building a breeder reactor on the Moon that, if successful, could provide fuel for spaceships, supply heat and power for Moon colonists, and possibly release oxygen from the Moon's mineral compounds and give the breath of life to that dead satellite.

No sooner does McCauley's rocket land than he makes dispositions to explore for more uranium ore. "Remember," he warns them, "we're a thousand miles from Moon Base and we have to depend completely on our own resources." Blythe pushes hard to go back to the rock face for a closer look and the colonel assures him it will be an added bonus once their work is done. Gazing at it through the porthole, Bush says with a smile, "Guess I wasn't so crazy talking about that ancient civilization, huh?" McCauley simply grunts, "Let's check it out," and, accompanied by the two scientists, they set out for where the tools were left. Major Blythe remains behind at the radio. En route, Coldwell points out that one of McCauley's trail markers had fallen down. "I thought you drove it into a rock to see it from a distance." McCauley counters, "We do. Obviously, I didn't drive this one deep enough." At length, the team arrives at the rock base, only to discover that the footprints made by McCauley and Blythe a month earlier are gone, as are the tools they left behind. The colonel radios Blythe and has him check the logbook; weren't the tools left behind at Marker 6? Blythe confirms that fact. "How do you explain it?" Bush asks. "Maybe there's been someone here," Coldwell conjectures. "There's been no one here," McCauley insists. "I don't know the answer now, but I know that there is one in natural terms." "Who knows what's natural on the Moon?" Bush slyly insinuates.

Walking along, the men are nearly sidelined by some falling rocks, which McCauley explains are a common occurrence. When Bush conjectures they might have been deliberately pushed, the colonel corrects him. "Let's not create difficulties. The real ones are tough enough." McCauley then demonstrates by taking some marking chalk from the doctor, lays it out in the Sun, and watches it melt. Another piece placed on the shade remains intact. This act highlights the wide temperature variations on the Moon's surface, which causes rock to expand rapidly and crack away from the cooler layers beneath. "If our space suits didn't have thermostatic controls, right now we'd be either fried or frozen stiff," McCauley explains. "Let's get back to work." Back at the ship, Major Blythe causally looks out the porthole at the stone face, only to see it brightly lit up from underneath. He immediately calls McCauley on the radio, but his transmission is cut off by the terrain. Meanwhile, the team splits up as the two doctors prepare to set explosive charges in the ground and McCauley lopes off to higher ground for better communications with the ship. Coldwell and Bush make several detonations, then the latter gets the urge to go visit the stone face on his own. "Won't Colonel McCauley be surprised if I bring back a stonecutter's chisel!" he declares. Meanwhile, Major Blythe finally contacts Colonel McCauley and informs him of the glowing light near the face. "I'll investigate after our geologists finish taking their sounding," the colonel assures him. Doctor Bush, meanwhile, perambulates towards the rock face only to glimpse a huge reflection of himself, then runs off in panic. He explains to McCauley and Coldwell about seeing a man, "But it was bigger than any man I ever saw on earth and it was coming right at me!" "How do you explain what's natural on the Moon, McCauley?" Coldwell wryly inquires. Back on the ship, McCauley, ever the skeptic, orders the men to remain onboard while he investigates what Bush "thought" he saw. Bush resents the inference and shoots back, "I suppose next you'll say I didn't see anything!" McCauley bristles and informs him, "If I thought that, doctor, I wouldn't be interrupting our mission this way." He also declines Major Blythe's invitation to take a pistol along. "I haven't used a gun on the Moon before," the colonel insists. "I don't think I need one now."

McCauley makes his way to the exact spot where Bush was startled and beholds a giant image looming ahead of him. Seconds later, he realizes it is his own reflection on a glassy stone wall and calls to the ship. "Tell Doctor Bush and Coldwell to join me. I want to show them their monster from outer space." The two scientists comply and are relieved to find what they feared is actually a large sheet of obsidian, or volcanic glass. "That explains the lights Major Blythe was talking about," McCauley adds. "I guess I'll never live this down," Bush confesses. "I'll make a deal with you," the colonel suggests. "You don't say anything about it, I won't either." Coldwell interjects, "Don't worry about my talking. I probably would have run faster than Doctor Bush!" However, retracing their steps to the ship, the men notice that their footprints and equipment have again vanished. The team is completely puzzled by their disappearance. Pushing forward, Doctor Coldwell begins sinking into the soil and has to be pulled out. He suddenly realizes the surface consists of sulphur, which partially liquefies in the extreme solar heat. It was normal to walk on while it was in the shadow of the mountain and Coldwell notes, "On the Moon, even shadows move." McCauley adds, "Yeah, and I bet if we probe down deep enough into that stuff, we'd find the instruments that disappeared, too." Bush smiles and states, "To quote you, colonel, there's nothing to fear on the Moon but the Moon itself."

Back on Earth, the four men prepare for their debriefing session. Bush hesitates and asks McCauley if he intends to mention his embarrassing little episode on the Moon and the colonel assures him he will not. Coldwell chimes in about not mentioning him and Bush taking that sulphur bath. Again, McCauley assures them that his lips are sealed. Then Major Blythe mentions the lights that he saw. McCauley again assures him that mum is the word. Bush asks with a smile, "Then what are you going to talk about?" The colonel matter-of-factly lectures them, "Well, the success of our mission, our finding the granite sulphur deposits... and that the Moon is our only enemy."

"Flash In the Sky"

(Aired April 6, 1960)

Starring: Joyce Taylor, John Lupton (Doctor Guthrie Durlock), Joan Marshall (Lorrie Sigmund), William Hudson, Mark Houston, Robert O'Connor

Script: David Duncan

Directed by: Walter Doniger

Technical advisor: Colonel Lawrence D. Ely, U.S.A.F.

The story you are about to see hasn't happened yet, but will happen when men such as these send rockets beyond the Moon, equipped with instruments that will bring back accurate descriptions of those distant worlds. This is the story of such a rocket, a rocket that will one day be launched from the Moon to survey our Earth's sister, the planet Venus.

Mary McCauley sits glued to her television set as her husband, Colonel Edward McCauley, makes a televised conference with Doctor Guthrie Durlock from the Moon. He is talking about using that body as a base to launch a rocket, which Doctor Durlock designed, towards the planet Venus. Suddenly, the doorbell rings and Mary's friend Lorrie Sigmund, an intelligent and comely blonde, strolls inside. Scanning the set, she asks, "Who is that interesting man with your Ed?" Mary tells her to hush, but she continues, "I could be interested in meeting a man like that... intriguing." "Ed tells me women frighten him," Mary warns her. "And a trip to Venus doesn't?" she purrs. "More intriguing."

> McCauley and the crew at Moon base had successfully built and launched a rocket from the Moon. Unmanned, it was on an automatic, programmed course to Venus.

As the Venus rocket lifts off from the Moon, Doctor Durlock dreamily watches it fly away, muttering, "There she goes. it looks like a perfect shot." McCauley, less impressed, brusquely orders the doctor to begin packing up his equipment for the return to base. Durlock hesitates, insisting he wants to watch the rocket disappear from view. "Our job is done," the colonel snaps. "Let's get packed and back to the base." Durlock, still engrossed, simply disobeys and scales a small cliff to get a better view. McCauley angrily strolls over to confront him when a sudden landslide knocks Durlock down and almost completely buries the colonel in Moon dust. McCauley orders the doctor to climb higher and radio the base to get help, but he insists, "There is no time for that." The colonel angrily declares, "Durlock, you heard what I said!" The doctor, however, insists, "If more dust comes down, you'll be completely buried. We'll never be able to find you." Durlock then disconnects and uses his emergency air supply over McCauley's protests and hoses the dust away, allowing the colonel to escape. "Let's get back to the base," he growls. Once inside the shelter, two of the crew present Durlock with a jury-rigged paper medal with the word "Hero" on it. Lieutenant Walker, in mock seriousness, recites, "For blowing up the biggest wind storm in recorded history on the surface of the Moon and thereby returning our illustrious commander, we present you with this Order of Space Hero." The laughter comes to a sudden halt when McCauley angrily snarls, "As commander of this mission, I will have no man as a member of my crew who disobeys orders!" He instructs the officers to arrange Doctor Durlock's return to Earth on the supply vessel arriving tomorrow. Durlock does not contest the order, but forewarns McCauley that he will definitely be aboard the spaceship that rendezvouses with the Venus probe after it returns in two months. "And I shall ask to be relieved of command," McCauley insists.

Durlock returned to Earth and McCauley followed three weeks later. Meanwhile, the Venus rocket soared onward, day after day, millions of miles through space. Even though it could not be seen, tracking stations on Earth could hear its voice as it told the story of its journey.

At Ground Control, Doctor Durlock examines a teletype print-out and notes that his rocket has stopped transmitting. Colonel McCauley asks what he intends to do next and the doctor explains that, since there is a good chance the vessel can still receive orders, it should continue on towards Venus as planned. "After that, we wait," he reasons. The colonel, seeking a rapprochement with the doctor since their Moon mission, asks him over to his house for dinner with himself and Mary. Durlock awkwardly explains that he wants to be present if the signal comes in and McCauley assures him he would be notified in the event. The doctor agrees and the colonel phones Mary that he is coming. That evening, the two men stroll toward the barbecue with Durlock complaining that not a peep has been heard from his rocket. McCauley tells him to quit fretting about it. Mary also approaches and makes nice; then Lorrie suddenly shows up, apparently unannounced. "Hey," she innocently feigns, "aren't you going to wait for me?" Mary introduces her to the shy Durlock, who strikes up an awkward conversation about space travel. Lorrie seems unusually well-informed on the subject and asks, "Is its course a parabola of a hyperbola?" The doctor begins illustrating the trajectory of his Venus probe with charcoal lines and fruits on the tablecloth. The colonel and Mary look on in disbelief, but the two seem to get along. "Why didn't you tell me?" McCauley asks quietly. "I tried to tell you," Mary whispers back. "Shall I put the steaks on?" he inquires of his wife-turned-matchmaker. "Not unless you want him to put an onion ring around his and call it Saturn," she merrily quips–then protests that the doctor is drawing lines in her tablecloth. "Oh, stop worrying about a paper tablecloth," McCauley insists. The phone rings and Mary shoos him off to answer it. Lorrie then points out that Durlock's etchings have inadvertently ended up in a "heart," possibly a manifestation of his longing for the goddess Venus. McCauley returns with news that the tracking center has picked up signals from the errant spaceship. "Headed for outer space, which means one chance in a thousand for interception," he explains. Nonetheless, a ship is being prepared to make the attempt. "Then we'll get it, even if I have to catch it with my bare hands," Durlock happily exclaims. However, McCauley's demeanor goes sullen and he says, "Your arms had better be long enough to reach it from Earth." The doctor insists on going, even if he has to go over the colonel's head to General Douglas. "Well, if General Douglas gives you permission," McCauley declares, "tell him you want permission to replace your commanding officer, who asked to be relieved."

The men traveled in a spaceship launched from Earth in an effort to rendezvous with the Venus rocket, an attempt to salvage the vital instruments which held important information about the planet Venus.

The spaceship, flown by Colonel McCauley, also contains Doctor Durlock. Even though he resigned as promised, the doctor nonetheless requested him to serve as flight commander. McCauley did not wish to antagonize General Douglas, so he accepted the mission without complaint. The colonel then asks how he intends to resolve any future conflicts between them. "You heard what the general said," Durlock states. "If there's any conflict between us relating to my work and in no way endangering the crew, then the decision is up to me." "Things are only that simple and clear-cut on paper," the colonel advises, "not in space." At length, their radar detects the Venus probe and McCauley begins maneuvering to intercept.

In the vacuum of space, a rendezvous is possible by matching the orbital speeds of two ships. McCauley carefully guided his ship alongside the Venus rocket, knowing that they would stay in position until some force was exerted on one of them.

No sooner does McCauley position the ship adjacent to the Venus probe than the instruments go awry due to a powerful magnetic field. Peering out the porthole, the men see their vessel being drawn toward the probe and McCauley immediately employs thrust rockets to pull away. Durlock deduces that it probably acquired a massive electrostatic charge in the Venusian atmosphere. "That's right," the colonel continues. "With our ship carrying an opposite charge, that rocket is going to jump at us every time we come within critical distance. One bump and we're all dead. We can't risk a collision. We'll have to check this one off." McCauley declares the mission over, but Durlock talks him out of it, citing that, during the next such mission, a new commander will have to make a dangerous choice that McCauley is now ducking. "I've never seen a man so eager to die," the colonel concedes, but he allows Durlock to venture over to the probe. "You can't do anything these days without takings risks," the doctor assures him, "even eat your barbecued steaks." McCauley still balks at granting permission, but Durlock insists in the name of science and the colonel relents.

Doctor Durlock, wearing a space suit and breathing apparatus, could leave the spaceship and travel through the vacuum of space, using his jet pack to propel himself.

Durlock suits up and jets over to the probe, only to become trapped to the hull by the electrostatic charge. He urges the colonel to leave him and McCauley tells him, "Sure, I'll leave you, Guthrie-just like you left me buried in the dust."

Colonel McCauley, fully aware of the hazards involved since he did not know the exact nature of the charge that the Venus rocket carried, cautiously approached it with a mooring cable in an attempt to rescue Doctor Durlock.

The colonel exits the rocket with a mooring cable to ground the electrostatic charge and he rescues the stranded doctor, but inadvertently transfers the charge to their own vessel. Both men then enter and retrieve the probe's instrumentation, then return. Their problem is whether or not the charge held by the invaluable cargo would ground itself upon entering earth's atmosphere or destroy the rocket. "We're going to find out. We'll come in over the ocean," McCauley orders. "Close the ports."

One hazard overcome, McCauley and the men in the ship faced still another—would the powerful charge they carried ground itself in the earth's atmosphere or explode their vehicle?

The reentry attempt is made and the charge grounds with an enormous flash, but the ship survives intact and successfully reenters the atmosphere. "We're clean," Durlock breathlessly exclaims. "Charge grounded." "Well," McCauley says, equally relieved, "now we can head for home."

Back at Lorrie's house, the colonel, the doctor, and Mary are enjoying dinner as she points to the "heart chart" Durlock drew, which she mounted on the wall. She claims it is a perfect example of the subconscious mind at work, while McCauley, noting who he drew it for, insists it was anything but subconscious. Mary quickly corrects him, stating, "It means that Guthrie was in love with the mythical Venus." Durlock insists that the design was purely accidental—at least he still likes to think so. He goes on to mention his next project is a probe of Mars and wishes to illustrate it on Lorrie's tablecloth, but she stops him cold. "No, Guthrie, not on my tablecloth," Lorrie insists. "This one happens to be made of linen!"

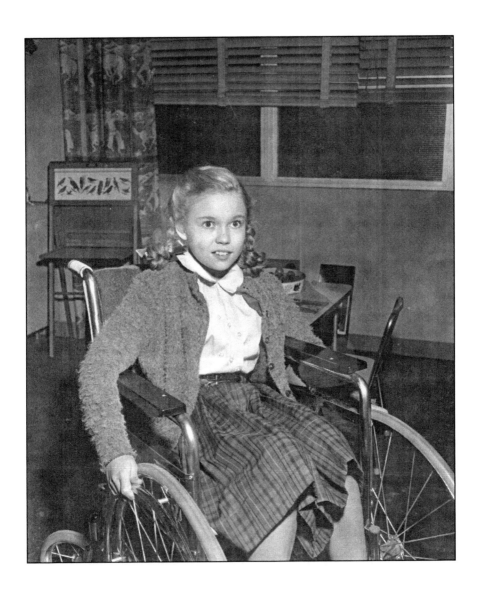

"Lunar Secret"

(Aired April 13, 1960)

Starring: John Hudson (Captain Kyle Rennish), Mimi Gibson (Jenny), Sally Bliss (Doctor Alice Roe), Kort Falkenberg, Robert Courtleigh

Script: Michael Plant

Directed by: Franklin Adreon

Technical director: Captain M. C. Spaulding, U.S.A.F.

> *As each man leaves the Earth to explore new and unknown areas of the Moon's surface, he will ask himself the question, "Is it possible that someone else has been or is now on the Moon?" This is the story of a group of men on a photographic reconnaissance mission who came close to death when they attempted to solve this lunar secret.*

At the Air Force Physical Rehabilitation Center, Colonel McCauley arrives and greets Doctor Alice Roe, a child psychologist who is treating Jenny, the daughter of Captain Kyle Rennish. Roe informs Rennish that, while Jenny is progressing fine physically, she thinks her mother, recently killed in a car accident, is still alive and talks to her. "That shock may be the very reason why she refuses to accept the loss," Roe lectures. Jenny is suddenly wheeled into the room and her father runs over to embrace her. "Are you going to take more pictures of the Man in the Moon?" she excitedly asks. "Take a picture of me!" Rennish promises when he comes back, then Jenny protests she thought he was taking her back to see her mother. Doctor Roe consoles the child, but the little girl insists she talked to her that morning and is helping her walk again. "Captain Rennish, I think this is your territory," Roe states. "Why don't you take Jenny into the playroom and have a little talk with her." In their absence, Roe asks McCauley if it is absolutely essential that Rennish accompany this trip. "Oh, very essential," he informs her. "In fact, the captain is the most experienced member of our lunar photographic team." Roe nonetheless is wary of the captain's mental condition, as losses of this magnitude usually result in acute stress. The colonel assures her that Rennish passed all his medical tests and "I believe in the screenings. I have to." Roe continues, "At the risk of sounding unprofessional, I believe that sometimes human instincts can be far more perceptive than a hundred computers." McCauley smiles and says he will remember her advice, then steps outside to wait for Rennish. Some time later, a rocket lifts off from the base and Doctor Roe calls Jenny to the window to wish them luck. Jenny, poring over a book about the Moon, simply declares, "Daddy doesn't need good luck; he's coming back safe. I know because last night Mommy told me." Roe states that Jenny promised not to talk that way anymore.

Once at the Moon photo outpost, Lieutenant Rudy Manton complains to McCauley that Rennish is very domineering of late. "I've been out with Kyle on two mapping trips before and I never saw him act this way," he protests. The colonel postulates that the recent death of his wife is the cause. McCauley assures him the major passed all his medical tests and instructs Manton to just ignore it and assist Rennish the best that he can.

McCauley and his crew worked on a carefully planned schedule to complete the vitally important mission assigned to them.

Rennish, having developed a photo, notices something shiny and round set against the background of the cliffs. He assumes it is not a natural object and excitedly bursts in on McCauley to relay his discovery. "Colonel, I thought no one else had been around here before," he states. McCauley insists he is correct, but cannot account for the glowing metal object on the cliffs. "One thing I'll swear,"

Rennish asserts. "Whatever that is, it wasn't made by nature!" He begins pressing McCauley for permission to investigate the object when Lieutenant Manton bursts in and is also asked to examine the photo. Manton correctly identifies it as spherical and metal, but when it does not show up in other photos, McCauley dismisses it as unimportant. Rennish storms back into his lab and McCauley, turning to Manton, asks if it were possible to fake such an image. The lieutenant remarks, "Do you think it's a gag or something?" and Rennish, who reentered, grows angry at the insinuation. The colonel finally allows both men to venture out and re-photograph the exact spot.

Captain Rennish and Lieutenant Manton returned to take additional photos, seeking a logical explanation to the mysterious object they saw on the previous photo.

"Sort of weird, isn't it?" Manton asks when new photos fail to show the object. McCauley shoots Manton a skeptical look, then Rennish explodes, "Mac, quit this, will you?" The colonel asks the captain for his theory. He speculates it might have fallen from a supply rocket, but McCauley notes that radar would have tracked it. Rennish volunteers to scale the cliff and retrieve the object, but the colonel dismisses the gesture as too dangerous. "Besides, you've got a job to do right here," he insists. Rennish angrily departs and McCauley, turning to Manton again, tells him, "You know, Rudy, I think we can settle this matter. I'll need your help–unofficially and off the record." The colonel and the lieutenant suit up and photograph the identical spot, only this time, their photo shows that the object has apparently moved quite a distance. "Mac," Rennish declares, "you know what this means!" "There's some object on the Moon that we don't know about," the colonel concedes, "something that moves." McCauley contacts Major McIntyre at the main Moon Base, who checks all official records and confirms that no supply rockets have passed over their site. "Definitely, it's none of our equipment," Major McIntyre declares. "Mac, are you sure about this?" McCauley then announces that he and Captain Rennish will attempt hiking to the object to ascertain its exact nature. In light of the rugged terrain anticipated, McIntyre tells him, "Good luck, Mac–better you than me." "Yeah, thanks," McCauley says.

The two men trek towards the cliffs and McCauley radios Manton to have him turn on the tape recorder. He then notes that the object has apparently moved back to the spot where it was first observed. Rennish calls out that he has found a way up to the top and two begin climbing it. Manton then radios their decision to Moon Base and McIntyre instructs him to ready spare oxygen bottles just in case. En route to the top, Rennish slips and falls into a crevice, but the colonel hauls him out. "You're lucky you didn't puncture your pressure suit," he tells him. "Are you ready to go on?" The captain agrees and the two continue upward. At length, they approach the object, which turns out to be the space suit of a long-dead astronaut. Rennish suddenly starts coughing and McCauley assumes that he must have punctured his tank while falling. The captain realizes he lacks sufficient air to return to base, urges McCauley to save himself, and, pointing to the lifeless suit, insists, "I'm in good company." "Shut up!" McCauley insists. "I don't care, Mac," he pleads with his superior. "I haven't cared for a long time." "Save your breath," McCauley barks. "You'll need it." The colonel then checks the air tank on the suit, but, finding it expended, admits, "He needed oxygen as badly as we do. Solve one mystery and you run into another." The colonel notes that the suit has no identification, as sunlight burned the name off the helmet. "Must have been the changing light that made his helmet seem to disappear," McCauley deduces. It suddenly dawns on him to try the victim's tape recorder and more facts are unveiled. The voice mentions Colonel Gould and McCauley realizes he has found a crewman from the MR-2, which vanished five years ago while attempting to land on the Moon. Fortunately, the anonymous voice speaks of leaving the wreckage behind and Rennish concludes it must be just over the hill. McCauley gambles that the oxygen bottles are still intact and, ignoring the captain's claim that his legs have given out, tells him, "Then learn to walk... learn to walk just like little Jenny is now." Minutes later, the pair arrives outside the derelict craft as Manton and McIntyre listen pensively to everything transpiring. As the colonel suspected, the salvaged tanks do contain air and the two men are saved. McCauley radios Moon Base and has McIntyre retrieve and read the log for the MR-2. The major announces: *"MR dash 2: Argonaut Type three-stage rocket. The sec-*

ond manned spaceship to attempt a landing on the Moon. Radio contact was broken one hour and thirteen minutes before achievement of Moon Orbit. Nothing was ever heard from them again, no trace of wreckage, survivors, was ever found. The MR dash 2 was manned by Colonel George Gould, United States Air Force." McCauley cuts in, "Captain Jeffrey Tuttle, Captain Kenneth Moresby, both United States Air Force."

Back on Earth, Doctor Roe greets Captain Rennish, who calls Jenny over. Standing erect, she hobbles over to her dad and receives a big hug and a kiss. Colonel McCauley, speaking low, congratulates her for "a tremendous job." Jenny exclaims, "And Mommy helped me, too." Rennish looks askance for a moment, but Doctor Roe has his daughter explain. "She talks to me because I can remember all the nice things she used to say. People can go on helping, even if they aren't here anymore." Captain Rennish, relieved, delivers anther bone-crunching hug while Colonel McCauley, smiling, exits through the door.

"Voice of Infinity"

(Aired April 20, 1960)

Starring: Myron Healey (Major Steven Hawkes), Charles Cooper (Doctor Thomas Ward), Ralph Taeger (Corporal Fred Jones), Charles Stewart, Rand Brooks, Barnaby Hale

Script: Ib Melchior

Directed by: Alan Crosland, Jr.

Technical advisor: Captain M. C. Spaulding, U.S.A.F.

The age of the conquest of space will be an age of men and machines probing far beyond our Earth. And just as some machines will probe deeply into space, others will probe the men who travel in space. Yet, put to the ultimate test, no amount of machinery will ever be able to determine the measure of a man's inner strength, for within each of us there is a voice of infinity.

A rocket ship docks into Space Station Astra and disgorges two passengers, Major Hawkes, a psychologist, and Captain Ward, a physician. Colonel McCauley greets them and introduces Major Canell, his executive officer. He declares, "You know, if that equipment you are bringing on board works as well on human beings as safety devices do on machines, it's going to cut our accident rate a great deal." Hawkes enthusiastically agrees, noting, "After all, the human body is a machine. If you can put safety devices on machines, you can put them on human bodies, too." Suddenly, an alarm bell blares and Canell orders all personnel to emergency stations. Something controlling the space station's spin rate has malfunctioned, so McCauley has a crewman immediately adjust his controls and the alarm ceases. The colonel and the major agree this incident has all the earmarks of human error. Hawkes and Ward feel it was an exciting "reception" that the colonel arranged for them and McCauley asks that they arrange a demonstration of their equipment for the crew when set up. Corporal Jones stops Captain Ward as he exits the door and asks what field he belongs to. Ward mentions that his specialty is space medicine, but that Major Hawkes is a psychologist specializing in bio-instrumentation. "Psychologist?" Jones jokes, "So where's his couch?" Ward assures him that he won't need one with the all equipment they are hauling aboard. Major Hawkes attaches his machine to Airman Jones and it begins correlating his bodily functions into units of stress, indicated by a row of blinking lights. "Gentlemen," Hawkes explains, "every man has his stamina limitation, beyond which he cannot function efficiently. A fatigue threshold, if you like, during which time he may become accident-prone." The major hopes that his transducers will allow accurate predictions of when personnel have reached their limits, at which point the wearer can be suspended from work. McCauley declares, "From now on, this equipment will be S.O.P for all on-duty personnel." The men are dismissed, but one confronts Captain Ward and says he better not try hooking him up. "Why not?" Ward inquires. "Because I run on D.C.," he says with a smile.

Some time later, Major Hawkes enters a room where McCauley and Ward are talking and pointedly asks why the civilian scientists are not scheduled to wear transducers. The colonel states they were exempted after a discussion he held with Doctor Ward. "Well, no offense, but how can Doctor Ward's point of view be important enough to cripple my experiments?" Hawkes demands. Ward explains that scientific research sometimes depends on the very tensions and hardships that Hawkes fears and "mistakes and errors sometime have a way of turning out profitably." McCauley politely but firmly chimes in, stating, "We cannot underestimate the human mechanism. I've seen men whom you would consider in the critical zone call on some inner strength to see them through, something your equipment can't measure." The major, unconvinced, insists this is the wrong approach, but McCauley gently upbraids him by stating, "It's been said that within every man there's a 'Voice of Infinity.'" Hawkes again disputes the colonel's decision and McCauley cuts him off, insisting, "My decision is final." The major continues angrily venting until the colonel orders him to his quarters to cool off "and learn to live with the restrictions I've placed on your work." Captain Ward jokingly remarks that, had the huffy major been wearing one of his own transducers, "I bet his panel would have lit up like a Christmas tree!"

As Space Station Astra revolves steadily in orbit, one thousand and seventy-five miles above the Earth, all personnel performing hazardous tasks were kept under constant check by instrumentation that would have immediately indicated whether each man was capable of completing his assigned duty.

As the various crewmen perform delicate work outside the space station, Hawkes and Ward carefully monitor their physical condition. They inform Major Canell that Sergeant Grinder has reached the critical zone and he is immediately replaced by Airman Saunders.

In the vacuum of space, small rockets on the rim of the space wheel ensured a constant spin, which provided the space station with a synthetic gravity. Work teams constantly checked and realigned the intricate computing devices and mechanisms that had to perform with unerring accuracy. So exacting was this work, there was no margin for error and technicians were immediately replaced when instrumentation showed them incapable of performing efficiently.

Saunders assumes his position behind Corporal Jones, who seems dazed for a few seconds before entering the work panel. McCauley radios Jones and asks when he will finish and he replies in about a half an hour. "I think I'll go out and inspect that job myself when it's finished," the colonel informs Hawkes. "I'll need to be wired." Meanwhile, Jones is becoming increasingly disoriented and Captain Ward notices his stress lights are flashing. Hawkes then asks Major Canell to recall Jones immediately, but the airman insists on taking a few more minutes to finish. McCauley steps up to the microphone and bellows, "Jones, this is Colonel McCauley; report back *immediately*." Once inside, the colonel berates the reluctant airman for delaying and asks why he did it. "I was practically finished, Sir; to have waited for another man to come out there would have meant a long delay." McCauley, skeptical but forgiving, tells him, "Well, there's no harm done this time, but the next time–" Suddenly, the station shudders violently as the outside jets begin firing out of sequence. The increased rotational speed boosts gravity rates far above normal and crewmen struggle to man their stations. Major Canell explains that his all monitors are out and McCauley directs him to contact Earth Control. He also orders his entire crew into space suits until the situation stabilizes. "This is Space Station Astra to Earth Control, we have a runaway rotation rocket," McCauley declares. "Station in jeopardy–situation critical. I repeat, situation critical."

As the station spins out of control, McCauley contacts Saunders and asks what happened. "Apparently, Jones hooked up the terminals backwards; that overloaded the circuits. When they blew, the whole panel burned out." The colonel orders him back inside and directs a new repair team out as soon as possible. Hawkes and Ward cannot help but notice that McCauley's transducer lights are flashing into the critical zone, yet his judgment seems unimpaired. The colonel is explaining their predicament to a crewman when the rockets inexplicably fire up again, increasing the spin rate.

Each time the thrust rockets on the space station fired, the spin of the wheel increased. If it continued, the space station and the men in it would be unable to withstand the tremendous forces being exerted on them.

"Gravity two-and-a-half times normal," McCauley announces. Saunders comes on the radio to mention that the repair team has stopped work and withdrawn. "If that rocket keeps firing..." Major Canell declares. "We'll have to stop it now–neutralize the spin before it's too late," McCauley advises, although this will be accomplished without computers or instrumentation. Hawkes and Ward, meanwhile, watch in alarm as McCauley's stress rises exponentially and they fear he can no longer make correct decisions. "I'm afraid we don't stand a chance," Hawkes says. The colonel then gets on the radio and explains the problem to his crew. "Right now, you weigh twice normal at 2.4 gravity. At three gravity, you'll weigh close to 600 pounds." With the computers down, McCauley will have to manually fire the retro-rotation rockets to counteract the spin. If his calculations are correct, the wheel should slow down. "I'll have to make a guess," he continues. "An educated guess, but nonetheless a guess. If I am right, we're okay. If I am wrong, I may set up a wobble in our spin that will tear this station apart. We have no other choice."

With his own body weighing more than he ever thought possible due to the increased gravity, Colonel McCauley summoned all his inner strength. His brain alone had to tell him what the dead computers could not: the correct rocket thrust needed to save the madly-spinning space station. While in the minds of the men who sat helplessly, crushed by the same invisible force, there arose the question: could McCauley, already strained far beyond his normal breaking point, make the correct decision?

The colonel strains to reach the retro-rocket control, but without warning, the outside jets fire again, heightening centrifugal forces within the station. Physical movement now becomes nearly impossible. "It's too late," Major Canell decides. "There's nothing we can do!" Major Hawkes also informs McCauley, "The indicator shows you far behind the top critical point." Summoning his last remaining strength, the colonel pushes the retrorocket button and the station begins gradually slowing. Several bursts ensue before gravity returns to normal and McCauley barks, "Get that repair party out there on the double!" Major Hawkes expresses to the colonel amazement that his stress levels could be so elevated, yet he made the right decisions. "Somehow, something brought you through that crisis," he concedes. McCauley refers back to their earlier conversation regarding the "Voice of Infinity" in every man. Captain Ward humorously mentions that his "inner voice" is telling him to get out of his space suit—*now*, to which McCauley replies, "Your 'inner voice' must be short-circuited because we are going to stay in them until the repair work is completed. Speaking of repair work, let's start right here."

Afterwards, Jones and Saunders are playing a close game of poker with Jones hooked up to the stress machine in the other room. Colonel McCauley and Doctors Hawkes and Ward closely observe them nearby. Saunders, also glimpsing Jones's tension lights flashing, assumes his bluff is fake and successfully calls him. "I used to be able to bluff you easy," Jones protests. Noting this illicit use of the machine, Ward jokes, "It's amazing how fast the human mind can figure out a way to quickly debase its finest achievements." McCauley chimes in, "That's going to make the odds on our success up here a lot closer to even."

"From Another World"

(Aired April 27, 1960)

Starring: Joyce Taylor, Russ Conway (General Devon), Edward C. Platt (Dr. Luraski), Alan Dexter (General Brereton), Rand Harper

Script: Beirne Lay, Jr.

Directed by: Herman Hoffman

Technical advisor: Captain M. C. Spaulding, U.S.A.F.

Is Man alone in the universe? The question is as old as the human race and as deep as Man's urge to discover the answer. Someday, as man achieves longer strides forward in his probings into space, he may find the truth—from another world.

Inside General Devon's office, the general explains to the president of the United States that a team led by Colonel McCauley has successfully landed on asteroid L78-1 and obtained rock samples. General Brereton, a doctor, enters and fidgets nearby. "It's like catching a needle in a cosmic haystack," Devon exults. "You know, doc, I can't give McCauley enough credit for this one." However, Brereton is anxious about his apprehension that the colonel is overworked and ought to be temporarily grounded. Devon feels that suspending McCauley is somewhat drastic. "Oh, not permanently, of course," Brereton assures him. "Still, I'd feel remiss as a flight surgeon if he didn't receive an extended leave from space flights–at least 60 days."

Devon warns, "He'll bitterly resent it, you know. There's something, well, indestructible about Ed." The doctor maintains that no one is indestructible and the two proceed onto the landing zone. There, McCauley highlights the valuable samples he brought back, although he mentions the mission was cut short when his oxygen failed and he temporarily passed out. "Can anybody use some sleep?" Brereton jokes. Devon also informs them, "Doctor Luraski and the other geophysicists won't be here until tomorrow, so we'll postpone the full dress debriefing until then if there are no objections!" McCauley gets in Devon's car and accompanies the two generals back to the office to give a taped deposition.

"Well, there it is, Chuck," McCauley states. "Quick and dirty. We didn't even have time to cover an asteroid that small. We may have to go back." Devon reminds him that everything depends on the orbit ultimately assumed by the asteroid. McCauley is about to leave, but he pauses to state, "There is something else I should report, although I kind of hesitate to report it." Devon encourages him to give a full disclosure and the colonel turns on the recorder, then slams it off, insisting, "Look, I don't want you and Doc to think that I'm around the bend or seeing things, but before I passed out from lack of oxygen I did see *something*. Now I warn you, it's going to be pretty fantastic." McCauley subsequently admits he saw evidence of life on the asteroid in the form of a fossilized pterodactyl. "Ed, you're positive about this?" an alarmed Brereton asks. The colonel draws an exact likeness of the creature, commenting that his crewmen did not see it and, by the time he regained consciousness, he was on the rocket back home. Devon wants to believe him, but his report constitutes unsubstantiated evidence, so he dismisses him until morning. The general is floored by the concept and informs the doctor, "Can you imagine how close we may be to the key to the universe? Life that had evolved like our own." Reflecting on the matter further, Devon agonizingly states, "About McCauley, Doc, I'll approve your recommendation." Brereton, greatly relieved, blurts, "I hope we're not too late."

Back at the McCauley residence, the colonel reclines on his couch while Mary fixes him a drink. "Did you remember to congratulate General Brereton?" she asks. McCauley does not know why and she exclaims, "Why, he got his star!" Surprised, the colonel concedes, "Oh, my aching back, I never even noticed it!" Mary then asks if he feels tired and suggests perhaps they should not have invited the general over for dinner that evening. The colonel insists he feels fine just as Mary reminds him that she has never pulled a "worrisome, military wife routine" like in the movies. Pulling her close, he admits she is prettier than any movie star, but Mary draws back and asks, "Ed, how long are you going to keep making those space flights?" She emotes how drawn he looks lately, but, again, he denies that anything is wrong. He confesses he saw "something" out there, but cannot tell her. The colonel still manages to sneak in a kiss as she laughs and calls him incorrigible. The doorbell rings and Brereton arrives. McCauley steps outside to put steaks on the grill while the doctor begins grilling Mary for information about her husband. "It's my job to look for the danger signs," he informs her, "and the wife's job, too." The phone rings and McCauley answers and says it's for Brereton, then asks what he and Mary were talking about. She plays it coy and assures him it was nothing. The doctor returns and declares that Doctor Parsons at the base hospital just told him that Sergeant Kelly's wife had triplets. "Hey, that reminds me," McCauley announces, "I've got three of the finest steaks you have ever tasted on the barbecue!"

The next day, Doctor Luraski conducts a high-level conference in General Devon's office. "These samples are priceless, Colonel McCauley," he lectures. "Although they cannot be compared to the far-reaching implications of your discovery or your report of the evidence of animate life." General Devon also states his belief in what the colonel saw, but any report by a single witness is not irrefutable evidence. Luraski agrees, but continues lecturing, "We can deduce from a fossilized flying lizard that the planet involved possessed an atmosphere and an ocean not too dissimilar to our own, with life evolving from the seas to the land and into the sky." He speculates that since the planet is obviously older than Earth, its life forms may be far more advanced than our own. General Devon assures Luraski that the Air Force will give top priority to revisiting the asteroid should a return orbit bring it back into range. The meeting adjourns, then General Brereton grabs McCauley just as he leaves. "Ed, you've had more than your quota of space flights without a rest," he says and mentions that General Devon wants him to avoid strenuous assignments for 60 days. "Are you *grounding* me?" McCauley asks in alarm, insisting that he *has* to go if the asteroid returns. "You don't think I'm going to stand here and authorize you to run yourself into the ground?" Brereton declares and maintains the decision is totally unrelated to his last mission. "Is this a decision or a recommendation?" McCauley asks before departing. "It's an order," the general brusquely informs him.

Back at Ground Control, General Devon analyzes the last trajectory figures for asteroid L78-1, which appears to be headed back to the Moon. "She might come in, within range, in three days," he orders his aide, "so please keep everybody on a standby basis." Devon walks head-on into Colonel McCauley, who informs him that the rocket is ready, then–after some hesitation–all that remains is the selection of the crew. "You'll hear from me," is all the general says. Back home, McCauley angrily fumbles through some easy golf putts while Mary, reading the newspaper, notes that asteroid L78-1 is returning and people are beginning to speculate something important has arisen from the initial flight. The colonel feigns ignorance, but Mary says, "Isn't it pretty obvious, Ed? There's only one thing you could have seen that would be important enough to account for all this hush-hush excitement in the way you've been wound up lately... well, you must have thought you saw some indication of life from another planet–your favorite dream." "I saw what I saw, Mary," he insists. "I didn't *think* that I saw it." He angrily sounds off about how people have been treating him lately, as if he were due some hidden sympathy, and says, "I think General Devon believes I'm off my rocker!" Mary sympathetically assures him that the general must include him in any flight back to the asteroid to confirm "whatever it is you saw." Suddenly, the phone rings and McCauley is summoned back to Ground Control on the double.

Reporting in, the colonel meets with General Devon at the space map and the probable course for the asteroid mission is laid out. The general orders the final countdown to commence; turning to the solemn-faced McCauley, he says, "Colonel, I've been talking with Doc Brereton. Do you think you've had a long enough rest?" "Too long," he responds. "Then take command," Devon says with a smile. "It's your baby. This time we'll wrap it up." Soon after, the rocket departs and begins rendezvousing with L78-1. Generals Devon and Brereton, listening to McCauley's authoritative voice over the radio, glance at each other and smile–they made the right decision. Eventually, the colonel and Doctor Luraski suit up and begin exploring the surface in the one hour available. "This is pretty close to where we landed, doc," he informs Luraski. "It all looks pretty much the same to me," the doctor replies. "Yeah, I know," McCauley concedes. "It's like trying to find a needle in a haystack." Luraski takes some rock samples and McCauley urges they move on. However, no trace of the fossil is found. The rocket officer radios in, declaring they have seven minutes left. "I know it was one of these two locations, doc," McCauley states. "I'm afraid we've had it. Let's start back." As the two men drift off to the spaceship, the camera pans over and focuses on the fossilized reptile only a few feet away. "Results negative," McCauley informs Ground Control. "Repeat, results negative."

Outside General Devon's office, McCauley and Mary sit impatiently and he frets about being surveyed before being permanently grounded. The colonel pensively enters and is told by Devon, "Doctor Luraski insisted that we wait for you, Ed, as he has an announcement to make." Luraski holds up one of the rock samples recovered, breaks it open, and shows the colonel an ancient cave engraving of a flying reptile. "In fact, this is not a fossil at all. The bird-like creature you see on this rock was made by some primitive artist," he says, beaming. The generals congratulate McCauley on his discovery. The colonel steps outside to meet Mary and Devon cautions him, "Ed, not a word of this to anyone." Once outside, Mary demands to know, "Well, what's new?" Leaning over to plant a kiss, McCauley murmurs, "That's a very good question."

"Emergency Mission"

(Aired May 4, 1960)

Starring: Donald Woods (Colonel Jim Benson), Anne Neyland (Annie Benson), John Baer (Major Hodges), William Leslie, Wayne Mallory, Edson Stroll, Taldo Kenyon

Script: Kalman Phillips

Directed by: Alvin Ganzer

Technical advisor: Captain M. C. Spaulding, U.S.A.F.

No matter how many voyages Man may make across the uncharted seas of space, on each journey, he will face unknown dangers. Some expeditions may even be lost in space, speeding through the vastness of the universe towards infinity. This is the story of an emergency mission to rescue an expedition that ventured beyond the point of no return.

At Project X-1000 headquarters, Colonels McCauley and Benson listen to a taped record extolling the virtues of the new X-1000 missile during a series of unmanned test flights. McCauley tells Benson, "You know, applying those figures to the requirements for a flight to Venus should give us a pretty good chance of success." Benson, however, mentions that the fuel consumption factor is still unsatisfactory and the report suggests that manned flights in the X-1000 be restrained to only 60 percent of thrust potential. Mc-

Cauley concedes that he will not be heading off to Venus anytime soon. He also mentions that Benson's son, Ron, has become a great communications officer, saying "I'm glad he's going to be with me." Suddenly, the intercom summons McCauley to report to the Control Room, where he learns that spaceship MR-28 has experienced technical failures. Apparently, a short circuit fired all the engines at once and now the ship is hurtling at high speed into deep space, unable to alter its course. Captain Ron Benson is on the flight and he informs McCauley, "We have no fuel reserve, Sir, the main tanks are empty." McCauley realizes they are beyond escape velocity, so he demands to know the flight status of rocket ship M-5. When told it could be ready in 30 minutes, he barks, "I want it in fifteen. Put every available man on the job!" McCauley comforts Colonel Benson, insisting they'll be rescued as soon as proper flight coordinates are readied. Benson hastily departs to draw them up, then McCauley is informed that Captain Benson's wife is in the lobby. Annie Benson happily greets the colonel, who relays the grim news. "They're all right now but, yes, there is danger," he tells her. "May I stay here," she pleads. "I'll keep out of the way." McCauley consents and returns to the Control Room.

Back inside, McCauley is told that the MR-28 will escape radar range in 20 minutes. Worse, Colonel Benson brings over computations on M-7's limited capabilities, noting, "It's the best she'll do." McCauley then asks about the new high performance fuel and is informed that M-7, an older ship, has not been converted to use them. McCauley dispatches Benson to Annie in the lobby, then he radios MR-28 to announce that the rescue flight will be launched in 48 minutes. The crew smiles in relief. However, an officer then presents the colonel with more bad news–his computations for the rescue leave no margin for error. The colonel regretfully aborts the attempt altogether. Major Hodges suddenly arrives and declares M-7 ready for boarding, but McCauley bellows, "I said we're not going! We have no chance to catch the MR-28 if these computations are correct." He orders Major Hodges to relay the bad news to the doomed crew, then snatches up the microphone to inform them personally. "Well, hello, colonel. We're looking forward to your visit," Captain Benson declares. McCauley drones on, "There's not going to be any visit. I had to cancel the rescue mission. Ron, we don't have a ship with the speed or range to overtake you." The colonel then asks him to increase his transmitter power to prevent fading and Captain Benson remorsefully states, "We got your message, sir."

Back in the lobby, Colonel Benson consoles Annie and tries to persuade her to go home. McCauley then steps up with even worse news: he is forced to cancel the rescue mission. "Why?" she demands to know. The colonel explains, "Annie, there's no possible way of catching up with them." "Well, how do you know if you don't try?" she insists. McCauley, glancing at Benson, assures her that computer figures do not lie. Benson nods sadly in agreement, then Anne angrily emotes, "How can you just stand there and let him die!" Benson tries reasoning with his daughter-in-law while McCauley, grim-faced, heads back to the control room and sits dejectedly. "Look, Mac, it couldn't be helped," Major Hodges emotes. "Somebody's got to make those decisions." He then asks if the X-1000 should be prepped for an unmanned flight tomorrow. A light flashes in McCauley's eye and he demands the top performance capabilities of the new ship. After reviewing them, he tells Lieutenant Peters, "Ask Colonel Vessel to get me authority to take off in the X-1000 right away!" Major Hodges then coyly reminds the colonel he will need a co-pilot and McCauley tells him, "It may be a one-way trip." "You'll still need a co-pilot," Peters insists. The colonel storms off to the dressing room and looks impatiently at Hodges, asking, "Well...?" "Yes, sir!" comes the response.

The X-1000 rocket sits on the gantry, attended by workers, while McCauley and Hodges sit in the cockpit awaiting permission to launch. Colonel Benson radios them, "Word just came through on the hotline, you have permission to take off!" Thanks, Jim!" McCauley says with a smile and workers begin clearing the launch area.

A launching countdown, which had always been the moment of truth for both man and machine, suddenly took on a new tension. The X-1000 had only been tested in robot flights; it had never before been flown by Man. Now, in a desperate attempt to rescue the crew of the ill-fated MR-28, Colonel McCauley would have to push it beyond the limits of its known capabilities.

As the X-1000 departs in a column of smoke and flame, Mc-Cauley warns Hodges, "Brace yourself for more 'Gs' than you've ever felt before." At that same moment, Annie phones Ground Control to apologize to Colonel McCauley and Colonel Benson happily mentions that he has just taken off after her husband. Annie still wants to come down there, but Benson dissuades her and promises to call once he has news. Aboard X-1000, the flight proceeds as planned, but McCauley discerns that liftoff consumed more fuel than anticipated. He informs Ground Control, "There's no margin for error–give us an approximate time to commence search at comparative velocities, will you?" Major Hodges, covering his microphone, mumbles, "And don't make any mistakes." Colonel Benson radios back that they should rendezvous with MR-28 in 72 hours, then inquires if they will have enough fuel for the return trip. McCauley concedes, "I don't know, Jim... I just don't know."

One by one, the tracking stations around the world lost contact with the MR-28 as it continued its headlong plunge into outer space, giving Colonel McCauley the almost impossible task of finding it before he, too, reached the point of no return.

On X-1000, McCauley orders Hodges to start the radar search, but the attempt is fouled by swarms of asteroids and the colonel declares, "We'll never find them in that." As an alternative, he orders Hodges to begin radio broadcasts to the stricken crew. "Well, there's no reason for the MR-28 crew to have their radios on. They don't even know we're up here after them," he lectures. "If they do, we have to have a signal going at that moment." Hodges begins endlessly repeating, "X-1000 calling MR-28–come in MR-28." Back on the stricken ship, the crew composes final letters to loved ones and begins squabbling over what information to record before dying. "Why are we kidding ourselves," one crewman laments. "This hulk won't be found for at least ten years after we're dead. By that time, they'll be out here making their own observations." Captain Benson orders the feuding to stop and the officers begin taking spectrographic readings.

The huge tracking stations on earth fell silent as contact was lost with the MR-28, which continued plunging further and further into deep space. Colonel McCauley in the X-1000 could only hope that the estimated point of contact with the MR-28 was correct or it would be swallowed up by millions of cubic miles of dark void.

Major Hodges continues calling to the MR-28, then asks Colonel McCauley, "How's our time?" The colonel wearily informs him, "Running out." Hodges hints that they will have to turn back soon, but the colonel mutters, "Let's hang on a little while longer." Meanwhile, the MR-28's crew resumes fighting amongst themselves, at which point Captain Benson asks, "Well, I wonder what sort of radio noise there is out this far." He turns the receiver on and hears Major Hodges' voice pealing through the blackness. "They're out here!" a crewman shouts. "They came after us!" A thankful Benson asks what X-1000 is doing out here and Hodges cracks, "What do you think we're doing!" He tells Benson to keep broadcasting so he can get a fix on their position and the three men begin reciting, "MR-28 to X-1000!" Hodges turns to Colonel McCauley and wonders if they themselves will get back home. "Let's take it as it comes," he remarks.

As each man transferred from the stricken ship to the X-1000, in his mind there was a question: Had the X-1000 stretched its capabilities too far to make a safe return to Earth?

McCauley, having guided his ship alongside MR-28, rescues the three astronauts, then states, "Now, let's see if we can get home." Colonel Benson, pacing nervously back on Earth, declares, "If they don't reach radio range in 10 minutes, it means they haven't enough fuel to get back into orbit." Suddenly, the radioman picks up McCauley's weak signals and transfers it to the loudspeaker. "Now listen carefully," McCauley explains. "We don't have enough fuel to land. We'll be making a five-thousand-mile orbit in 20 hours. Track us and have a tanker rendezvous with us." Colonel Benson nervously grabs the microphone and says, "Ed, did you... did you reach the MR-28?" "Mission accomplished," is the response. "Everything's fine."

After refueling, McCauley radios Ground Control and asks for new reentry data. Colonel Benson also informs his son that, since he will not be based on the Moon, Annie has plenty of work for him to do at home. "She's the boss," the captain admits. McCauley, cracking a smile, deviously asks, "Are you still glad we found you?" McCauley radios back, "Captain Benson will follow instructions." He also observes that, since the X-1000 checked out so well in flight, testing can be suspended and the two colonels can take some time off for fishing. Benson sympathizes, but informs McCauley that, since the X-1000 was out of telemetry range for most of the flight, the testing schedule will have to be resumed as planned. Captain Benson smiles and tells McCauley, "Well, Sir, looks like you and I are both in the same boat!"

"Beyond the Stars"

(Aired May 11, 1960)

Starring: Joyce Taylor, Gene Nelson (Major Charles Randolph), James Best (Lieutenant John Leonard), Sally Fraser (Donna Talbot)

Script: David Duncan

Directed by: Jack Herzberg

Technical advisor: Captain M. C. Spaulding, U.S.A.F.

To say there is life in space is one thing; to take contact with it, another. The day will come when explorers in space will set up an outpost far from man-made radio interference on Earth. This is the story of three men who kept a lonely vigil on the far side of the Moon, listening for a signal from beyond the stars.

At a remote listening post on the dark side of the Moon, Colonel McCauley begins taping his daily log entry, including an account of the injury which may cost the life of Major Charles Randolph. A distressed Lieutenant John Leonard interrupts, insisting, "You might add, Colonel McCauley, the whole mission was fouled up because of me. It was all my fault." McCauley points out that their mission is not "fouled up" and that they will wait to see if the major recovers enough to survive the journey back to Earth. Leonard continues insisting that the accident was his fault, to which the colonel snarls, "Slow down! Stop blaming yourself for the accident and get back to work." The lieutenant resumes mapping segments of the sky with the giant radio telescope outside, mumbling, "Did you ever realize, colonel, that in the entire history of astronomy, every new theory about the universe has had to make it bigger and more complex than the theory that was discarded?" McCauley muses, "Is that going to happen again?" Suddenly Major Randolph starts moaning incoherently from his bed, causing both men to stop. Leonard then asks if the colonel would mind if he finished the taped log entries. "No, go ahead," McCauley acquiesces. "Get it out of your system." Leonard begins his narrative at a gathering at the colonel's house, just prior to departure.

A small party consisting of McCauley, Mary, Lieutenant Leonard, and his fiancée Sally are reveling when the phone rings. Mary answers and it turns out to be the latest woman trying to say goodbye to Major Randolph, a womanizer replete with a little black book the size of the Yellow Pages. She duly records the name on the ever-growing list of callers, then rejoins the party in progress. "You know," McCauley speculates, "he must have some special technique of saying goodbye!" The doorbell rings, Mary answers, and in pops the rakish Randolph, handing her a bouquet of roses. "I know I'm late. Don't try to deny it, but I forgive you with these!" he confidently asserts. Randolph also hands Donna roses, in his word, "a token of farewell." "Where have you been?" McCauley pointedly inquires. "Walking by myself," he answers, "thinking how sad that I go to the Moon and leave no woman waiting." He agonizes why he cannot settle down and Donna pooh-poohs the idea, asserting, "Because you'd hate it so, Charlie." He emotes about ending up a "star-gazing old bachelor" with everybody staring at the lipstick on his forehead. "Well," McCauley mutters, "you sound pretty convincing–except for this!" As he wipes Randolph's forehead clean, he mutters, "Uhhh, my niece, she told me goodbye. She's getting to be quite a little lady." The phone rings and the colonel sends Randolph to answer and–sure enough–another woman wishes to bid him adieu. The major grabs his guitar case and offers to sing–then the phone rings again. "I'll get it, Casanova," the colonel tells him. "It *might* be for me." The colonel, of course, misjudges and he says, "Hold the guitar, Charlie. I have a Susan here." McCauley then explains to Donna that they will be on the dark side of the Moon to conduct star mapping and listening for intelligent signals from beyond. "Well," Mary insists, "that's not so good for us girls at home. The whole time you're gone, you'll be out of contact with Earth." The colonel suggests they all eat and notes, "*Romeo* can join us when he finishes talking with Susan." McCauley mockingly states, as he passes Randolph, "I don't think he will be ready for a 6 AM takeoff!"

The next day, a rocket launches for the Moon and it successfully lands at the remote radio telescope base. Leonard continues narrating that the equipment worked so well that the men had too much time on their hands, so Randolph suggested taping a radio show for the folks back on Earth. "All right," McCauley declares, "so long as I don't have to tap dance." The major gleefully appoints him the announcer and, in a sonorous voice, the colonel invites Leonard to describe what he sees from the observatory window. "I see nothing but desolation," he drones. "It is the Devil's nightmare–not a blade of grass, not a tree, nothing moves out there. This is a land of death." The colonel shuts him up before he scares the kids, then asks Randolph if he would care to sing. "Naturally, I'm going to sing," he smirks. "You're my captive audience!" Picking up his guitar, the major strums along with facility and warmth:

Darling, to you, I sing from the Moon, into the void of sky—
Here from the stars, forever my love, words that will never die—

His two compatriots applaud with McCauley gesturing, "Charlie, you touched me!" Suddenly, the lights start flickering and Randolph traces a short circuit to an azimuth drive control on the radio telescope. The three men begin suiting up and venture over to the ailing device to repair it. Strolling over to the microphone, the major jests, "Sorry folks, the show is interrupted. We're all going outside to get a nice, fresh breath of *vacuum!*" En route, Randolph notices that the wire insulation is like peanut brittle, which McCauley attributes to extreme temperature fluctuations on the Moon's surface. "Be glad your suits are insulated so that you can take either extreme," he lectures. Their work completed, Randolph gazes wistfully upwards, murmuring, "I like it out here. Look at that sky." The dour Leonard fires back, "Well, you can have my share... this lifeless terrain." They tramp on back to the igloo until Leonard snags part of the auxiliary power cable on a rock. Pulling hard, he partially strips it of insulation and Randolph, reaching over to free it, is stunned by the charge and falls down into a crevice. "So, Charlie," Leonard continues narrating, "who'd always been so full of life, has been unconscious for three days–probably dying. Dying because of my stupid blunder." McCauley, discovering that Randolph's temperature and pulse are approaching normal, still determines to cancel the mission and return him to Earth. Leonard protests that the major might not survive the trip, but is overruled. "We don't know that for certain," McCauley insists, "but we do know he needs a lot more medical attention than we can give him." The colonel instructs Leonard to start packing while he goes out and inspects the ship for takeoff. Leonard complies, then listens to the tape recording one last time. Randolph's forlorn love song comes up and it rouses the singer to semi-consciousness. "The sound from the stars..." he murmurs, "I want to hear it." McCauley has Leonard turn on the radio telescope and an unusual wave pattern is discerned. The colonel finds the focal point on a star, 200 light-years away, and the signal remotely sounds like music. "Do you think that it could be an intelligence from somewhere in space?" Leonard asks. "It's almost like a question," the colonel speculates. "Like someone asking if there is anyone listening who understands arithmetic." The signal fades and the major, struggling to sit up, demands to know where the sound went. McCauley assures him the senders are awaiting an answer and he decides to reply to Randolph's love song. Leonard plugs in their transmitter and focuses it on the star in question. "We've heard your signal," McCauley broadcasts, "and with this song we are answering you. We are Earthmen who live on the third planet from the Sun. And now here is our song." The music rouses a groggy Major Randolph to consciousness and he asks, "What kind of nonsense are you guys pulling?" He confesses feeling like he has been hit by a 10-ton meteor, then asks if there is anything to eat. "Yeah," McCauley assures him, "I think we can scrounge up something. After that, we head for home." However, Randolph refuses to have the mission scrubbed for his sake and insists on lying back while they wait on him hand and foot. "In your spare time, you can finish the work we came up to do," he declares. McCauley agrees, noting, "I think he's too ornery to take back to Earth right now, anyhow."

Back at the McCauley residence, another party winds on and the colonel expresses astonishment at how Major Randolph juggles all his girlfriends. "He must use a computer!" Randolph gets off the phone and asks what's so funny. The colonel says he had a tragic thought about all the women from space who will begin calling for him from that distant planet once they've heard his song. "I should think that a 400-year delay would cramp a man with even your style," he notes. The phone rings again and Randolph, flashing his devilish smile, informs him, "I'll find a way!"

"Misson To Mars"

(Aired May 25, 1960)

Starring: John Van Dreelan (Colonel Tolchek), Jeremy Slate (Captain Jim Nichols), Jack Hogan (Major Ingram), Don Either (Major Ralph Devers), Tyler McVey (General Miles), David Janti, Wil Hufman, Ted Roter

Script: Lewis Jay

Directed by: William Conrad

Technical advisor: Captain M. C. Spaulding, U.S.A.F.

For centuries, the histories of Earth-bound men have been filled with conflicts. Within the not-too-distant future, when descendants of these men leave Earth and begin to conquer space, will they carry these age-old hostilities with them? Or will this great scientific step at last teach men to stand shoulder-to-shoulder, united, when confronted with the unknown?

Captain Jim Nichols enters from the airlock on Moon Base and hands Major Devers his completed work report. Devers, however, passes him a revised schedule and, scrutinizing it, the captain complains that the proposed modifications to the fuel pumps will require an extra three days. "And maybe make the difference between us getting safely back from Mars or not," Devers assures him. Exasperated, Nichols slams his note board down and insists that the boosters

249

are plenty powerful enough, but the major, handing the slate back, declares, "Colonel McCauley didn't think so." The captain, working himself into a lather, declares that these changes might cause them to miss the favorable time frame to launch for Mars. "Furthermore," he spouts, "it practically guarantees the Russians beating us!" At that point, Colonel McCauley passes through the airlock and skeptically inquires, "Who's trying to beat the Russians?" Nichols replies, "I am, for one, Sir!" The colonel calmly saunters over, announcing, "Well, I don't object to that as far as it's secondary to something more important, and that's getting to Mars and *getting back*." Captain Nicholas continues sputtering against the modifications, but McCauley sternly orders the new work to commence immediately. Major Devers confesses that when the Russians set up their Moon base three months ago, he liked the idea of having neighbors. "Yes," McCauley reflects, "and they've been *good* neighbors, too." Major Ingram then mentions the morale problems all this created. "Seems like all our guys can think of now is beating the Russians–never mind the care and the safety factors, just beat the Russians!" Glancing out the base viewport, McCauley espies a Russian cosmonaut approaching the base and announces they are about to have visitors. Ingram notes that this is the first time they visited since the first exchange of courtesies three months ago. Devers also points out that their respective radio operators are in daily contact with each other. "Pretty interesting dialogue, too, like 'How's the weather over at your base?'" McCauley states, grinning.

At length, Major Gulyt enters, salutes smartly, and inquires, "Colonel McCauley?" The colonel greets him, introduces Majors Devers and Ingram, then asks how he can help. "My commander, Colonel Tolchek, presents his compliments," he continues in accented English, "and would like the American commander and two of his officers to come to dinner at 22 hundred hours this date." McCauley warmly thanks his counterpart for such hospitality and assures him that he, Devers, and Ingram will appear as planned. "Thank you, sir, I will deliver your message," Gulyt states with another smart salute, then departs. "Now, I wonder what that was all about," McCauley speculates. "I have a feeling it's not just a courtesy invitation."

Suddenly, Captain Nichols radios McCauley that he has devised a shortcut that would save time on the waste recycling system and wants the colonel to inspect it. "Save time?" McCauley declares, casting a baleful glance at Devers and Ingram. He nonetheless suits up and visits the rocket. "Yes, if you'll okay this change, I can spend the rest of the time on the fuel pump modifications," Nichols excitedly tells him. McCauley casts one glance at the makeshift arrangement and declares it unsatisfactory. Nichols protests that it would save time and enable them to beat the Russians. "I understand why you did it," the colonel lectures. "When you're off duty, report to my quarters." Later, McCauley chews out Nichols for being in such haste. When the captain harps about the Russians again, McCauley bellows, "You know it! And don't you think for a minute that they've overlooked any single item which would help to ensure the success of their expedition!" Constraining his anger, the colonel simply tells the captain, "Now keep that in mind for the future, will you?" A contrite Nichols departs, pausing only to blurt out, "But I still hope we beat the Russians!" "Well, I'll tell you a secret," McCauley confides. "So do I." Major Devers then jests about not having any formal wear for their dinner engagement at the Russian base. McCauley, taking the jibe in stride, informs him, "Well, I think your space suit will be adequate for street wear and your coveralls passable for inside." Pointing to the door, he motions to the major. "And *you* may be excused, too."

The three American officers trudge their way over to the Russian base, where they are warmly greeted by Colonel Tolchek, an ebullient man speaking excellent English. "Come in, gentlemen!" he exclaims. "Colonel McCauley, it is good to see you!" Pleasantries are exchanged, then Tolchek inquires of his guests how, in American parlance, to make a date. "We will meet on Mars and have a picnic!" McCauley smiles and informs his host, "Some other time, colonel, we are not stopping there this trip–just reconnaissance, then we're heading home." "Same with us," Tolchek informs his guests. Major Devers rather awkwardly asks Major Gulyt if they have set a date yet. The Soviet officer starts to answer, halts, and shoots an anxious glance to his commander. Tolchek, taking the cue, simply announces, "Only tentatively. *Have you?*" Devers fires off an equally anxious look to McCauley, who lectures, "Well, colonel, we're calculating, as I am sure you are, that the best possible relationship between the

Moon and Mars is in the next 48 hours and lasts for a four-day period. We hope to get off before the end of the four days." The smiling Tolchek nods in agreement. "So do we." McCauley then continues, "We've been delayed slightly because we're making modifications on the fuel pump systems on our main boosters. It's an extra margin of safety; otherwise, we would have taken off at the beginning of the four-day period." "Modifications?" Tolchek incredulously asks. "At such a late date?" McCauley says he felt that the changes were necessary and his host informs him, "With us, the die is cast. We are making no engineering changes; otherwise, we may lose the favorable period altogether." McCauley congratulates Tolchek that his engineering is adequate and the Russian beams, "Thank you. Gentlemen, I propose a toast–to our mutual success!" McCauley brings the glass to his lips, pauses, and exclaims, "Vodka?" Tolchek, smiling, announces, "Naturally!" McCauley smiles warmly at his host. "May we both have a successful trip," Tolchek declares, "and may the best crew win!" The men drink, then McCauley asks, "Colonel, do you feel your effort is in competition with us?" "Not at all," Tolchek insists. "Not at all. I admit that some of my younger officers have tendencies in that direction, however." McCauley nods and concedes, "Yes, I've experienced the same difficulties." Tolchek continues, "Now for a time, let us forget the cares and perplexities that mutually beset us." The men raise their glasses again and drink.

Back at Ground Control, General Miles radios Colonel McCauley that the analysis he submitted for the coming flight checks out. "We confirm your findings," Miles assures the colonel. "You *are* ready to go." Before signing off, the general assures McCauley that his will be the final judgment whether or not the attempt should be made. "We don't expect you–we don't want you to go–unless you feel completely confident and comfortable on every detail," the general states. McCauley thanks him, then signs off. "You know," he confides to Ingram and Devers, "I'm a little envious of that Russian commander." "You can't like vodka that much!" Devers quips. The colonel continues, noting how nice everything is down pat for his counterpart, no changes, no worries. A skeptical Ingram states, "I think it's probably just a front for our benefit." McCauley almost regrets ordering all those last-minute modifications; otherwise, he would have a three-day lead on the Russians. "The responsibility of command is producing some last-minute doubts, I'd say," Devers interjects. When McCauley jests that maybe Captain Nichols was right, Devers insists, "No, colonel, Nichols himself wouldn't bet on that."

The following morning, the Mars 1 rocket prepares for liftoff and Major Ingram informs them that the Russians are likewise readying to launch, ten minutes behind them. "Not much of a head start," Nichols whines. Mars 1 shoots skyward amidst flame and smoke and Ingram pronounces it a perfect launch. Within minutes, he also informs McCauley that the Russians have also launched. Major Devers then observes them on radar, noting that their deviation is six degrees off course and increasing. McCauley observes, "They're in trouble." Ingram suddenly declares that the Russian rocket has exploded and the crew failed to eject. Nichols blurts out, "I wanted to beat them, but this is overdoing it!" McCauley also learns that the Russian crew is still alive, but neither Soviet nor American rescue rockets can arrive before their air gives out. Nichols nervously states he is going aft to inspect the life support system, but McCauley tells him not to bother. "Mars 1 to Moon Base," he calls out. "We are abandoning the Mars expedition." "No!" Captain Nichols gasps. "As soon as you have a good analysis of their orbit, please pass it to me," McCauley continues. "We're going to attempt to rendezvous with the Russian ship."

Back at Ground Control, General Miles is on the phone attempting to explain McCauley's actions to the president of the United States and he subsequently contacts Mars 1. The general informs him, "I must say, you've succeeded in pushing every red button we have down here." "Yeah," McCauley drawls, "I imagine so, Sir." The general instructs him to remain in contact and keep him posted of any rescue attempt. At length, Mars 1 pulls alongside the stricken Russian ship and McCauley suits up and floats over to retrieve the survivors. Meanwhile, General Miles again explains to the president that he is out of radio contact with McCauley and the commander-in-chief orders him directly back to Earth once the rescue is finished. "To *Earth*, Sir?" an incredulous general exclaims. "I understand."

Back near Mars 1, McCauley announces that both Russian pilots are alive and that he will retrieve them. Meanwhile, Captain Nichols motions to Major Devers to switch off his radio and he asks, "What do you think they'll do to the colonel back on Earth?" Devers says, "Well, if I had the say, he'd get a medal." Nichols counters with, "But you don't have the say." "No, I haven't," Devers deject-edly concludes. Soon after, McCauley and Nicholas revive the bat-tered Tolchek and Gulyt with oxygen masks. The groggy colonel asks McCauley how he managed to change direction to rescue them and learns that the Americans abandoned their Mars mission to do so. "You threw away a perfect shot at Mars?" he asks. "Not completely, colonel," McCauley assures him. "We gained a lot of valuable expe-rience." "So did we," Tolchek concedes. "We felt a need for haste." McCauley, casting an icy glance at Nichols, exclaims, "So did we." The colonel excuses himself and goes forward, whereupon General Miles informs him he is to proceed directly back to the space sta-tion, where another rocket will take them all to Earth. "Say again, please?" the colonel asks in astonishment. Miles repeats his order while McCauley, glancing at Major Devers, admits, "Well, I guess they can't wait to nail my hide to the wall, eh?"

Once on Earth, McCauley reports directly to General Miles' of-fice. He wants to call his wife, but the general instructs him to don his dress uniform and board a jet waiting for them. The colonel angrily protests such treatment and Miles assures him, "I have my orders, too. One of them is to keep my mouth–and yours–shut." McCau-ley reluctantly complies and soon finds himself before the president. The commander-in-chief lauds him for his heroic efforts and informs him, "By abandoning your mission to save human lives, you have at once done more to make the American position clear than anything that has been done in the last fifty years." He shakes McCauley's hand and points him across the hall, where his wife and children are waiting. General Miles likewise snaps a salute and departs.

Back at Moon Base, a gathering of Russian and American space-men enjoy a round of drinks being passed around. "Now this is all very pleasant," Colonel Tolchek declares with his infectious smile. "My comrades and I are all very happy to be invited to your base for dinner." "Just being neighborly," McCauley replies. "Splendidly said, Colonel," Tolchek emphatically announces. "A toast to neighborli-ness between us–may we always treasure it!" The men drink up and Tolchek, taken aback, mutters, "Lemonade!" "Of course," McCau-ley assures him and all are seated for another friendly interlude.

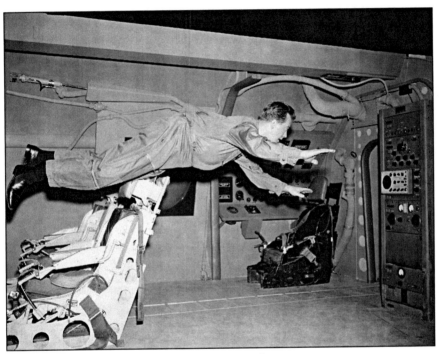

Courtesy Landov Media.

"Moon Trap"

(Aired June 1, 1960)

Starring: Dan Barton (Major Tom Jackson), Richard Emory (Doctor Parker), Don Burnett (Captain Dick Jackson), Robin Lorry (Harriet), Mike Keene, Jim Cody

Script: Lewis Jay

Directed by: Otto Lang

Technical advisor: Captain M. C. Spaulding, U.S.A.F.

The deeper into space Man travels, the more severe the requirements will become, and the more complex the equipment needed for his safety. But machinery and computers, no matter how carefully engineered, cannot surpass Man and his ability to meet and cope with unforeseen situations. This is the story of two men who, when deprived of the protection of their complex machinery, fought for their lives when caught in a Moon Trap.

Harriet Jackson, a vivacious teenager, answers the phone in her house by going, "Blast off, Mac, it's your fuel!" Her tone instantly changes when the caller turns out to be a senior military figure asking for Colonel McCauley. The colonel is in the den with Major Tom Jackson and his brother, Captain Richard Jackson, discussing the major's upcoming Moon flight. His sister excitedly interrupts, exclaiming, "Tom! The base called! You're going to take off!" Glancing over at McCauley, she blurts out, "Like wow! A bird colonel!" Tom corrects his kid sister for being so informal, then introduces her to the boss. "I get it," McCauley says with a smile. "Tom... Dick... and *Harriet*." Tom asks her to repeat her message and, somewhat calmer, she informs them that Colonel Swenson wants Tom to report to the base at midnight. The major then momentarily leaves to call in, Dick departs to get McCauley another drink, and Harriet corners him to declare, "Look, Colonel, I want to go to the Moon!" McCauley explains that is a mighty tall request for a young girl and she counters with, "Why for a girl? After all, several women have been to the Moon." The colonel notes that they were only sent on an experimental basis and she replies, "I don't mind going experimentally." Fortunately, Dick arrives with McCauley's drink and shoos her off. The colonel, in a tone equal parts admiration and exasperation, admits, "She's quite a gal." He next assures a jittery Tom that he will do just fine as a newly-minted spaceship commander. "Besides, you'll have Captain Henry as a co-pilot. You can't do better than that," the colonel reminds him. "*Ahem!*" Dick intrudes. "Except me, of course." Tom still admits to feeling nervous, but McCauley consoles him with, "I'm glad you do. If you didn't, I'd have to think you were numb and would have to scrub you from the mission!"

The next morning, McCauley and Captain Jackson are at Ground Control as Major Jackson prepares to launch MR-34. They wish Tom good luck and he departs as planned with Captain Henry and geologist Doctor Parker. That evening, Harriet chews out boyfriend Harvey on the phone when he asks her out and she is worried about her brother landing on the Moon. She promises to go out the following evening. "Once I've gotten Tom safely there, I'll take *you* to the movies." Later, Harriet carefully plots Tom's trajectory on a Moon map and her brother Dick corrects her. "Look," she tells him, "you guys do your navigating, I'll do mine." The captain jokingly declares, "I'll tell the Air Force to get rid of all its computers and let you take over." Not missing a beat, Harriet counters, "That would be a very good idea." She then pleads with Dick to take her to the control room, which he cannot, but he promises to phone once Tom has landed safely. Meanwhile, McCauley tracks MR-34's flight path, pronouncing it perfect for a lunar landing. Colonel Swenson gets on the radio and declares, "Ground Control to MR-3-4. Your position is excellent; at your option, start rotation and go to auto-control for landing." Major Jackson acknowledges his orders, but no sooner does the procedure begin than the rocket suddenly loses power. "Prepare for emergency landing," he tells the crew. "Get your helmets on!" Just as he informs Ground Control his estimated position, the radio falls ominously silent. McCauley fails to raise them, so he orders Dick to get the best possible estimate of their location while he prepares a rescue mission. "If we can get a fix on them, a rescue team from Moon Base might do some good," he informs Swenson. The estimated crash zone is near the Straight Wall, 200 miles from Moon Base and, as Swenson painfully points out, "Under the best possible conditions, it's a four-day march." Dick then asks to be excused so he can phone Harriet and McCauley lets him go.

On the Moon, Tom and Doctor Parker pick through the wreckage of MR-34 and discover the body of Captain Henry. "Dead," Parker mumbles. "The blast caught him. Now what?" "Maybe the blast should have caught us, too," Tom laments. "Two hours of oxygen and Heaven knows how far we are from Moon Base." Suddenly, Parker recognizes the Straight Wall, which he surveyed last year. Tom suggests they get to the top of the formation in the event it boosts the range of their helmet transmitters. Parker also recalls that there is a cache of supplies left from the previous survey and that it might contain oxygen bottles. Tom agrees, thinking that the rescue expedition would likely check there for them first. "I'd rather die trying something, wouldn't you?" he asks. The doctor agrees and they amble onwards. At length, the two men encounter the supply cache, but the only available oxygen is in liquid form. "Doc," Tom suddenly exclaims, "maybe we can use one of the caves at the Straight Wall as a temporary igloo!" Parker warns they would have to seal off the entrance and Tom insists they could boil off enough of the liquid to last a long time. "Not a long time," Parker somberly explains. "The rising level of carbon dioxide would probably kill us before we ran out of oxygen." Tom refuses to remain idle, so Parker, just before leaving, takes out a pen and scribbles where they are to all prospective rescuers. The two men then work a large oxygen canister into the entrance of a cave and begin sealing it off when a landslide completely covers the opening. "Open the valve and see if it will build up any pressure in here," Tom states. "We've got it made," Parker exults.

Back in his office, McCauley phones to General Robert that the MS-9 is fueled and ready for launching. Colonel Swenson bluntly reminds him, "The odds are steep. Moon Base reported a shock wave from the Straight Wall area two and-a-half minutes after the transmission ceased–that means an explosion. So even if they got out of the wreck alive, there couldn't be enough oxygen." At this juncture, McCauley motions Captain Jackson to see Harriet, then entering the room. "Tom will think of something," she murmurs. McCauley explains that he is waiting for permission to launch a rescue mission, saying, "I guess you probably overheard Colonel Swenson estimating their chances." Suddenly, the phone rings; McCauley answers, then tells General Roberts that Captain Jackson will be his co-pilot. Swenson also declares he will get the countdown started. A pensive Harriet grabs Dick by the arms and instructs him, "I have faith. You just go up there and bring your brother back."

MS-9 takes off while Tom and Parker are alive, but begin exhibiting carbon dioxide poisoning. Meanwhile, as McCauley approaches the Moon, he informs Swenson that he and Captain Jackson will depart upon landing and that their helmet radios will be tied directly to Earth Control. Moon Base also informs the colonel that two more days are required for the rescue expedition to reach the wreckage. McCauley advises, "We'll be there in ten minutes." The ship executes a flawless landing and the two men debark. Sifting through MR-34's wreckage, they find the body of Captain Henry and Dick, espying his brother's footprints, deduces, "Tom and Doctor Parker are still alive." McCauley cautions, "They were–two and a half days ago." He feels that their only option is to visit the supply cache at the Straight Wall, the most logical place they would have gone. Arriving at the cache, they find it vacant and Dick solemnly exclaims, "Nothing!" "Did you expect to find them standing here, waiting here for us?" McCauley sarcastically jests. "I thought we'd find some kind of a sign," Dick insists. The colonel, gazing upon Parker's written message, exults, "We did!" Back in the cave, Parker begins growing delusional and mentions dreaming about going outside, opening his suit, and ending it quickly. Tom calms his friend, noting, "We're not dead yet." "Aren't we?" Parker maintains. "How long has it been?" Tom informs him 61 hours. "If they're going to rescue us, they should have been here by now," Parker concludes. "We're kidding ourselves. I doubt if they even know where we crashed." He repeats his desire to go outside and die in the light, "where they can at least find our bodies one day. I'm getting out!" The desperate Parker begins clawing at the seal around the tank, but Tom drops him with a single punch. "I'm sorry, Doc," he murmurs.

Outside the cave, McCauley and Captain Jackson look vainly for the cave entrance until a small landslide uncovers the oxygen tank. The colonel begins tapping Morse code to see if the two men are alive and they respond in kind. McCauley instructs them to put on their helmets. "Will do," Captain Jackson reads back. Back at the Parker residence, McCauley informs Major Parker that the board of inquiry could not establish the cause of MR-34's malfunction. "Well, at least it wasn't pilot error, so your name is still on the availability list for future command assignments," he states. Harriet then enters the room, dressed to the nines, so McCauley asks her to join them for dinner. She declines, stating a date with Harvey is in the offing, then the doorbell rings and Harriet departs. Dick jokingly states it's a good thing they invited her anyway or she would have howled like a hyena. McCauley, grinning ear-to-ear, states, "Well, I think you're about to find out that your tomboy kid sister has suddenly discovered that it's better to let the boys do the howling."

Courtesy Landov Media.

"Flare Up"

(Aired August 17, 1960)

Starring: Werner Klemperer (Major Kralenko), Edgar Barrier (Russian general), Skip Ward (Captain Webb), Preston Hanson (Captain Rumbough), Larry Thor (Major General Mallon), Jay Warren (Russian captain), Eric Feldary (Colonel Alexandrov), Lee Raymond

Script: David Duncan, Sidney Kalcheim

Directed by: Herman Hoffman

Technical director: Captain M. C. Spaulding, U.S.A.F.

When the nations of the world move forward in their exploration of the blackness of outer space in search of new and distant frontiers, they will be confronted by the unknowns of an ever-changing universe. Only one thing will always be the same—human behavior. This is the powerful story of one man, whose behavior almost changed the future relationship of two nations and their desire to live peacefully on a distant planet.

Colonel McCauley and Captains Rumbough and Marlowe are on the Moon's surface, taking seismic readings, when Captain Webb, radio operator at their advance base, informs them of an unidentified object approaching. "Unidentified?" McCauley declares. "Keep me advised." Meanwhile, inside Russian spaceship NK-1, Major Kralenko orders their course altered eight degrees and to prepare for landing. When his subordinate angrily protests the procedure, the major insists, "Alter course 8 degrees!" Neither subordinate complies, so Kralenko makes the adjustments himself. The captain loudly objects, telling him, "Major, you've gone way off course! You'll destroy the ship and us, too!" Kralenko reminds him who is in command and silences him. "It won't help you," the captain notes. "The course recorder is keeping a record of the way you are handling this ship." The major nevertheless orders them to prepare for landing and to worry about the course recorder later. Their rocket suddenly shudders violently. The captain, thoroughly alarmed, declares, "I warn you, Sir, I am filing a separate report of this affair as soon as we land." Back at the advance base, Captain Webb informs McCauley that the mystery ship is landing at coordinates C-4. "C-4?" the colonel exclaims. "Well, if it's Russian, they're way off course." An explosion in the distance indicates that something has crashed, so McCauley orders Webb to have the Main Base contact the Russians and inform them that a ship is down and might be one of theirs. The colonel then tells Rumbough and Marlowe to stop testing and accompany him to the wreckage.

At the impact zone, Kralenko recovers in the cabin, only to see his two compatriots dead. He then radios the Russian base that NK-1 has crashed and that sabotage is suspected. "Our landing radar was deliberately jammed," he insists. Colonel Alexandrov instructs him to secure the course recorder, then report to the American base as they themselves are too distant. The colonel then states, "Major, for many reasons, you are to say absolutely *nothing* about what you believe has happened. Is that perfectly clear?" Kralenko acknowledges his orders, then grabs a crowbar and tries removing the course recorder, but it is stuck fast. After several more failed attempts, he rises from his seat and meanders outside just as McCauley's team approaches. The major dodges behind an outcropping and remains hidden as the colonel picks through the wreckage and radios that the ship is indeed Russian. There are apparently no survivors. Low oxygen levels force the Americans back to their advance base and they enter the airlock, whereupon Captain Webb asks, "Where's the Russian?" "What Russian?" McCauley snarls. "There were only two men in that ship." Webb then hands him a communiqué from the Russian base, which had contacted the sole survivor. "There were only two men in that ship," the colonel notes. "Well, there's something wrong here," Webb comments. "Yeah, there sure is!" McCauley exclaims and he gets on the radio to Main Base.

The scene switches to Major General Mallon's office in the Pentagon, where he is in an intense discussion with a senior Soviet general. "I agree with you, Sir, that, above all, we should try to prevent this incident from growing to proportions that would be difficult to handle." "We should get at the whole truth, and quickly," the Russian insists. "Our ship's course recorder would be an impartial observer, so to speak." Mallon wishes to have Americans present when the recorder is examined and suggests that a joint Russian/American team proceed to McCauley's advance base to investigate the wreckage. Colonel McCauley will also be ordered to redouble his efforts to find Major Kralenko. The general insists that the Americans do not disturb any part of the wreckage. "This McCauley, how do I know he can be trusted?" he inquires. Mallon insists, "I would never question his reliability, nor will I allow you to, sir." "Fair enough," the Russian declares, "but I think we both understand from what we already know that someone in this affair will be proved to be unreliable, to say the least." He solemnly departs Mallon's office.

Back on the Moon, Captain Webb passes along a Top Security communication to McCauley from General Mallon. Glancing over the sheet, he murmurs, "Oooh, we have a beauty here." He instructs the men that whatever happens on their mission from now on is strictly confidential and mentions that the sole surviving Russian, Major Kralenko, has accused the Americans of sabotaging his ship. Moreover, they are to find the missing man and escort him safely back to base. "Tell General Mallon there was no sabotage!" the colonel angrily insists as the three men depart for the airlock. Back at the Russian wreck, Kralenko again tries removing the course recorder, pounding on it furiously with a crowbar, but it remains wedged tight. He heads back outside and again dodges McCauley's team as it inspects the vessel. This time, McCauley notices that Kralenko has removed spare oxygen tanks from the dead men and also tried removing the recorder. "Mac," Rumbough inquires, "do you think this is part of a deliberate attempt to provoke an incident?" "I hope not," McCauley states. "I think the Russians are cooperating with us. But the sooner we find Kralenko, the better I'll feel about it."

The colonel advises Captain Webb to keep an eye out for the errant major and to report immediately should he appear at the base. The three men then spread out and search for him nearby.

Meanwhile, Kralenko limps off to the advance base, pistol in hand, and enters. He orders Captain Webb to stay away from his radio and, when Webb declares, "My orders..." Kralenko pulls his gun and murmurs, "Have been changed!" The captain dives towards the radio transmitter, whereupon Kralenko shoots him dead. Suddenly, McCauley calls for Webb on the radio, so Kralenko answers and calmly declares, "Colonel, I am now in charge of your station." He orders the Americans not to enter, but McCauley protests that they only have a limited supply of oxygen left. Kralenko warns him that Captain Webb has been wounded and placed in the airlock without a space suit; he will die instantly if the door is opened. McCauley's team strolls up to the base window and the colonel informs Kralenko that a joint Russian-American team is en route to the base. "Now stop and think," he entreats the major. "You panicked, you hid, you ran. That's all. If we die, if Webb dies, you'll be a murderer." Kralenko smugly assures him, "No colonel, I will not be a murderer. My report was sabotage and you and Webb died attempting to destroy the records of my course instruments to conceal your guilt." Furthermore, Kralenko informs them he will take explosives from the American base and destroy the course recorder once McCauley and the others are dead. "I will say that you did it to cover up your own sabotage," he smugly declares.

Checkmated, McCauley and his team retreat behind an outcropping, which blocks their radio signals. The colonel warns that they must somehow get inside the base; otherwise, if they die, Kralenko's scheme may very well work. "I keep thinking of that course recorder," Captain Marlowe opines. "If we could get it into the hands of the Russians intact, that would at least cook this guy's goose." "Yeah," Rumbough concurs, "that would be the only taped record that could speak for us, even if we *are* dead." Suddenly, McCauley gets a flash and has the men turn on their own tape recorders. "If we could only get Kralenko to repeat what he just said, we could record it," he muses. The men step back to the viewing screen and McCauley asks, "Kralenko, what's so important in your life that you must kill all of us?" "Success is a hard master, colonel," he lectures. "An occasional failure would remedy that," McCauley assures him. "Not for me," Kralenko shoots back. "The fact that we didn't sabotage your landing attempt will become known eventually," McCauley continues. "Never!" Kralenko insists. "I will have destroyed the course recorder and you and your friends will be dead." He also admits to having shot Webb. The colonel then informs him that they have recorded every word Kralenko just said and, when the major scoffs at the ploy, McCauley says, "You don't have to believe me–just listen." The recording rattles Kralenko and he offers to trade the tapes for fresh oxygen bottles, but McCauley simply declares they are heading for the main base with the recordings. As hoped for, Kralenko panics, dons his space suit, and ventures outside in pursuit. Rumbough reminds McCauley that they will be out of air in three minutes, so the colonel says they will wait 30 more seconds, then try and rush the station. "Maybe one of us will get through alive," he states. Fortunately, Kralenko carelessly walks near the outcropping and the three Americans subdue him. Once inside, McCauley radios the main base to say, "I regret to report that Captain Webb is dead, but we have Major Kralenko, his tape-recorded confession, and the course recorder on the ship is still intact. There won't be anything for those investigators to do but carry off their mission. Out."

Back at the Pentagon, General Mallon, his Soviet counterpart, and Colonel McCauley are discussing recent events. The Russian laments that Kralenko was a man obsessed with "a ceaseless drive for perfection." Mallon concludes that the thought of failure–any failure–terrified him and the Russian correctly adds, "But a good soldier must learn to face failure as well as success." McCauley points out the bitter irony that the investigation concluded that mechanical failure, not Kralenko's poor piloting, caused the crash. "I commend you for your handling of this affair, colonel," the Russian states. McCauley states his hope that, hereafter, "other differences between us can be satisfactorily resolved."

Courtesy Landov Media.

"Into the Sun"

(Aired August 24, 1960)

Starring: Paul Picerni (Bob King), Harp McGuire (Major Tex Nolan), Nelson Leigh (General Adams), Mack Williams

Script: Lewis Jay, Fred Freiberger

Directed by: Jack Herzberg

Technical director: Captain M. C. Spaulding, U.S.A.F.

*Increased government and industrial use of atomic energy for power
has intensified the problem of disposing of atomic wastes. Present
methods of burying this waste deep in the Earth are satisfactory,
but there will be a time in the future when a more ideal method of
disposal will be needed. This is the story of a group of dedicated men
who conducted the first tests that might enable man to send atomic
wastes back to its source: into the Sun.*

At a meeting of high-ranking politicians in General Adams's office,
the issue of safely disposing atomic waste is a matter of growing concern. Mayor Clark insists, "A more ideal method for disposing of ac-
cumulating atomic wastes should be found." General Adams informs
them that the Air Force shares his concern and has a possible solution to the problem. The firm Space Engineering Associates has been
contracted to develop the means of shooting atomic waste into the
Sun. Colonel McCauley explains the program as envisioned by the

military. "Well, our project is simple to explain," he lectures. "Atomic waste will be loaded into rockets and fired into an orbit which will either draw it into the Sun or circle it forever." Adams then demonstrates how the project will unfold in two stages. First, four capsules full of waste will be placed in orbit near the Moon; second, a team of astronauts will hook them up into a "train" and attach an atomic-powered rocket, which is then fired off. McCauley notes that, inside the rocket, the waste material is surrounded by fuel, which acts as a shield to protect ground personnel and astronauts from radiation. "We will be watching this experiment with the greatest interest and the highest hope," Clark assures them. As the mayors depart, General Adams mentions that the chief engineer selected is Bob King, a former Air Force officer and astronaut, who left the service after a reentry accident. McCauley, who sat on the board of inquiry, recalls him as a fine officer and how no blame was attached to him. "He's done very well," the colonel notes. "It will be a pleasure working with him."

At that precise moment, the receptionist calls and informs Adams that Mr. King has arrived. He enters the room and shakes the general's hand, but appears standoffish towards McCauley. King's office is right next to McCauley's and it is apparent from the onset that he still resents his presence on the board of inquiry. Later, when the colonel informs him that he dislikes the way the valves function of the fourth stage rocket, King bristles, insisting, "That's nonsense! I checked those valves myself half a dozen times during the past few weeks. They worked perfectly." He then sounds off about the board of inquiry that prompted his resignation and McCauley reminds him that no blame was attached. "Then how come I sat around a whole month without a space assignment," King demands to know. "*A month?*" McCauley incredulously exclaims, "I've been three months between assignments." King's anger, however, only intensifies. "Look, McCauley," he insists, "I've got a new career now—no mistrust, no suspicion, no lack of confidence. And I am going to tell you right here and now, I am not going to let anything in this assignment hurt my reputation with my company!" The colonel angrily advises King not to invent problems that do not exist, shoves the design papers into his chest, then bellows, "You'd better get checking on those valves!"

The work of building the waste capsules and delivering them to the Air Force Test Center proceeded on schedule. There, after exhaustive checking, the capsules were air-shipped to a remote Pacific island for launching, where there would be no danger from contamination in case of an accident.

McCauley and King arrive in the office of Major "Tex" Nolan, who states, "Bob King? Didn't you used to be in the Air Force?" King identifies himself as that same officer who was mixed up in a reentry accident "and left the Air Force after the investigation." Nolan is taken aback by his apparent bitterness, claims he heard of no such rumors, and offers to show them around. Later, in King's quarters, McCauley shows up and talks to him about his attitude. "Bob, we're coming down the home stretch," he lectures. "Pretty soon, we're going to have a payoff date for all the hard work we've put in." King accuses the colonel of not thinking he has done a competent job. "Oh, don't think I haven't been aware of you going along behind me every step of the way, double-checking everything I do!" McCauley angrily tells him, "Sit down and relax!" He then reminds King that, as a former officer, he knows that everything in this line of work is checked and re-checked, without exception. "The only person that seems to lack confidence in the job that you're doing, Bob, is you yourself!" King goes into a tirade about the colonel giving him this pep-talk so that he will be less of a burden to him when they fly into space. McCauley, his own temper flaring, abruptly tells King he will see him tomorrow morning for the test launch, then angrily storms out.

At the launch site, McCauley, Nolan, and King anxiously watch the test vehicle as it prepares for takeoff. The colonel gets on the intercom and warns ground personnel to take cover, for, in the event of a self-destruct, the debris is highly radioactive. "Don't be too quick with the destruct button, Tex," King cautions Nolan. "Give her all the leeway you can." McCauley assures him they have no plans to destroy the missile. However, the rocket's ascent is very wobbly and the colonel has Tex arm the self-destruct mechanism. "Not yet," he cautions. However, King panics and yells, "It's no good. Destroy it. Destroy it!"–then lunges for the button. McCauley pushes him back as the rocket self-corrects and enters orbit. King storms off and Nolan observes, "Boy, that guy is really hurting over something." Mc-Cauley informs him, "He has no confidence in himself and, what's worse, he thinks nobody else trusts him." Nolan questions the wisdom of carrying him into Phase II of the project, but McCauley is reluctant to drop him, for "if I ask the SCA to replace him now it would cook his goose, not only with the company, but with himself for sure."

The phone rings at Ground Control and General Adams answers, pleased to hear McCauley's voice at the other end. The general is satisfied with progress so far, but wonders if his issues with Bob King continue. "Yes, sir, there's no change," he admits. "We take off from here in an hour." McCauley then saunters over to King, who is still analyzing the clamps for the atomic motor, and asks how he is doing. King mentions that clamps are designed to handle 20,000 pounds of strain, with anticipated forces not to exceed 5,000 pounds. "That's a four-to-one safety factor," he brusquely informs King. "I suggest you report to the ready room. We take off in an hour."

The first task, that of gathering the waste capsules together and securing them into a single unit, was performed by a specially trained crew of space technicians. Now it was up to McCauley and his men to handle the most critical phase of the operation—that of attaching the atomic engine to the space capsules and firing them into Sun orbit. Like the crew that had gone up earlier, it would be strictly limited in the amount of time they could spend on the job because of the atomic radiation.

In the TR-1 cabin, Major Nolan locates the capsules on his radar and McCauley begins positioning their ship astride them. General Adams then radios the colonel, "Ed, I give you this last warning. Watch the radiation exposure time very carefully. Under no circumstances, repeat, under no circumstances are you or any of your crew to exceed the time limits set for you." King suits up and is carefully instructed not to exceed his 14 minutes. "I'll be finished before my time runs out," he confidently asserts. King floats over and begins putting the atomic engine in position, but with six minutes left, the final clamp refuses to take hold. McCauley orders him back inside once his limit expires, then suits up to finish the job himself. That done, the colonel returns and orders the rocket fired, but silence results. "There's nothing wrong with this equipment," King insists. "I am getting good, strong output." McCauley deduces that something must be wrong with the engine's receiving equipment and he prepares to return outside. Upon closer investigation, McCauley notes the control rod has slipped from its receptacle and he orders Major Nolan out to assist him. Nolan complies, but as the two men reset the rod, the engine suddenly roars to life while the major's helmet is still lodged in the work bay. "Colonel!" King shouts. "You'll soon be out of sight! Let go, let go! You're headed for the Sun!" Minutes pass before McCauley wrests Nolan's helmet free and they drift along at high speed. The colonel instructs King to fire up the TR-1 and follow them while he and Nolan use their jet packs to close the distance. King panics when mentioning their speed differential, but the colonel assures him, "Just figure the difference in mass and take into account the difference in thrust between your engines and the A-rocket." King nervously makes his computations, then eases TR-1 forward. He soon locates the two men on radar, then coasts alongside to rescue them. Back inside, McCauley and Nolan congratulate King on the fine job he did. "That was a very tricky problem of navigation that you handled under tough conditions," the colonel asserts. "Better start checking the course of the waste capsules. Make sure they're headed into the sun."

Back on Earth, General Adams congratulates the men for their efforts and notes that the waste materials are passing Mercury and on course. "Going back to the Sun where it came from," McCauley states. "To give us more energy here on Earth." King also mentions that his company has slated him for a new project, shakes hands, then departs. When Nolan slyly comments that they finally straightened him out the "hard way," McCauley adds, "And the next time, I am going to try and find a less dangerous rehabilitation technique!"

Courtesy Landov Media.

"The Sun Never Sets"

(Aired August 31, 1960)

Starring: John Sutton (Air Vice Marshal Terry), David Frankham, (Neil Bedford-Jones), Robin Hughes (Captain Tom Hetherford), Mavis Neal (Lady Alice), Roy Dean, Sidney Smith

Script: Lewis Jay

Directed by: Alvin Ganzer

Technical director: Captain M. C. Spaulding, U.S.A.F.

Space and the celestial bodies belong to all Mankind, not to any one nation. Yet each nation is pushing its space program, looking for its place in the Sun. But speed in this race does not always make the winner. This is the story of the men of two nations, working together in an attempt to conquer outer space, and of an experiment which almost brings them to the brink of disaster when they try to find a shortcut to the universe where the Sun Never Sets.

A spaceship enters the Earth's atmosphere, then successfully lands on a dry lake bed. Some time later, Colonel McCauley trots into the office of a senior general, apologizing that his recent work on the Moon ruined his chance to work as an exchange officer in England. "The assignment's still on," the general declares. "We intended to send someone else in your place, but your friend Air Vice Marshal Terry wouldn't hear of it." The mission commences the day after tomorrow, at which point McCauley groans, "Goodbye, fishing trip…" However, the general assures him, "You can thank Mary for your one day's delay. She badgered me!" The general also mentions British plans to use an American Neptune first-stage rocket as a second-stage engine, greatly enhancing the lifting capacity of the overall machine. "If this idea works," he notes, "it will put the British in the forefront with one giant step." McCauley agrees, conceding, "And I might come back with some information that might help our space program." The general wishes McCauley off and extends Air Vice Marshal Terry his best regards.

In England, McCauley arrives at Air Vice Marshal Terry's office and the old friends exchange pleasantries. At length, Lieutenant Neil Bedford-Jones takes him next door, where he is introduced to Group Captain Tom Hetherford, leading officer of what is revealed as the Vega Project. He next encounters Flight Lieutenant Sopwith, Hetherford's smarmy co-pilot for the upcoming test flight. "I expect this whole thing must be very boring to you, Sir," Sopwith sneers. "Boring?" McCauley counters. "No test flight is ever boring." "Really?" Sopwith drolly remarks, drawing a surprised look from his superior. Hetherford goes onto explain that the Vega Project consists of two Neptune rockets for the first stage and a third for the second stage. "It's that second stage that I'm interested in," the colonel informs him. Arrangements are made to visit the test center on the morrow, but for the present, Hetherford wishes McCauley to be properly billeted for the evening.

The next day, McCauley, Hetherford, and Sopwith arrive at the test center, where the colonel leisurely examines the engineering blueprints. He expresses some concern as to the viability of the project, whereupon Sopwith brusquely interjects, "I take it you don't approve, Sir." McCauley simply informs him, "Well, let's just say that I'm here as an observer and to prove myself useful, if I possibly can." Sopwith sarcastically agrees, stating, "*Very* well said, Sir." Hetherford then explains the firing mechanism for the second state to a skeptical McCauley and Sopwith chimes in, "We've tested it many times. It works perfectly." McCauley's irritation mounts, but he maintains his composure, declaring, "Lieutenant, success on the testing stand and success in outer space are two entirely different things." Hetherford then questions why the colonel is so unsure about the Vega project and McCauley states his doubts over the Neptune rocket's reliability as a booster. "Well, that's a pity," Sopwith rudely interrupts, "because the thrust of a Neptune in second stage gives the Vega a remarkable overall performance." McCauley, fed up with such insolence, bellows, "Lieutenant!"–then Bedford-Jones cuts him off by suggesting that he spend the weekend at his country estate. Hetherford orders him off to collect resumes and Sopwith, judging the time right, excuses himself. McCauley expresses his admiration for Bedford-Jones and asks if he will be part of the Vega test program, but when Hetherford informs him that Sopwith is his sole co-pilot, the colonel simply scowls.

At the spacious estate of Bedford-Jones, McCauley is introduced to his mother, Lady Alice, and pleasant conversation ensues. "Well, now, what are your impressions of England so far?" she asks. McCauley states his admiration and that he has performed service here previously. He mentions he has two sons, nine and eleven, and Lady Alice says, "Oh, how wonderful. But isn't a pity that you couldn't have brought Mrs. McCauley and the boys with you." The colonel states he will probably do so once the Vega program testing concludes. Lady Alice mentions that she's heard nothing but the Vega program from her son, although she's glad he will not be on the first test flight. McCauley asks if she has tried steering him in other directions, but she exclaims, "Oh, good Heavens, no. Why, his father and grandfather were in the RAF. Why, he's planned his career since his earliest school days." She also warns that his own sons will put him through similar paces one day and he mentions they already demand going to the Moon with him. At that juncture, Bedford-Jones reenters and suggests that the colonel change out of his uniform and he agrees.

The work of bringing Project Vega to its climax went steadily ahead. Colonel McCauley worked closely with the British team, learning new techniques and methods that would be helpful to the U.S. space program and, if possible, making contributions to the British effort out of his own vast knowledge and experience.

McCauley is working in his bedroom when there's a knock at the door and in steps Group Captain Hetherford. The latter informally plops down on the colonel's bed and the two begin discussing the Vega program. "I'm not surprised," Hetherford concedes. "I've known your opinion on this for some time." McCauley still intimates that the program should be postponed until the reliability of the Neptune rocket is verified. "Tom," he reasons, "I was sent here to observe and help. I know the national importance placed on the Vega Project. That's why I am urging, as strongly as my position permits, that you abandon the whole project until the second stage of the Vega can be revamped." Hetherford counters that too much national capital has already been invested in the project. McCauley warns that the Neptune has not been tested in outer space in such a capacity, to which the group captain insists, "There hasn't been a single failure in all our test-firings." Hetherford further relates that the potential of this project is so promising that Venus and Mars might be targets "not for tomorrow, but today!" He insists that, as far as the British government is concerned, the gains outweigh the risk.

The next day, Air Vice Marshal Terry confirms that the Vega lifts off on the morrow as planned, piloted by Hetherford and Sopwith. Bedford-Jones strongly suggests that he be allowed to go onboard as an observer, then Terry asks of him, "Exactly what do you expect to observe?" The lieutenant shoots back, "Well, sir–whatever there is to observe, sir." The Vice Air Marshal shrugs off the suggestion and politely reaffirms that Bedford-Jones will remain assigned ground control duty as his assistant. McCauley then wishes Hetherford and Sopwith good luck. The Vega rocket lifts off as planned as McCauley, Terry, and Bedford-Jones monitor the ground instruments. "Go! Go!" the lieutenant mutters as it climbs into the sky. McCauley, for his part, simply crosses his fingers and watches the monitor, declaring, "A beautiful takeoff; couldn't be better." "Maybe you could be dead wrong, Sir," Bedford-Jones chides. "I sure hope so," the colonel remarks. First-stage separation occurs as planned, but when Hetherford hits the second stage button, the Neptune engine stays inert. "No response," he informs Terry. "I repeat, no response!" McCauley approaches the Vice Air Marshal and suggests, "Sir, why don't you have them separate the second stage and try to ignite the third stage? That will get them into orbit." The stricken crew complies, then reports, "Vega to Ground One–Vega is out of control. We are tumbling." McCauley suggests that he take one of the training MRs up to rescue the crew before they are completely disoriented. "Your ship will be ready in an hour," Terry assures him. Then, turning to Bedford Jones, he announces, "Colonel McCauley will need a co-pilot. Report to the ready room as soon as possible."

The MR lifts off shortly afterwards and McCauley starts bringing his vessel along the Vega, whose crew no longer responds. Bedford-Jones suggests that attempting to board a tumbling vehicle is dangerous and that he should go. The colonel asks him how many times he has been in space–only once–which effectively negates the gesture. McCauley also remarks he has prior experience trying to enter a tumbling vehicle. "One more question, sir: did you succeed in boarding that tumbling vehicle?" the lieutenant asks. "No," McCauley declares, then suits up. At length, the colonel succeeds in entering the wayward vessel and he removes the unconscious crewmen by hand. "They may drift some distance, so keep tracking them with your radar," McCauley orders Bedford-Jones. Once inside the MR, a groggy Hetherford declares, "That Vega would certainly make a good roller-coaster ride." McCauley assures him, "You both should be all right by the time we land." Sopwith blurts out that "I've never felt so dizzy in my life." The colonel, unable to resist a jab, unleashes a mock-British accented, "*Real-ly?*" Laughing ensues.

Back at the estate, the colonel informs Lady Alice that he is flying his family to England for a few days. "How wonderful," she exclaims. "Oh, I do hope that for at least part of the time you can be our house guests." The colonel gratefully accepts her offer. Bedford-Jones then announces that he has been accepted for advanced training at the U.S. Moon base. A pensive Lady Alice states that she is sure it will be a wonderful assignment. "And 100 years ago it would have been India or Australia, I suppose," McCauley reassures her, "which, to my way of thinking, would have been a far more distant journey."

Courtesy Bonestell.org.

"Mystery Satellite"

(Aired September 7, 1960)

Starring: Brett King (Major Tim O'Leary), Charles Maxwell (Colonel Frank Bartlett), Edward Mallory (Captain Don Miller), Mike Steel (Major Vic Enright), Harry Ellerby (Major General Albright), Mel Marshall (Sergeant Tucker), George Diestel (Major Bob Williams)

Script: Lewis Jay

Directed by: William Conrad

Technical advisor: Captain M. C. Spaulding, U.S.A.F

> *To the best of our knowledge, Earth has not yet been visited by any type of intelligent life from another planet in the vast universe. Yet it is within the realm of possibility that Earth has been under observation by beings from some of these distant worlds. A time will come when men who travel through the vast reaches of outer space may encounter a stranger. This is the story of a group of space travelers whose paths crossed a mystery satellite.*

As rocket ship MR-37 drifts towards the Moon, its crew engages in ide banter to pass the time. Captain Don Miller becomes the butt of good-natured ribbing when he inquires if "desolation" is spelled with one 'T' or two. The rancor increases when Colonel McCauley and Major O'Leary discover he is writing to his bride-to-be. "Colonel, can you recall any previous trips where part of the crew members got moon-struck before we got to the moon?" O'Leary jests. "Well, I supposed we have to make allowances for bridegrooms," McCauley fires back a smile. Suddenly, O'Leary notes he has a blip on his radar scope, closing in on MR-37 from abeam and apparently placing it at a distance of 14 miles. He speculates it must be a meteor, but Miller expresses that it might be "something else." McCauley reports the situation to Major General Albright at Ground Control and asks for permission to close with the object. Albright signals his approval, but cautions the colonel to watch his propellant reserves. McCauley orders the requisite course changes, but to everybody's surprise, the object changes its course and speed, maintaining a parallel course. "Must be something wrong with the radar, sir," O'Leary declares, "or we're dealing with something besides a meteor." An incredulous McCauley orders Miller to do a service check on the radar system while he informs General Albright. The general orders him to resume his course to the Moon while he investigates the possibility that the strange object is a satellite belonging to another nation. As MR-37 makes yet another mid-course correction, the visitor apparently loses interest and gradually disappears from the scope. O'Leary reflects, "Now we'll never know if it was a meteor, one of our old dead satellites, or something else." Miller sits up sharply and asks, "What do you mean, *something else?*"

No sooner does McCauley arrive at Moon Base than discussions about his encounter commence with newly-promoted Colonel Frank Bartlett and his crew. "You know, Mac, in your shoes, I would have been tempted to use some of my reserves," Bartlett declares. "Yeah, I know," the colonel reasons. "I'm on the curious side myself, but in space I've learned it's safer to keep it in check." "Yeah," Miller chimes in, "we might find something we wished we hadn't." More speculating ensues and Miller continues rambling, "I keep thinking about that professor who said there might be beings on other worlds who would consider us humans to be First-class beef animals." O'Leary scoffs at the notion and assures the captain, "Not you, certainly–you'd be too tough." General Albright eventually informs McCauley that the object does not belong to any nation on Earth and he mentions it might be an old satellite, although the object's evasive maneuvers are unprecedented. He consequently orders him to hand over his ship's course recorder and logbook to Colonel Bartlett for closer scrutiny back at headquarters. Before departing, Bartlett is advised to keep his radar on for the mystery object and he jests, "I'll tell you, Mac, if I detect it, I'll run it down, take it home, and have it stuffed." McCauley subsequently orders O'Leary, Miller, and Sergeant Tucker outside to commence a geological survey of specific points nearby. The colonel also confesses to Major Vic Enright how the strange object has occupied his thoughts lately. "Do you think it *was* something?" Enright ponders. McCauley reflects for a cold moment. "I do think that someday a human being is going to make contact in space and when it happens, it's going to be the greatest thing in the history of Mankind. I have to admit that... I'd kinda like to be that man."

En route to Earth, radar on the MR-30 picks up a blip which closes with the vessel and, as before, it begins pacing them from astern. Bartlett makes frantic efforts at full power to maneuver and close with it, but the stranger keeps its distance. "Stand by gyro controls," he mutters to his co-pilot. "I told Mac I'd take this thing home and have it stuffed." The colonel keeps closing the distance, disregarding orders from General Albright to abort–and his rocket is approaching the atmosphere too fast. Bartlett nonetheless persists, approaches within camera range, and blurts, "I can see it on the TV scanner! It's–" Radio contact suddenly terminates. Agonizing minutes pass, then Albright solemnly informs McCauley that MR-30 apparently burned up in the atmosphere; its crew did not eject. The loss of the ship triggers more speculative banter back at Moon Base and Miller questions if the object deliberately lured them to their deaths. "I don't like the use of the word lured," McCauley thunders. "Colonel Bartlett and his copilot died trying to find another answer. It's the price we pay for the knowledge we gain." The subject is quickly dropped. Subsequently, Miller and Sergeant Tucker, working outside, report a "round and silvery" object passing overhead. McCauley immediately assumes it is the visitor. Sensing an opportunity, he abruptly orders MR-37 placed on five-minute standby launch status over Major Enright's protests. "What does all this mean, Colonel?" he demands. "I want to go hunting on a moment's notice," McCauley insists. "Now get that ship ready."

All of the resources of the vast Skywatch network on Earth, as well as the radar facilities on the Moon, were thrown into the hunt for the elusive and mysterious object which had already caused the loss of two men and their spaceship. At Moon Base, tension mounted as the men realized that, should the object be sighted again, Colonel McCauley intended to make a determined effort to close with and identify it.

Affairs at Moon Base are disrupted again when Ground Control informs McCauley that Earth radar is tracking an unidentified object, apparently heading for the Moon. The colonel immediately requests and receives permission to intercept. When Albright questions the utility of a head-on approach, whereby the rocket would flash by the object in mere seconds, McCauley assures him, "I intend to swing out from the Moon in a wide ellipse and come in on the object's course more or less parallel." Soon after, MR-37 hurls itself into space and the hunt is on. En route, O'Leary bemoans that all they have sighted is three meteors. "I keep worrying whether or not I'm a good beef animal," Miller interjects. O'Leary counters with, "That's a switch. I figured you'd have written three letters by now." Suddenly a blip registers an object behind them, apparently closing fast. McCauley speculates the stranger has crossed the ionized trail of their exhaust gases and is homing in on them. As MR-37 bores in towards the Moon, McCauley cuts power to eliminate his gas trail for a few seconds to confuse the pursuer. The object approaches to within seven miles and is finally observed on the TV monitor. It is long and silvery, but no indication of its origins. Meanwhile, their own vessel is on a collision course with the Moon and O'Leary warns, "At that speed, we impact in 90 seconds." McCauley holds his course steady for what seems like an eternity, then suddenly orders full power. His rocket only skirts the lunar surface while the mystery object barrels directly into it. "It's disappeared, colonel, I don't have it at all," O'Leary informs him. "I had hoped that by changing course at the last possible moment we would avoid hitting the Moon and the object wouldn't," the colonel declares. McCauley orders Moon base to check its seismic monitor for a recent shock wave and to fix map coordinates of the epicenter. That done, the colonel and his crew land, debark, and approach the mysterious satellite on foot, beholding only wreckage. McCauley examines a few parts and pronounces, "This came from Earth... you know, I'll bet that this object that has caused so much trouble is a robot that had been launched from the Earth ten or fifteen years ago, maybe longer." O'Leary and Miller then query him on the object's bizarre nature. "There are only two explanations for its behavior," he deduces. "Either it was being controlled by some intelligence or it had been in space so long that it picked up a tremendous charge that repelled it whenever another object came too close." Miller expresses relief about not having to worry about being a good beef animal and the colonel concedes, "Well, not this time, anyway."

Back on MR-37, now heading back to Earth, the light-hearted banter resumes. Miller asks if "anticipating" has one 'T' or two and is immediately pounced on. "You can always tell the direction this guy is heading by the words he can't spell," O'Leary chides. McCauley cannot fathom why he writes at all, seeing he will be reunited with his girl in six hours. "That's beside the point," Miller insists. "I promised my wife that I would write to her every day, so I've got to write whether I'm getting home or not!" Laughter ensues.

"Flight To the Red Planet"

(Aired in syndication)

Starring: Marshall Thompson (Major Vic Devery), Michael Pate (Doctor Morrow), Tom Middleton, Harry Ellerbee, John Zaremba

Script: Lewis Jay

Directed by: David Friedkin

For years, Man has looked at Mars with the one hope that someday he could travel to the one body in the solar system where there are some indications of life. He has asked himself the questions, "Is there life there? Are the canals of Mars there man-made? Can Man live there?" Only a manned spaceship landing on Mars could answer these questions. This is a story of the future, when a group of dedicated men risked their lives on the first flight to the red planet: Mars.

The American rocket Mars 2, presently on its 236th day of flight, is coasting its way toward the red planet. A fatigued Colonel McCauley, ready for his scheduled nap, summons Major Vic Devery into the flight cabin as his relief. "Well, did you enjoy your nap, buddy?" he jests. The cheery Devery, smiling as always, agrees and asks, "Only 236 days... Ed, can you remember being anywhere except on the way to Mars?" "Vaguely," he grunts, unbuckling his seat. "Have a nice nap!" Devery sarcastically jests. "Thanks," McCauley sputters. Once in the crew quarters, the colonel is surprised that time never seems to bother Doctor Morrow. Casting an envious eye at Captain James Nichols, fast asleep in his bunk, he mutters, "He's got the best idea." Suddenly, Devery announces a meteorite strike on the ship and all hands come forward. No serious damage is sustained save for a skin puncture and McCauley and Nichols don suits and venture outside to fix it. Meanwhile, Devery mentions this is the third such strike in 24 hours and asks Morrow for a reason why. The doctor confesses he has no scientific explanation, but he likes to compare their efforts to Columbus's voyage of discovery, as when he espied land birds, indicating a close proximity to shore. "You know, there is a good deal of opinion holding that as a comparative large body like Earth or Mars moves through space, it sort of sweeps up space junk–meteorites–like a vacuum cleaner, drawing them into its gravitational field." "Yes, we're being drawn into that gravitational field," Devery chimes in, "and the traffic is getting terrific." "Exciting, isn't it," Morrow says with a smile. Meanwhile, McCauley and Nichols complete their repairs and return inside.

Back at Ground Control, Doctor Tor marvels over the reality of the ongoing flight, emoting, "As a boy, I used to dream of just such a flight to see Mars at close range. How many generations of stargazers before us have dreamt of just such this moment? Without even such fulfillment." The general he addresses concurs and mentions that, thanks to Doctor Tor, the flight is made possible by a total velocity budget he devised. "I am already looking forward to the day when we will have fuel that will enable us to use hyperbolic orbits and thus to make this trip to Mars in 100 days instead of the 237 that this is taking! That day will come," he declares. At precisely this moment, McCauley makes his scheduled status transmission to Earth, which includes a time lag of four minutes and five seconds. "Well," he drones on, "since there's no time lag aboard this ship, we'd better start making preparations for landing on Phobos." This remark engenders simmering resentment from Doctor Morrow, who desperately wants to land on Mars itself. Captain Nichols jokingly points out that they will only be 3,700 miles from the surface, which is still pretty close. "Well, doctor," Devery adds, "I'd rather land on Phobos and get home again than land on Mars and maybe not get home." "That's where we differ, major," Morrow bristles. "Colonel McCauley, I've spent my whole life in preparation for this trip.

I'd be bitterly disappointed if we don't make a landing on Mars." "Sorry, doctor," McCauley states as the latter storms back into the aft chambers. At length, McCauley and Devery work the rocket into a landing position over the jagged landscape of Phobos. Owing to the magnetic properties of the moon, Mars 2 is suddenly drawn into a nearby rock pile and makes a hard landing. Damage appears slight, but McCauley and Nichols will go outside and inspect the ship's hull. Doctor Morrow also quips that due to the high iron content and magnetic attraction, they can probably traverse the surface without magnetic boots.

A large tear is discovered on the vessel's underside, which McCauley orders fixed. Back in the cabin, Morrow remonstrates that the repairs are delaying his observation equipment from being unloaded. "Safety of the ship comes first, Doctor," McCauley quips. Additional grousing draws another sharp reply from the colonel, "We'll have time to get your work done, doctor!" Morrow asks Devery to open the observation port so the latter can at least start studying the planet's surface. Waxing philosophic, Morrow murmurs, "You know, those markings on Mars are really beginning to mean something. Perhaps we'll learn even more about the canals and the changing of colors. Maybe even some form of life." His demeanor becomes hostile once McCauley returns and pronounces Mars 2 sound and Morrow sarcastically quips, "Well, it would appear that we have a fine, well-functioning ship. Maybe we should make a few test flights now, then start for home." Suddenly, Captain Nichols informs the colonel that they have a leaking fuel tank in the rear and McCauley advises, "Doctor, that crack of yours about heading for home right away *might* just happen." Upon examination, the fuel tank for the return trip is losing 14 pounds per hour and cannot be fixed. This accident effectively ends the mission, yet Morrow explodes into an angry diatribe. "Getting home? Did we spend all this time and effort and money to sit cooped up in this ship for 237 days, all this only to turn and run from the first little problem that we encountered?" "It's not so little, doctor," Devery calmly reasons. "It's literally a matter of life and death for all of us." Morrow fires back, "Did you think this trip was going to be all peaches and cream? Our purpose is scientific, our goal is to conquer the universe that we live in. What are a few lives, even yours and mine when we stand on the brink of the greatest discoveries that Man ever made?" McCauley, listening dispassionately, finds himself agreeing with the doctor. "Vic," he declares, "you and Jim start unloading the equipment."

Back on Earth, Doctor Tor and the general debate why McCauley is not abandoning the mission, given the dire circumstances. "I know Morrow," the doctor declares. "His very dedication to the goal of exploring Mars could make him extremely persuasive in a situation like this." The general, who knows McCauley equally well, opines that he will figure out how to get home safely. Meanwhile, the Mars 2 crew begins unloading monitoring equipment as Doctor Morrow goes traipsing off with his telescope. McCauley cautions him to remain in line of sight lest he lose radio contact with the ship. "Pretty easy to get lost around here," he warns. Morrow, dumbstruck by the visage of Mars looming in the distance, blithely ignores him and wanders off. "Phobos is an amazing rock pile," he exclaims to McCauley. "Yes," the colonel warns, "and we don't want it to become a graveyard." At length, once the monitor is functioning, the men need Doctor Morrow to calibrate it, noting only an hour remains left. When Morrow cannot be raised by radio, McCauley walks off to find him. As expected, he finds the doctor intently observing Mars, consumed by his work. The doctor apologizes for the lapse, then excitedly explains, "Colonel, I've got invaluable information on the canals and I believe that they are waterways. Those green areas on either side suggest irrigation and that rock over there, you see, it's fused and it's obviously of volcanic origin. Now I want several samples to take back." McCauley apologizes, but he must refuse permission and orders him back. "I'm sorry, time is running out," he explains. "Later, if possible." The two meander off to the ship.

The adjustments are completed with only 25 minutes to go and, once the crew returns to the cabin, Morrow remains outside for some final fine-tuning. At length, McCauley calls for him to return, but the doctor fails to respond. The colonel realizes that Morrow has again wandered off and he resolves to retrieve him. "Ed, we have less than ten minutes," Devery warns. "I know. Take off on schedule," he declares. "But what if you're not back?" the major ponders. "Take off on schedule," McCauley repeats. The colonel finds Morrow near that fused rock pile that so fascinated him, only now injured by a rock slide. Freeing him, another slide damages their radios, cutting them off from the ship. The two begin walking back to the Mars 2, but Morrow can only hobble. With three minutes to go, Devery begins frantically calling for McCauley as the precious seconds tick by. Nichols remonstrates about leaving the colonel behind, but Devery reminds him that if they fail to launch, "None of us will get back to Earth." The major opens the observation port and continues pleading, "Ed! Come in, please! Our time is up!" The 30-second mark is reached before the two men amble into view and the countdown stops. Nichols is ordered out of the ship to assist them and Mars 2 is last seen departing Phobos for home.

On Earth, Doctor Tors exclaims, "I must return to the lab. The mass of data on Mars that the monitoring equipment on Phobos is sending back is fantastic!" The general concurs, adding, "What's fantastic is the trip that these men are returning from." Back on Mars 2, Major Devery announces that the ship has left Mars orbit, "in case anyone is interested." Doctor Morrow subsequently apologizes that McCauley had to rescue him and is bewildered by why he did so after all the trouble he caused. The colonel matter-of-factly consoles him with, "Doctor, we were all just as anxious to land on Mars." Morrow conjectures, "Well, maybe next time, we'll find out if there is life on Mars." "Next time, doctor?" McCauley bristles—then smiles, hinting, "Maybe…"

APPENDIX I
Interview with Anastacia Lundigan, July 2012

JF: Tell me, what are your earliest impressions of your father?

AL: He was kind and gentle, happy-go-lucky, and he doted on me very much.

JF: In other words, he spoiled you rotten.

AL: Yes... I have no complaints.

JF: How old were you before you realized your father was a famous movie star and that you could watch him on television and in the movies?

AL: I guess I must have been three or four because he was always taking me along to various movie sets. Or my mother would take me down there to visit him. And when I saw him on the TV screen, I always shouted, "Look, there's Daddy!"

JF: What was your most lasting memory of *Men Into Space*?

AL: It's kind of hazy–I very young, but I recall walking around the Moon set, definitely.

JF: So did you have a sense of wonderment, like you were actually on the Moon?

AL: Yes, Mother would take me down there occasionally and Dad would buy me an ice cream and we would take long walks around this big, impressive set. I remember that vividly to this day. I recall seeing Dad in his silvery space suit and his helmet, which he sometimes let me wear. It was kind of spooky and dark, although the stars were pretty. The only other memory I have was in carrying my *Men Into Space* lunch box to school.

JF: I read that you apparently mentioned that your father took you to the Moon while riding the school bus a day or so later and the driver began wondering exactly who your father was.

AL: Yes, I remember that. It did get something of a big laugh when they actually realized who Dad was and what he was doing. More than anything, I looked forward to the ice cream cones he bought me on every visit to the set.

JF: Well, tell me, what is your single best memory of your father?

AL: The fact that he was always there for me. He'd be easy to talk to and tell me stories and I could talk to him about anything. He did not talk about his career that much, just everyday living.

JF: Did he continue taking you to sets as you got older?

AL: Yes, I remember visiting the *Marcus Welby* set, where I met John Travolta, and *Here Come the Brides* with Bobby Sherman. I also met David Soul while filming *Starsky and Hutch* when I was fourteen.

JF: Did he try to interest you in the movie biz?

AL: Not really. I had a bit role in *The Way West* (1967) when I was about 12, but I never pursued it. But I did get to meet

Kirk Douglas, Robert Mitchum, and Richard Widmark. Sally Field and I also used to skip jump ropes on the set!

JF: It must have been a tremendous blow when William died.

AL: Yes, I was only 21. It was all over the newspapers, walking out of the church and the cameras would be in your face and then they would follow you to the cemetery. I remember Cesar Romero read his eulogy. When he was sick, Robert Mitchum would call every day to see how he was.

JF: Thank you for taking the time to speak with me.

AL: You're welcome.

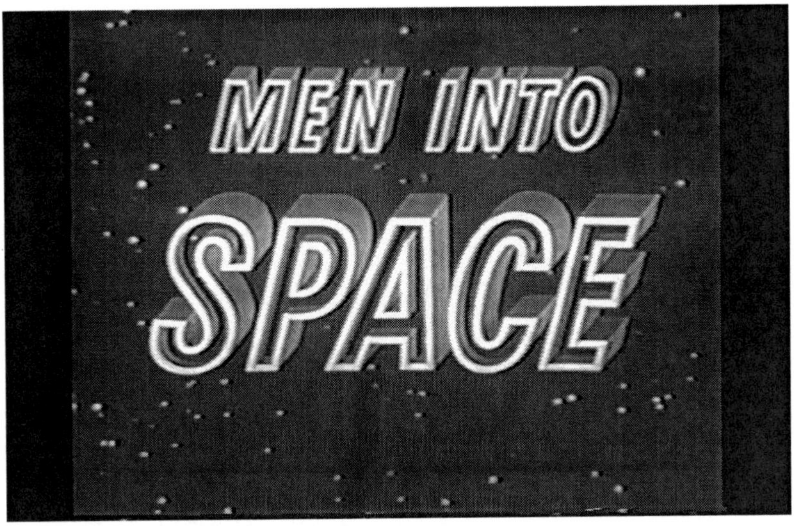
MEN INTO
SPACE

APPENDIX II
Men Into Space Merchandise

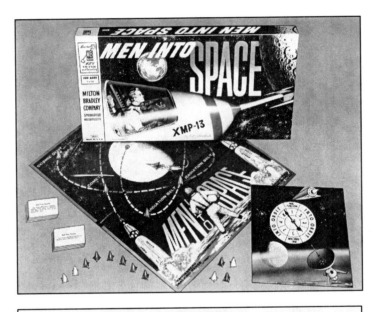

4203-6 COL. McCAULEY SPACE HELMET

© Copyright 1960, Ideal Toy Corporation

About the Author

JOHN C. FREDRIKSEN holds a doctorate in history from Providence College and is the author of 30 reference books on various topics. He is depicted here in the backyard of his Warwick, Rhode Island, home in August 1960, the same month that "Flare Up," his favorite episode of *Men Into Space*, was broadcasted.

ENDNOTES

1. Two erudite overviews are James Evans, *The History and Practice of Ancient Astronomy*. (New York: Oxford University Press, 1998), and John North, *Cosmos: An Illustrated History of Astronomy and Cosmology* (Chicago: University of Chicago Press, 2008).

2. Reviews of the interaction between space and culture are William E. Burrows, *The New Ocean: The Story of the First Space Age* (New York: Random House, 1999), and Howard E. McCurdy, *Space and the American Imagination* (Baltimore, MD: Johns Hopkins University Press, 2011).

3. Technical discussions of this important weapon are in Gregory P. Kennedy, *Germany's V-2 Rocket* (Atglen, PA: Schiffer, 2006), and Norman Longmate, *Hitler's Rockets: The Story of the V-2* (New York: Skyhorse Publishing, 2009). For broader historical context, consult Michael J. Neufeld. "The Nazi Aerospace Exodus: Towards a Global Transnational History." *History and Technology* 28, no. 1 (2012): 49-67.

4. A recent interpretation of these trends is Sean N. Kalic, *U.S. Presidents and the Militarization of Space, 1946-1967* (College Station: Texas A&M University Press, 2012). Sadly, a comparable text on Soviet military practices during this early period is lacking. A good overview of the beginnings of nuclear deterrence is Evan Thomas. *Ike's Bluff: President Eisenhower's Secret Battle to Save the World* (New York: Little, Brown, 2012).

5. A popular discussion of UFO hysteria is Frank C. Feschino, *Shoot Them Down! The Flying Saucer Wars of 1952* (Morrisville, NC: Lulu , 2007); a less sensational approach can be found in Jacques Vallee and Chris Aubeck, *Wonders in the Sky: Unexplained Aerial Objects from Antiquity to Modern Times and Their Impact on Human Culture, History, and Beliefs* (New York: Jeremy P. Tarcher/Penguin, 2010).

6. Two informative treatments of this topic are Karal Ann Marling, *As Seen on TV: The Visual Culture of Everyday Life in the 1950s* (Cambridge, MA: Harvard

University Press, 1996), and Lynn Spigel, *Make Room for TV: Television and the Family Ideal in Postwar America* (Chicago: University of Chicago Press, 1992).

7. The best overview of these programs is Cynthia J. Miller and A. Bowdoin Van Riper, *1950s "Rocketman" TV Series and Their Fans: Cadets, Rangers, and Junior Space Men* (New York: Palgrave Macmillan, 2012). Scholarly analysis can be found in a forthcoming essay by Margaret A. Weitekamp, "Setting the Scene for Human Spaceflights: Men Into Space and The Man and the Challenge," to be published in *Spacefarers: Images of Astronauts and Cosmonauts in the Heroic Age of Spaceflight.* Edited by Michael J. Neufeld (Smithsonian Institution Scholarly Press, forthcoming).

8. Recent discussions of Von Braun's controversial past are Wayne Biddle, *Dark Side of the Moon: Werner Von Braun, the Third Reich, and the Space Race* (New York: W. W. Norton, 2009), Michael J. Neufeld, *Von Braun: Dreamer of Space, Engineer of War* (New York: A. A. Knopf, 2007), and Dennis Piszkiewicz, *Nazi Rocketeers: The Dreams of Space and the Crimes of War* (Mechanicsburg, PA: Stackpole Books, 2007).

9. For more on the classic *Man In Space* animated series, from which ZIV probably derived the title for their own TV series, see J. P. Telotte, *The Mouse Machine: Disney and Technology* (Urbana: University of Illinois Press, 2008), and *Learning from Mickey, Donald, and Walt: Disney's Edutainment Films.* Edited by A. Bowdoin Van Riper (Jefferson, NC: McFarland, 2011), 84-102. See also Randy Liebermann. "The Collier's and Disney Series." In: *Blueprint for Space: Science Fiction and Science Fact.* Edited by Frederick I. Ordway III and Randy Liebermann. (Washington, DC: Smithsonian Institution Press, 1992), 135-146.

10. A useful discussion of space-related products and popular attitudes is in Eva Mauer, et al. *Cosmic Space Culture: The Cultural Impact of Soviet Space Exploration Since the 1950s* (New York: Palgrave Macmillan, 2001).

11. Good overviews of Sputnik and its impact on United States space policy are in Paul Dickson, *Sputnik: The Shock of the Century* (New York: Walker Books, 2001) and Matthew Brezinski, *Red Moon Rising: Sputnik and the Hidden Rivalries that Ignited the Space Age* (New York: Times Books, 2007), and *Reconsidering Sputnik: Forty Years Since the Soviet Satellite.* Edited by Roger D. Launius, John M. Logsdon, and Robert W. Smith (London: Routledge, 2000).

12. A lucid review of the most important spaceflight movies of the 1950s is Gary Colville and Patrick Lucanio, "Reaching for the Stars!" *Filmfax* No. 21 (July 1990): 54-57.

13. Frederic W. Ziv (1905-2001) was a giant of American syndication broadcasting and producer of countless iconic programs of the 1950s. See Irv Broughton, *Producers on Producing: The Making of Film and Television* (Jefferson, NC: McFarland, 1986), 17-22, and Linda Vaccariello. "Fred's World." *Cincinnati Magazine* 37, no. 7 (April 2003): 46-51, 161-162.

14. Martin J. Collins, *After Sputnik: 50 Years of the Space Age* (New York: Harper Collins, 2007), 64; Gary Colville and Patrick Lucanio. "Men Into Space." *Filmfax* No. 21 (July 1990), 59.

15. According to Lundigan's wife, Rena Morgan, "When they did the pilot, they didn't have any flying harnesses, so Bill was given Mary Martin's old harness, the one she used to fly around in *Peter Pan*. Bill would come home every night, very sore and uncomfortable. Once the series was sold, they made more comfortable harnesses." Mark Phillips, "William Lundigan: TV Space Pioneer's Wife Remembers." *Filmfax* No. 120 (Spring 2009), 89.

16. "His Wardrobe is 'Way Out.'" *TV Guide* (Sept. 26-Oct 2, 1959), 16. This breaks down into a space suit, $750; a helmet, $260; magnetic shoes, $75; summer and winter Air Force Uniforms, $520 apiece; three flight jackets, $150; and coveralls, $125. However, Lundigan's "long, winter underwear" cost a paltry $7.

17. "As an Astronaut, He's Way Out." *TV Guide* (April 2-8, 1960), 11. The noted sci-fi writer J. Stuart Byrne, who contributed two scripts to *Men Into Space*, recalls the difficulties this emphasis on realism had on casting: "Bill Lundigan met me once in the studio bar and he said, "I hear you're one of the guys that writes this turkey." I said, "Yeah," and he said, "How come I can never rescue a woman or something in this thing, I am always fighting nature." I said, "Well, if I told you, you'd want a pretty stiff drink." He said, "What is it?" I said, "Well, under the auspices of the Air Force, they want everything absolutely accurate." "Well," he continued, "what's that got to do with what I'm saying?" "Well," I said, "They have not yet invented a catheter tube for a woman's space suit–that's why there are no women in space." He said, "Oh, my God–give me a straight whiskey!" Audio interview courtesy of Jean Marie Stine of Renebooks.com.

18. For a producer of Tors' stature, surprisingly little has been written about him. A useful overview is Patrick Lucanio. "A Man and His Challenges: The Life and Films of Ivan Tors." *Filmfax* No. 29 (October/November 1991): 46-55, 94.

19. Chuck Fries, *Godfather of the Television Movie* (Beverly Hills, CA: Monte Cristo Publications, 2010), 59. He continues, "It was one of the, if not the most ambitious, undertakings of that time in television. Gotta give Fred Ziv credit for taking the shot." E-mail to the author, June 6, 2012.

20. Patrick Lucanio and Gary Colville. *Smokin' Rockets: The Romance of Technology in American Film, Radio, and Television, 1945-1962* (Jefferson, NC: McFarland, 2002), 193; Mark Phillips and Frank Garcia, *Science Fiction Television Series* (Jefferson, NC: McFarland, 1996), 210-214.

21. For the full range of issues broached by this show, consult Gary Westfahl, *The Space Suit Film: A History, 1918-1969* (Jefferson, NC: McFarland, 2012), 54-73.

22. The travails encountered by female astronauts during these early years were anything but humorous. Consult Margaret A. Weitekamp, *Right Stuff, Wrong*

Sex: America's First Woman in Space Program (Baltimore: Johns Hopkins University Press, 2005). See also Westfahl, *Spacesuit Film*, 63-65.

23. Weitekamp, "Setting the Scene for Human Spaceflight," 14.

24. "Men Into Space." *Variety* (October 2, 1959), 16. The reviewer continues, "Walter Doniger's direction gets much greater mileage from special effects than from actors and actresses. William Lundigan is capable, but doesn't seem to be straining himself. Angie Dickinson has one of those worried wife roles and she looks pretty worried." Another maven pronounced, "Director Walter Doniger appears to have done the best he could in light of the script's deficiencies. While comparisons are odious, "Men Into Space" needs a lot more velocity before it catches up with Disney." *Variety* (October 9, 1959), 29.

25. "'Men Into Space' Iffy; Gulf Out." *Variety* (February 17, 1960), 18; "Network Vidfilms: Midseason Score," *Variety* (Jan 27, 1960), 23; "55 Web TV Shows Axed This Season; CBS Hit Hardest." *Variety* (April 27, 1960), 10.

26. John Sinn. "The Public Interest–An Interested Public." *Variety* (August 2, 1961), 30. One source sums up the program's demise this way: "Technically, the series presented the best special effects for TV at that time. However, the characters and human drama often failed to reach orbit, thanks to the dry plots." Garcia and Phillips, *Science Fiction Television Series*, 210.

27. Literature on the defining Apollo program is extensive, but more modern interpretations include John M. Logdson, *John F. Kennedy and the Race to the Moon* (New York: Palgrave Macmillan, 2010); Asif A. Siddiqi, *The Soviet Space Race with Apollo* (Gainesville: University Press of Florida, 2003); and Deborah Cadbury, *Space Race: The Epic Battle Between America and the Soviet Union for Space Domination* (New York: Harper Perennial, 2007).

28. Roger D. Launius. "Reconsidering the Foundations of Human Spaceflight in the 1950s," http://launiusr.wordpress.com, and Matt Novak. "How Space-Age Nostalgia Hobbles Our Future." www.slate.com.

29. An oblique critique of all this is William D. Atwell, *Fire and Power: The American Space Program, A Postmodern Narrative* (Athens: University of Georgia Press, 2010).

30. All is not lost, according to several writers. See Benaroya Haym, *Turning Dust Into Gold: Building A Future on the Moon and Mars* (New York: Springer, 2010); Claude A. Piantados, *Mankind Beyond Earth: The History, Science, and Future of Human Space Exploration* (New York: Columbia University Press, 2012); Neil DeGrasse Tyson, *Space Chronicles: Facing the Ultimate Frontier* (New York: W. W. Norton, 2012); and Matt Doeden, *Human Travel to the Moon and Mars: Waste of Money or Next Frontier* (Minneapolis: Twenty-First Century Books, 2012).

31. James E. Wise, Jr., and Anne C. Rehill, *Stars in the Corps: Movie Actors in the United States Marines* (Annapolis, MD: Naval Institute Press, 1999), 117-122.

32. Thayer Soule, *Shooting the Pacific War: Marine Corps Combat Photography in WWII* (Lexington: University of Kentucky Press, 2000), 160.

33. Sterling Mace and Nick Allen. *Battleground Pacific: A Marine Rifleman's Combat Odyssey in the K/3/5.* (New York: St. Martin's Press, 2012), 223-224.

34. Quote is from Richard Lamparski, *Whatever Became Of...?* Fifth Series (New York: Crown Publishers, 1974), 73.

35. Westfahl, *Spacesuit Film*, 35-39.

36. "TV's Traveling-est Salesman." *TV Guide* (July 21-27, 1956), 17-19; "As an Astronaut, He's Way Out," *Ibid*, (April 2-8, 1960), 11.

37. Martin Grams, Jr. *Science Fiction Theater: A History of the Television Program, 1955-1957* (Albany, GA: BearManor Media, 2011), 130-134.

38. Ed Misurell. "Bill Lundigan Solar 'Floater' In New Series." *Milwaukee Sentinel* (September 6, 1959), 12.

39. "As an Astronaut, He's Way Out." *TV Guide*, (April 2-8, 1960), 11. "McCauley represents one of those quiet, heroic figures which have now gone out of style. As the series developed, McCauley evolved into almost a perfect paradigm of the way America was then pleased to view itself." Colville and Lucanio, "Men Into Space," 64.

40. Ed Misurell. "Bill Lundigan Solar 'Floater' In New Series." *Milwaukee Sentinel* (September 6, 1959), 12.

41. "As an Astronaut, He's Way Out." *TV Guide*, (April 2-8, 1960), 10.

42. Phillips, "William Lundigan," 88. The actor freely admitted, "I don't know a logarithm from a rocket sled, but I do play a lot of golf. The last time I went to the country club, someone had hung a sign on my locker-'Way Out Willie.' It's the sort of thing that makes you stop and think." "As an Astronaut, He's Way Out." *TV Guide*, (April 2-8, 1960), 11.

43. Quote is from Richard Lamparski, *Whatever Became Of...?*, 73.

44. No formal biography of Lundigan exists, but additional information can be gleaned from the Wikipedia and Internet Movie Database entries about him.

45. Quote is from Tom Weaver, *Monsters, Mutants, and Heavenly Creatures* (Baltimore: Midnight Marquee Press, 1996), 229-230.

46. "Miss Taylor from Taylorville." *TV Guide* (September 10-16, 1960), 29.

47. Quote is from Tom Weaver, *I Talked with a Zombie* (Jefferson, NC: McFarland, 2009), 166.

48. See also the Charles Herbert entries in Wikipedia and the Internet Movie Database and Paul Parla, "Hollywood Eats Its Children." *Classic Images* No. 258

(December 1996): 18-23.

49. Murray Schumach. "Going Far Out on Television." *New York Times* (November 15, 1959), Part II, 12. Unger continues: "We just could not afford to be caught napping. We wanted scripts that were more than just an adventure. We wanted our writers to answer such questions as reentry, about the families of astronauts. We were asking for theater and we chose space as our arena."

50. "As an Astronaut, He's Way Out." *TV Guide*, (April 2-8, 1960), 10-11. Rachmil explained: "We decided against a landing on Venus. That was a little far away from the mind's grasp. Of course, if our series runs long enough–and we hope it does–we may get to Mars." Murray Schumach. "Going Far Out on Television." *New York Times* (November 15, 1959), Part II, 12.

51. "Ziv-UA Ups Rachmil." *Variety* (June 7, 1961), 20; see also Colville and Lucanio, "Men Into Space," 58-60, and entries in Wikipedia and the Internet Movie Database.

52. See biographical entries in Wikipedia and the Internet Movie Database.

53. Colville and Lucanio, "Men Into Space," 59-60. See also Bonestell Space Art at www.Bonestell.org.

54. There are no biographies of Rose existent; this information was gleaned from the Wikipedia and the Internet Movie Database entries. See also the Oxford Music Online, Encyclopedia of Popular Music essay, and his official website www.davidrosepublishing.com.

55. Fries, *Godfather of the Television Movie*, 69.

56. The Music Division, New York Public Library, maintains a small file of David Rose clippings, some of which were consulted here.

57. This information was gleaned from the Atlas entries of *Encyclopedia Astronautica* (www.Astronautix.com) and www.AviationHeritage.blogspot.com.

NAME INDEX

CPSIA information can be obtained at www.ICGtesting.com
Printed in the USA
BVOW021345280213

314359BV00010B/230/P